AMERICA
IN THE
DARK

DAVID THOMSON , 1941-

AMERICA
IN THE
DARK

HOLLYWOOD
AND THE GIFT
OF UNREALITY

WILLIAM MORROW AND COMPANY, INC.

NEW YORK   1977

Printed in the United States of America.

1   2   3   4   5   6   7   8   9   10

Library of Congress Cataloging in Publication Data

Thomson, David (date)
  America in the dark.

    Bibliography: p.
    Filmography: p.
    Includes index.
    1. Moving-pictures—United States.   2. Moving-
pictures—Social aspects.   I. Title.
PN1993.5.U6T46   791.43′0973   77-3978
ISBN 0-688-03210-9

BOOK DESIGN   CARL WEISS

FOR

RACHEL

AND

LUCY

CONTENTS

It only works in the dark.
>—BETTE DAVIS in *Hush, Hush . . .*
>*Sweet Charlotte*

I'm as mad as hell, and I'm not going to take it anymore.
>—The Lament from *Network*

I've never been excited by movies as movies *the way*
I've been excited by magic or bullfighting or painting.
After all, the world existed for a long time without
people going to movies.
>—ORSON WELLES

AMERICA
IN THE
DARK

A CHILD'S GARDEN
OF HOLLYWOOD

> *Are you talking to me? You must be,*
> *'cause I'm the only one here.*
> —TRAVIS BICKLE, in *Taxi Driver*

HOLLYWOOD WAS A FRAUDULENT EDEN THAT REACHED AS FAR
as the shabby gentility of my childhood in suburban London.
It eased any regrets that the "real" Eden was unimaginatively
described and my corner of London pale and matter-of-fact.
At the time I was not conscious of it, but now I recognize
how far Hollywood was the most influential source of fiction
for me. I had had stories read to me, and I learned to read
for myself at about the time I began seeing movies. But those
stories were as palpable as type and paper; tear a page and
you interrupt the tale—throw a ball of paper at a screen and
it bounced off the heedless image.

The serene persistence of film mystified me. I sat in the cinema looking this way and that, wondering whether there were people in or behind the screen illuminated by the shaft of light. Or could there be anything to my father's offhand explanation that somewhere in the building a man was turning a handle that unwound images on the screen, like yards of cloth in a draper's? For years I could not grasp how the movies worked, and the miraculousness of such wonders went hand in hand with what a cautious child knew must be a trick. I felt as I did in front of a magician: enchanted by the illusion and the delicious worry that it was fake. Years later this mixture of beauty and dishonesty still seems the secret of cinema. The magic of photography is not quite dead yet, and in the movies the conjuring still transforms us.

My parents remembered when South London had been countryside gradually spoiled by sedate suburbs. But in my childhood the only breaks were where bombs had cleared buildings out of the way. The ten miles into the heart of London were otherwise solid with construction: tenement houses like matches in a box; small shops, all different but all versions of one calm view of trade. There were few large buildings other than churches, and the most glamorous places were the bus garages where the red monsters whose numbers I craved stewed the smell of rubber and petrol in the gloom.

Except for the cinemas. They seemed exotic places, and many of them were very large. They were ornate, decorated, and extravagant, whereas the rest of South London gave no hint that anyone designed or decorated buildings. Cinemas were immune to the gray sprawl surrounding them; and they might have been designed by stay-at-home English who dreamed of Granada, Morocco, Samarkand, and Macao. The sprawl was anonymous, somewhere for everyone and anyone to live, where anyone became everyone. Years later when I read novels about the universal, featureless city, I knew it already from London. A Joseph K. could easily go astray

between Clapham, Balham, and Streatham, and those suburbs are still as consistent as the frayed yellow strips along
the edge of the street that forbid stopping to the jammed
traffic.

In the stretch of sprawl I knew, there were three cinemas
and they were cavernous, gaudy, and always changing. This
last quality was very compelling for a child, and before I
measured changing time I knew that what the cinemas offered was always altering. Did they therefore deal in change?
The shops rarely changed ownership or line of business; their
window displays were locked in place and had not much
"display" about them. But the cinemas were restless and
volatile, lively yet unstable. I learned the pleasure of looking
for the week's fresh posters, but I also found that, inside the
cinemas, excitement with the movie I was about to see was
surpassed by the raised expectations of the coming attrac-
tions. I always wanted it to be next week, and I see that it
was in the cinema that I began to be discontent with now and
immediate reality and felt the perpetual longing that is the
lasting imprint of advertising.

The movie houses I knew catered to the middle and lower
middle classes in an area that did not own up to workers.
But they had a daily rhythm different from that of their
audience. In the mornings when the shops were busy the
cinema stayed closed, asleep even, like a brothel where the
girls lie in late. There was no sign of life except for drab
women polishing the heavy glass doors. This dark sheen did
not offend the workaday street, even if a breath of perfume
wafted from the cinema into the fresh and innocent air. The
interiors of cinemas were as sweet as hairdressing salons; and
if the building was asleep, then its sleeping breath was fra-
grant with Turkish-delighted dreams. So the child thought.
But adults too, I suspect, were in awe of the cinema then.
The housewives buying fish and cabbages might sometimes
modestly resemble Dorothy Lamour or Esther Williams.

They had the same unassuming prettiness, but would not have dared emulate the sultriness of Hedy Lamarr in *Samson and Delilah*.

Amid small tea shops, ironmongers, and greengrocers, what could *Samson and Delilah* mean? There was no temple to pull down, only several smoke-gaunt churches built in economical mock Gothic and persisted with on Sundays. The world did not seem religious: It was too proper and settled to need moral justice, and the English are as alarmed by the spirit as they are by unrestrained feelings. A war lately won only encouraged placidity. *Samson and Delilah* seemed to have very little to do with God, though no doubt he (or He) is called upon several times and may shine out of its clouds. It plunders the Bible for graphic incidents and the resonant fable of the strong man whose hair was cut short by a wanton. I can only remember the red-meat swagger of Victor Mature and the unhealthy allure of Hedy Lamarr. As to the story, my impression was of indistinct humiliation of the slow Samson by supine, idly depraved Delilah. I responded to the daft splendor of the imagery, the contrast of nobility and wickedness, and, before my time, suspected that the movie was about the intimate exchanges of sex.

At that age I did not understand that *Samson and Delilah* was a film made by Cecil B. De Mille. Like the multitude audience, I attended to the title of a film and the names of the people in it, and worshiped the imagery of posters. My own name, and the names of everyone I knew, seemed as sober and useful as the numbers on houses. But the creatures in suspended movie metamorphosis had descriptive names: Samson is nearly a metaphor for strength, so that any Sam feels confident. Delilah was lovely to say; it opened the mouth —for a French kiss, perhaps—and played with "delight" and "liar." As for Victor Mature and Hedy Lamarr, they were not just names but meretricious poetry, announced lies. What sort of man could overcome a mature victor? What headiness was there really in *l'amour,* even if this Hedy might mar it?

I never noticed directors because I was lost in the anagrams of Delilah and Hedy Lamarr. That began as childish perplexity, but the movies have always thrived on such confusion; it is an aspect of their obscuring fact with fantasy. The names in films are expressive but unreliable. Adults too were caught in the subterfuge. I heard them talking about films in which "Joan Crawford did this . . . and then Zachary Scott told her . . ." When my grandmother took me to see *The Third Man,* and I had difficulty following the plot, she turned to me and said helpfully, "Orson Welles is the Third Man." When Harry Lime, or Welles, or number three eventually appeared—in a doorway in a dark street, a fond cat nuzzling his shoes, his face suddenly exposed by a light in an upstairs window—it was not a hardened face, such as the film's Vienna was peopled with, but a boy's face. And Welles looked like a youth still, dressed up in his father's overcoat and hat, pretending to be raffish. I thought he looked like me, and when he smiled knowingly into the camera I suspected he thought that too.

That sort of suspended instant had always attracted me to the movies, though it was years before I found a need or the means to begin to explain it. One of the first films I ever saw was Olivier's *Henry V* and I have always "recalled" an image from it that is not actually in the film. When the French raid the English camp, and set fire to it, I believed I had seen a molten dissolve of burning tents and agonized faces. The horror of anyone being burned alive moved me to tears, but some calm voice within my tears said, "It can't be so," and my mother took me on her knee and said, "It isn't real." How could men be burning to death on or in the screen, otherwise why did the cinema not catch fire, and how was their pain so easily replaced by Henry on horseback roaring that he was not angry since he came to France till this moment? The cinema regularly transformed itself, and perhaps I doubted a fixed nature of things or myself because of that slippery ease.

The image I thought I saw was itself a suspension—a dissolve or a superimposition; but more profoundly I was intrigued by what was clearly so and what might be so. Film was lifelike. It did not lie visually, and I believed in it. But did that mean that its images were true, credible, or even possible? Fiction bloomed in my head with so many lovely manifestations of things outstripping common sense or cause and effect. Feeling, and feeling's hope of fulfillment, fantasy, generated movies. Films were the materialization of daydreams, but as clear and factual as the photograph. The theater as a storytelling medium seemed ponderous when, in *Red River*, one fade could move forward fifteen years and transform the child Mathew Garth into the somber, lean figure of Montgomery Clift. There, in a few seconds, was the perfect example of a movie whispering to a child, "You, you can become this hero." Years later I called my son Mathew and noticed that the adoptive father in *Red River* was named Tom Dunson, a muddled echo of my own name.

I was not alone at the cinema, even if I make it sound like something made for me. Millions went, millions more than go now, but millions fewer than had gone in the 1920s. It struck me that whereas traveling fairs came around once or twice a year, football matches were played on Saturdays, and plays were produced in theaters (remote buildings I had very little knowledge of), the cinemas were open every day and to be found beside all the other shops providing necessary goods. They were not like the other shops, but did as steady a trade. After dark they found their time. By then the shops were closed, and the cinemas alone stayed open, twinkling with lights and turning the night into dark velvet. The cinema comes to life with dark—like Dracula.

On many evenings one had to leave home early and queue

to get in. Regularly the cinema was more full than empty, and I used to wait for the darkness preceding a film to shelter me from the strangers in whose midst I was sitting. It was an experience made for a crowd. I was often unwilling to laugh at jokes made by people who were not really there, no matter that their images uttered the biting asides or fell down the stairs. But I felt the crowd laugh, and I laughed with them, helpless but happy to be sharing a response. At the same time, the darkness was a concealment for the depth of feelings that might overtake one with a movie, and under cover of darkness every individual was having a private experience. Fantasy is the loneliest reach of the imagination where we are desert-island monarchs, torn between the perfection in which everything yields to our whim and the terrible lack of company.

I was not a discerning or discriminating moviegoer until well into my teens. For years I wanted only bright spasms and the darkness. That arrangement was itself thrilling and passionate, allowing speculation, reverie, and imagination to flourish. The going there quickly became a habit. Films of "adventure" appealed to me more than "kissing" pictures. But as childhood sharpened into early adolescence I was more tolerant of ladies on the screen, and more susceptible to romantic episodes. Both action and love beckoned me. They were experiences unlike my own: The child feels remote from adventure and the adolescent yearns for a splendid love. It was the cinema that indicated their absence for me, and made the images more lustrous and vivid than anything in reality. I was a shy but inquisitive intruder at the entrance tunnel to a hall of desirable things. The movies were a secret garden that only I had discovered, because the flashing change of imagery was exactly suited to my own nervous apprehension. Every time I blinked in wonder the screen was transformed.

The screen impressed me enormously. In the half-light between films I sometimes went down the aisle to a blonde girl in white, flush pink with spotlight, who was selling ice cream. She was as impervious as plastic, and as pretty as a doll. Dazed by the spotlight and the task of counting out change, she seemed in a trance, as if she had stepped out of the screen behind her. There it was, rising up, sheer and daunting, like the side of a battleship to someone in a rowboat. A great white wall, unflawed and tranquil, but bearing the frenzy of every film. Such promiscuous actions apparently left no mark or infection on the screen. What if screens had memories, like humans, and stored all the images flung at them?

There were satin curtains that were drawn backward and forward, with brocade patterns on them: mosques, flamingos, and minstrels—impossible companions in harmony. Before a film was shown the curtains writhed slowly: I was never sure whether draft or the color changes in the footlights made this motion. I studied the movements as if they were part of the ritual and waited for the dimming of the lights. It came so slowly that I was uncertain whether the lights were altering or night had slipped into the building like smoke. But as darkness was fully appreciated and the footlights remained the only light (the glow of dawn on the horizon), we all sighed with expectation and fell silent. It was dawn at midnight, a reversal of the natural order of life, and an effect that most films of that period employed—of shooting nocturnal scenes in sunlight—called day for night in America, and in France *la nuit Américaine*.

I did not know that term as a child, but I would have accepted that the night was American. The films I saw, so many of them American, reached out to the far corners of the world and made them American locations. The first time I conceived of Paris was when Gene Kelly, without duress or rehearsal, had French street kids join him in a pavement "I Got Rhythm" in *An American in Paris*. Not that I had a clear sense of what was going on, but I was dazzled by the picturesque animation of "Great French Painters" in the concluding dream sequence. Throughout that film I loved the deft passage between reality and fantasy. It was as if an American transformed Paris with his glance: And I noticed a name—Vincente Minnelli—because it was florid and because I had seen it before, attached to *Meet Me in St. Louis,* a film that made me wish for older sisters, a large fond family, and the precious aura of St. Louis in 1904. Very powerfully, I wished that I had been there then: Not many movies gave me as strong a sense of wanting to be other than myself. American films offered that invitation: Long before I heard the word *escapism* I made the journeys the films allowed. It may have trained my imagination to travel.

But wherever it went, Americana gilded the scenery. *The Flame and the Arrow* said that it was occurring in Lombardy, but the characters were Robin Hood and Maid Marian as embodied by Burt Lancaster and Virginia Mayo. Everyone spoke American, moved with comprehensive grace, purpose, or villainy, and lived in the nick of time. Not the least beguiling thing was the directness with which the forest outlaw, Dardo, wooed and won the aristocratic lady. The smooth leaping of social distance was accomplished with the same confidence as Lancaster swinging acrobatically on the battlements of a cardboard castle. In literature, lowborn lovers had to be proved as foundling princes, but in American movies the light equalized without such convenient explanations.

No matter the period or the setting—*Yankee Pasha* or *The Prisoner of Zenda, King Solomon's Mines* or *Ivanhoe*—there was an emphatically valiant hero who had whatever prowess was required of him by great journeys, desperate ordeals, or cunning problems. He matched circumstances and villains, gravity and logic, and finally allowed a flimsy woman, hitherto held back by fate, to subside in his arms. Every part of the world sustained this simple pattern; all disasters could be overcome without hurt or loss. The convention that had

Americans play Saxon knights, Arabian sheikhs, or British gentlemen did not trouble me. I took it for granted that differences of language had to be ignored, and I never flinched from the imperialism of the movies.

In Britain after the war there was bitterness toward America. *Objective Burma* was banned because it implied that Americans had solved a jungle war the British were proud of. *Yank* was a derogatory term, inspired by so many Americans in England waiting for D-day, better fed, less devious perhaps, more uninhibited certainly. Britain was hurt that the war had required America, just as it resented America's lateness in coming and its shocking wealth in goods. There were clouds of disapproval of Americans above my head, bitter with the suggestion that American culture was materialistic, shallow, and vacant. I was warned off American comic books, chewing gum, and movies, and grown-ups looked anxious when I talked about the films. As I understood their fears, they seemed to me mistaken. American movies were not material, but imaginary, fantastic, and expansive. The simple-mindedness of the stories did not impede the complex mingling of actuality and artifice. I guessed even then that the movies were doing the one thing my elders hoped for: educating me, enlarging me, making me wonder.

As I grew up, my education advanced. At school I was studying history and literature with every thought of going to university. My school took pride in the thoroughness of its academic approach; it had fine teachers from whom I benefited. I read F. R. Leavis and learned the importance of "moral seriousness" in literature, as well as detailed textual analysis as a way of proceeding not just to scholarships, but even to understanding. This method took it for granted that literature was about life, and that there was an easy bridge between the two. My faculties were sharpened, and I began to notice more in the cinema. A crucial event was seeing Alfred Hitchcock's *Rear Window*.

I remember queuing for that film and knowing even then that Hitchcock was an attraction equal to the film's stars, James Stewart and Grace Kelly. That suggested some method was involved in the filming; hitherto I doubt if I had thought of method when so much else was dreamlike. The form seemed so phenomenal that I never considered an author: That has always been the attitude of an audience in a cinema, and it runs counter to English literature's respect for the author as a choice-making moral sensibility.

Rear Window absorbed me, and I went back to see it again, to prolong the pleasure, for I wanted films to go on forever. It was not adventurous in the sense of galloping horsemen, fistfights, and shootings. Nor was it expansive: All the action took place in a city courtyard, where apartment windows confront one another and a section of the crowd is torn between curiosity and the tactful need to ignore other people. A photographer sits in his apartment while his broken leg mends. He is not a patient convalescent. He specializes in action pictures and the broken leg is the result of getting too close to danger. While he remains home with his leg encased in plaster, he has the visits of a nurse, Thelma Ritter, and his beautiful girl friend, Grace Kelly—or Lisa-Carol-Freemont, she says, turning on a lamp with each name to blow away the darkness in the apartment.

But the photographer often leaves the lights off and sits in the dark, concealed, watching the life going on in the window frames of the courtyard. This begins as an alternative to boredom; but it persists because he is inquisitive, a natural spy. He becomes caught up in what he sees and, one rainy night, as he sits by the window, half-dozing, half-awake, he believes he may have seen the circumstances of a murder. In one window, there live a man and his invalid, nagging wife. The husband is busy all one night and in the morning the wife is nowhere to be seen.

At first the photographer is regarded as foolishly suspicious by the ladies and his policeman friend: Too many dramatic pictures have given him a taste for melodrama, they say. But here Hitchcock's method intervenes. We know no more than the photographer, and helplessly we share his speculations, because we watched with him. For the first time, I realized that seeing and being seen were the subject of movies as well as the mode. My eyes had been opened, and henceforth I was an analytical observer, aware that the compulsiveness of film lies in the form: The spectator is required for the melodrama to function; his credulousness sustains it; the movies are a trap for the voyeur.

Rear Window moralizes on this topic, whatever Hitchcock may say to the contrary. The photographer plots to get evidence against the imagined murderer. The climax comes when, having lured the agitated man away with a fake phone call, the photographer sends Grace Kelly to the apartment to look for the wife's wedding ring—if she had really gone on holiday, she would not have left the ring behind. Grace Kelly knows that, since she wants to marry a reluctant James Stewart. The man returns before Kelly can escape, but not before she finds the ring. The man threatens Kelly and the helpless but distraught Stewart calls up the police to protect her. In the confusion, she gestures across the courtyard with her hand to Stewart, who is watching through one of his telephoto lenses: The ring is on her own finger. But the "murderer" notices this gesture and follows it across the way to Stewart and all the others sharing his dark.

Melodrama anticipates that he will now turn on Stewart. We have "seen" him as a killer and expect murderousness. But when he comes to the apartment he is hesitant, pained as a bull waiting for the kill. "What do you want of me?" he asks. It is one of the most touching moments in the work of a cold-blooded director, and it is a question that pierced me as I watched, even if it is posed by a director who has had enormous success depicting murder, suspicion, and guilt.

The windows that Stewart spied on were, approximately, cinema screens; the film was a model of what occurs in any cinema and—speciously or responsibly—it wonders about the ideological relationship that may accompany the visual link of spectacle and spectator.

I have begun in a very personal vein, and there are risks in that. No filmgoer wants to be thought of as typical, and yet I hope that this book will address the general experience of watching movies. I have made a large part of my life out of the cinema, and I have taught and written about "the art of film." Some of the people I taught were as uneasy about that title as the audience packed around me would have been. That there is a deep appeal to the imagination in the movies seems beyond dispute. But the movie industry and most of its audience have resisted the term *art,* which is sometimes defined by artists as a deep appeal to the imagination.

I think that many people had a childhood sense of the movies like mine, that the impact was powerful beyond description. And I think that the imagination of our time has been shaped and tempted by the movies. The dilemma in this book is in wondering whether that influence has been for good or bad. It may still turn on the answers one finds to the murderer's question in *Rear Window,* or to a version of it, "What do we want of the cinema?" To begin to answer that I need to go on a little with autobiography, to show how quickly in my life "art" rose up to cultivate the profuse garden of Hollywood.

The 1950s confirmed my love of film: By the age of nineteen I was articulately enthusiastic about the form that ten years earlier I had followed in rapt adoration. Ironically, these were the years of breakdown in the structure of moviemaking that had my allegiance. It was during the 1950s that people talked about "the death of Hollywood," and cinemas emptied, closed, or yielded to the dreary pleasures of bingo and ten-pin bowling. In the same decade, television became a necessary focus in the majority of households; it may even be the instrument that turned homes into households.

By now it is a commonplace to see cinema subsiding and television growing at its expense. So it is worth testing that relationship a little more closely. The bulk of time on television is occupied with film; many of the people who work for it—in front of and behind the cameras—once worked in movies; and many television shows are made in studios built for film companies. The most striking instance of this shift came in the 1950s when Lucille Ball purchased RKO, the studio that had never fully believed in her as a movie actress, and turned its premises into a factory for television and herself into one of the first household names on the "box" in the living room.

Hollywood is not dead, even if there are only ruins left of the Babylon that existed between *The Birth of a Nation* and *Gone With the Wind,* an enclosed civilization of rival studio-states, the conventions of genre films and the figurehead stars, all set against the sunshine of California and the luxury in which movie people were alleged to live. That is no more; only yesterday, Adolph Zukor died, 103 years old, the longest-lived founder of that civilization. But television perpetuates its ethos, just as it employs its veterans. It still relies on moving images and genres; it still inhabits Hollywood and other suburbs of Los Angeles. And whatever it was that Hollywood offered as a way of thinking while our bodies went about their monotonous lives, that is insisted on by television.

Still, television made important refinements in the experience of watching moving images. It destroyed the sense of community. Marshall McLuhan once claimed that television had made a "global village" out of the audience. I think that is too neat. In the cinema, no matter the vital element of being addressed intimately by the film, one was part of a crowd. Laughter and tears alike were shared in. Television isolates the spectator: It is the time killer of someone living alone, and it may make people living together feel lonely. This seems a minor distinction. But its subtlety should not conceal television's adding to our feeling of being helpless, alienated individuals no longer belonging to an impossible mass. When an advertisement insinuates that we are not like others without this deodorant or that cigar, the solitude of watching television aids the suggestion. Whereas, in cinema, the cynical lie can still be laughed to scorn by the group response.

Hollywood the cinema empire might have owned television if it had had more business acumen; but it is one of the many fallacies associated with Hollywood that it was shrewd and farsighted. It was years before I acquired the historical perspective to see the process, but all through the fifties old Hollywood was shuddering at its own disintegration. There is still an accepted wisdom that the era is both the end and the worst of Hollywood. I think that is mistaken. It was an end, but it was also a transition painfully embarked upon. As the commercial system foundered, so the subjects of films became more penetrating and disturbing. Of course, there was rubbish being made; there always had been. There were vain attempts to defeat television—3D and Cinema-Scope. But the parables in genre pictures rose nearer the surface; and there was no longer the same adherence to happy endings or the muffling of uncomfortable realities. Some people said the cinema was becoming realistic, others saw a first advance on sordidness. I sometimes recognized my own life, rather than just a merchandise prairie into which my restricted sense of myself could ride at night.

In the fifties I discovered two names to go with Hitchcock; I had one shattering experience that I could relate to nothing else, and I found a film that helped me order my own past. The two names were Nicholas Ray and Anthony Mann; the shock was a film called *Citizen Kane*; and the film that made me remember was *Rio Bravo,* made by Howard Hawks, the director of *Red River.*

I will write about *Kane* more fully later. For now it is enough that I wandered into it because it happened to be showing at a local cinema. I had not heard of it, I was stunned by it, I did not follow or understand it. But it was like seeing the ocean for the first time: I had not guessed anything could be so large and compelling.

The two names crept up on me. When I was very young I was bored by credits and never read them. But some names recurred, and I noticed that some were more reliable than others. In particular, Anthony Mann directed a series of films that had the added identity of James Stewart: *Winchester 73, Bend of the River, The Naked Spur, The Far Country, The Man from Laramie.* They were westerns; Stewart wore the same hat in all of them, and they were film records made in the 1950s of men dressing up as cowboys and pretending to inhabit the 1880s.

The genre had a set of codes and habits that had very little to do with life in the West. Foremost among these was the theme of honor and duty, and the way violence was redeemed by integrity. I was already dissatisfied with white-horse westerns and heroes as bloodless as Roy Rogers, Gene Autry, or Hopalong Cassidy. But Stewart was a believable person, as selfish and suspicious as he had been in *Rear Window.* He played a solitary man, able, adroit, and canny, but reluctant to do anything for anyone else. Yet the action of these films drew him into helping others, and into a final trial of arms that was a test of character.

I was riveted by the way character and action merged in these films, and I loved the visual particularity that Mann brought to them. Never before had the open spaces of the western seemed as precise. Mann was a landscape film-maker; by another standard he used deep focus and a moving camera

—an artist of spatial relationships. The visible distance between people in his films *was* their relationship. It did not
express it. It *was* it. Today, Mann looks a rather academic
director, a little too composed to be urgent, but he taught
me that there could be style or what in a few years I learned
to call *mise-en-scène*. When I saw a war film, without Stewart,
called *Men in War,* I recognized it as Mann's before I found
out that he had directed it. No one else could or would have
made combat so lucid or beautiful.

Nicholas Ray did not impress me as a stylist, and he may
be a finer director because of that. He did not keep to one
actor or genre, like Mann; he did not even make films that
were clearly of a particular genre. But he was the director
of *The Lusty Men, Run for Cover, Johnny Guitar, Bigger
Than Life,* and *Rebel without a Cause. The Lusty Men* and
Johnny Guitar, for instance, are examples of two genres
shuffled together: the western and the women's picture. They
both stress something overlooked in most westerns—certainly
in Anthony Mann's—that those men in hats knew women
who were sometimes more intelligent than and as interesting
as themselves. *The Lusty Men* is about the traveling life of
rodeo performers and the tension between a loner, Robert
Mitchum, and another cowboy and his wife. The wish to be
settled, the skepticism with rodeo heroics, the cramped trailer
life, and the risk of death in the arena—these things were
wonderfully realized, and in a way that sited "the West" in
American social and domestic realities. I had never guessed
that a cowboy's hat did not protect him from pain and
ordinariness.

The revelation of drama in everyday things came most
clearly in *Rebel Without a Cause.* In hindsight, no one would
praise that film for realism. Melodrama throbs in it, as it
does in adolescent anguish. It is a film about rage, yearning,
and reconciliation. Its wide screen and colors are vibrant
with emotion, and Ray's visual imagination never mocks, or

forsakes, a vein of teen-age opera. But that is proper, for the film is true to adolescent experience—perhaps especially the experience of an adolescent brought up on movies. Despite the undoubted star presence of James Dean, *Rebel* suggested that many teen-agers felt as his character did—about parents, school, growing up, and love. This California adolescence was unlike my own in many ways, but the identification it called up was new. Whereas with other movies I had been taken out of myself, *Rebel* was a thrust into me. Star appeal and the new teen-age market—simultaneously provided for in rock and roll—altered my attitude toward movies. The underlying danger I had always felt in films—that at any instant I might be shown something unbearable—was confirmed. Not only could a movie invent feelings for me to trip in, but also it could disclose my own latent sensations to me.

That, I knew, was what education expected of art. It was what Wordsworth had done in *The Prelude,* a work I was studying at the time I saw *Rio Bravo.* That anyone should encounter these two at the same time, and with the same kinds of pleasure, baffled the school master teaching *The Prelude.* That poem was an authentic masterpiece, as monumental as any of the Cumbrian mountains Wordsworth knew and possibly as long-lived. I recall the terms in which we were taught to admire it: It was childhood "recollected in tranquillity," and recollection "made poetically concrete" by the wealth of linguistic expression we learned for examination questions. I liked the poem, despite its worthiness and the indicated scheme for liking it; and I liked *Rio Bravo,* despite the dismay my delight brought to the teacher of Wordsworth. I do not recall tranquillity playing much part —and I think it is more a condition teachers and critics like to attribute to artists than anything they know—but in *Rio Bravo* I remembered *Red River.* It was the same river, granted ten years, color instead of black and white, a different narrative situation, and only John Wayne and Walter Brennan staying in the cast.

In both, there was fondness with stories and an ear for conversation. There was an abiding friendship that could overcome most difficulties, sudden, succinct action, and talkative girls who got under the skin of otherwise sufficient men. *Rio Bravo* was a long western with a shoot-out at the end and set pieces like meals on a summer weekend. But it rolled, like a great river. There was a situation that gave it current, and after that, what transpired were the shapes of the river during the day. There were songs, jokes with cigarettes, discussions about what was happening, the sense of someone sitting near the camera talking to the cast as they worked, and the unquestionable knowledge that this was not 1878 but 1958. *Rio Bravo* was almost a film about grown men, some shrewd and amusing, playing with the schoolboy genre, the western; the professionalism in its code of values applied not just to how this sheriff was going to guard his prisoner, but how these men would spin out this story. It gently teased itself and its basis. Ward Bond appeared in the movie, leading and repeatedly being called on to stop and start a wagon train: *Wagon Train* was then a lumbering and successful TV series featuring Bond. Angie Dickinson bore not the slightest resemblance to a saloon girl: She was evidently one of the best new girls in pictures, doted upon by her director, eating up her scenes. Dean Martin was Dino, Ricky Nelson was probably wearing his own clothes, and John Wayne was quietly going about his business of being one of the most telling personalities in movies. *Rio Bravo* made me want to make films, for it suggested that the art or craft or trade was as much fun as a day on the river.

But how could I tell the Oxford college at which I sought entrance that *Rio Bravo* was the most stirring event of my year? Still, I told them, and they did offer me a place. But

I said thank you, no, and chose to go to film school. My school was astonished and never even owned up to having already educated Clive Brook, Raymond Chandler, Leslie Howard, and Michael Powell.

My veering away was not quite as abrupt as it sounds. It had been swayed and changed by art and poetry. In the school magazine I wrote three breathless articles on the cinema: on James Dean, Hitchcock, and Ingmar Bergman. That Bergman was not today's but the maker of such pretentious allegories as *The Seventh Seal,* which had a half-baked seriousness capable of convincing anyone a la mode that film was an art. I went to film school filled with Bergman and the small, righteous band of uncompromising Artists of Integrity who made difficult films the way they wanted. I regret that I put Howard Hawks temporarily on a shelf and succumbed to the pressure that if I was determined to make a fool of myself over cinema, then at least let it be respectable, demanding, highbrow "art house" cinema.

In the fifteen years or so since then so much has changed. Even British universities are cautiously admitting film studies; in the school system the subject is making rapid strides and now sits with English language and biology at "O" level. In America, it is being studied by over one hundred thousand at any one time in college. Much of that teaching concentrates on "professionals" like Howard Hawks, and sometimes compares them with Wordsworth. Hollywood cinema was reclaimed from oblivion, during the 1950s in France and later in the rest of the world. The garden I knew had been explored by many others, and their debt to it showed. François Truffaut, Jean-Luc Godard, and Jacques Demy, for instance, in France; Peter Bogdanovich, Francis Ford Coppola, and Martin Scorsese in America—a generation of directors who knew the history of cinema, who refer to it in their own work, and who are conscious, with different degrees of tolerance, of the way movies have been the central form of fiction in our time.

Yet Coppola and the others are not Hollywood so much as American cinema. They may live near Hollywood, they often work for the companies and in the ways established in the years before 1950. Still, they work for themselves in a way that would have shocked the old system, and causes heartache for them and the financiers they still need. Hollywood is so pervasive a culture that its influence is as great now as ever; it is only proper that a source of make-believe should be more potent when not actual or material. Hollywood is a memory for a nostalgic culture, and now that cinema faces at least three paths—the respectability of serious films, the notoriety of exploitation, or amateur movies—we can see how far it has lost to television the middle ground of regular, mass entertainment based on narrative fiction. The light still shines, wanly, in every living room, and the masses are huddled, if not together. This book is an exploration of what that relationship has meant to America, and the way "America" has become an imaginary future for the rest of the world, as it was for those original huddled masses ushered in beneath the shining light of liberty.

II

THE SYSTEM

> *One doesn't mix motives in Holly-*
> *wood—it is confusing. Everybody un-*
> *derstands, and the climate wears you*
> *down. A mixed motive is conspicuous*
> *waste.*
> —SCOTT FITZGERALD, *The Last Tycoon*

THE TITLE OF THIS CHAPTER SEEMS THREATENING, AND I concede a loss of innocence in the move from a garden to a system. As a child, I had no idea that the profusion of delight was calculated and organized. But even Eden had its author, a Hitchcock-like god coldly arranging paradise, Adam, Eve, the tree, and the serpent and waiting for melodrama to take its course. That god is the first director of performances to discover the equation of thunder sheets and wrath in the air, and guilt and smothered nakedness on the ground. Our legend of paradise begins with the place being put off limits; presumably no one lives there now except for a complacent serpent. Or is he only a prop monster at the foot of god's parlor door to keep out the draft?

We are aggravated by the shadow "system" throws over us; and yet we sometimes seek it as shelter. The worst nightmare of nuclear war is that we might survive in a world deprived of all those comforts we steadily resent: Internal Revenue, the FBI, the post office, the telephone, social security, Chevrolet, Budweiser, apple pie, the Rose Bowl, and Harry Reasoner. Without them, we would be back in that perilous American genesis: the wild continent of space, danger, and opportunity, a trackless land to fulfill or destroy every ambitious outsider escaping the ledger-book system called Europe.

That Eden of forest, river, and prairie was soon fenced off. The waywardness and energy were controlled by sheriffs, politics, and the propriety of capitalism. Even the Hollywood western has acknowledged this, though with customary equivocation. In *Cimarron,* the pioneer who builds a house on the raw land becomes a drifter, always moving on, while his wife stays at home, a pillar of the community, displacing him at the center of society. That story dodges family breakup: The audience is able to divide its response, enjoying the man's urge to be away adventuring, while respecting the wife's homely instincts. A story that begins in the exuberance of a land rush ends in the development of a city, and the spectator is allowed to participate in both. He is like the prospective purchaser, bemused by the specious atmospherics of real-estate jargon, looking over "a ranch-style residence" on the edge of Detroit.

Many American films of the last ten years are belligerently hostile to the system. As if guilty for four decades of obliqueness and simplification, they challenge set ideas of American history; they oppose the dogma of flag and country with personal values; they do not always skirt difficulty or exploit unpleasantness; there are concessions to doubt, pain, and the confusion that real Americans experience from day to day. *Taxi Driver* depicts the effects of unwholesome cities and available guns; *All the President's Men* exposes the White House as a den of inept crooks; *Five Easy Pieces* shows the difficulties people have in being with one another for long; *The Godfather* is nearly a satire on the authoritarian nature of family life; *Little Big Man* deprives glorious legend of its glory; *Dirty Harry* suffers the impossibility of a policeman matching the public's image of infallibility, skill, and integrity.

Indeed, the "sheriff" figure has not stayed to face the crisis, as Gary Cooper did in *High Noon*. Dirty Harry abandons his badge; Pat Garrett rides sadly away—to historic death at the hands of those who hired him to dispose of Billy the Kid; and in *The Chase,* Marlon Brando leaves the town to its own degeneracy after he has been beaten bloody trying to protect a prisoner from the mob. Only on television, now, is the policeman optimistic and successful: How oddly that reassurance backs up the claims of insurance plans and California burgundy.

In all these films, American systems are regarded balefully. Yet most of them cost more than two million dollars to make and were subsequently profitable. That means that a company structure made, promoted, and sold them to an audience of several million. Even shorn of its former size, the crowd in the American cinema is of a magnitude that constitutes a system. The movie director in America has never been as liberated as he is today, but that does not leave him free. It is as un-American as it ever was to make an entertainment film so disturbing to its audience that it keeps them away. "Disaster" films are as acceptable as their returns indicate. It may be part of the system that the audience in cinemas is beyond taking any offense, other than boredom.

In this chapter I want to look at the effect of "system" on

art and imagination in America; on the way film was turned into an industry; and on the role of the industry's leaders. The most useful purpose in this is to mark out the obstacles to accepting film as an art form and to ensure that we take the movies more seriously.

Because America is the first man-made nation in the world, it is an invented place where imagined ideals were invoked as a structure for reality. It is the product of artifice, not nature. No country conscious of its roots stretching out of sight and knowledge could have the same confidence in purpose and design. Whether one regards America now as an Eden or a Poisonville, it is still a country concocted from men's imaginations. Even countries that have undergone decisive changes in direction—like Russia or China—live with a past that must be amended. In America, without such a past, there are earnest efforts to embalm recent history. There is still more imaginative emphasis on the future and more encouragement to idealism and fantasy. The beauty of American cities is in the way imaginative aspiration, wealth, lack of tradition, and a willingness to be fantastic have sometimes transcended the merely brutal or grotesque. Reyner Banham has described how well Hollywood has epitomized this reckless ambiguity in buildings of solid structure and phantasmagoric meaning:

> Both Hollywood's marketable commercial fantasies, and those private ones which are above or below calculable monetary value, have left their marks on the Angel City, but Hollywood brought something that all other fantasists needed—technical skill and resources in converting fantastic ideas into physical realities. Since living flesh-and-blood actors and dancers had to walk through or prance upon Hollywood's fantasies, there was much that could not be accomplished with painted back-cloths

or back-projections; much of Shangri-la had to be built in three dimensions, the spiral ramps of the production numbers of Busby Berkeley musical spectaculars had to support the weight of a hundred girls in silver top hats, and so on. . . .

The movies were thus a peerless school for building fantasy as fact, and the facts often survived one movie to live again in another, and another and others still to come. Economy in using increasingly valuable acreage on studio-lots caused these fantastic facades and ancient architectures reproduced in plaster to be huddled together into what have become equally fantastic town-scapes which not only survive as cities of romantic illusion, but have been elevated to the status of a kind of cultural monuments, which now form the basis for tourist excursions more flourishing than the traditional tours of film-stars' homes.

This feeling of walking in a vast set is not uncommon in America. Design and landscape are both regarded as states of mind and sometimes they change as quickly. New York once influenced Fritz Lang's *Metropolis* but now exists in helpless debt to it: The street in Manhattan is the European street taken to a demented conclusion in which the vertical dominates the linear until a Kong tames it. Those streets are expressionist manifestations of man's awe, and if he doubts the readiness of the city to engulf him in wonders, then the streets spout steam, like a magician's grotto. And there, out in the harbor, is a female statue-building named Liberty, past which so many immigrants sailed.

That surreal embodiment of an ideal is as characteristic as the era of American cinema that created every sort of setting as verification for fantasy dramas. To crave the imaginary and the real is contradictory, but it underlies the Hollywood movie and is a knot running through American history.

Identity in America is often self-conscious: So cinema's playful confusion has a nagging relevance to the American. He is preeminently someone aware of his own enterprise, pain, or dissatisfaction. He has the distinction or glamour of the elective outsider. That compensates for a voyage into the unknown, fearful of toppling over the horizon, foundering in the tempest, or landing among savages. Some Europeans were received in America as gods, and they behaved like the tyrants who "represented" God in Europe. But the godlike sensation must have been heady: To have survived gave man belief in his prowess and his destiny; to have survived to find such resources, gold, land, and credulous natives only stimulated grandeur; above all, the men who settled could make rules and systems anew and live as they hoped.

Something of that reward waited for the classical immigrant in the nineteenth and early twentieth centuries. He was at a more lowly level. But once admitted to America he could look forward to a job, somewhere to live, and freedom from persecution, pogrom, potato famine, institutional poverty, feudalism, and the suffocation of family and tradition. The ordeal of transit left only the lucky and the innately resistant as survivors. The immigrant had to obtain elusive permits, save passage money, and get to a port; he had to endure the slow sea voyage and the bureaucratic inspection at Ellis Island, or whatever port he came to. That mixture of energy and courage must often have depended on the vitality of his imagination—his will to go on believing that America would be better, that he would be so much more himself there that every sacrifice was justified. America is a country of the Romantic age, carrying the hazardous promise that we can find ourselves.

America opened its arms to a decent screening of "all" of them and called the huddled masses frail, oppressed, and weak. But the masses were really the toughest and most intransigent, determined, or compelled to get away from

Europe: That included criminals, madmen, and others in whom determination meant lack of scruple, gentleness, or politeness—Al Capone or Louis B. Mayer. Famous photographs show the immigrant as an apprehensive peasant. But in practice he was self-interested, durable, and imaginative. There is a fine scene in Part II of *The Godfather* in which our latent memory of hundreds of sepia photographs of immigrants is realized in a shipload of Sicilians coming to New York, among them the child Vito Corleone. This tender face grows into the pasta-white hatchet grin of Robert De Niro—whose future we had already met in the sagging makeup of Marlon Brando, and now glimpsed again in the taxi driver haunted by himself in his own mirror, so angry with the spoiled world that he exterminates spoilers. The cinema dissolves faces and times, and every immigrant anticipated his own circumstances turning magically to prosperity and happiness once he was in America. That some such change worked for enough people helps explain the conservatism of the country now. A society established through change fears further upheaval.

With so many disparate peoples to unite, the American system sought to convey optimism in itself: "We hold these truths to be self-evident, that all men are created equal. . . ." That might appease prickly individualists and bring about the massness of America. Yet the idealism is treacherous. The urge to institute equity makes sure that two hundred million people remain a huddled mass. So long as citizens are determined equal, the cinema audience is an accurate model for the American public. Created equality can order us all alike, forming an amorphous whole in the dark. Indeed, we can live in the dark, and there is no need for government ever to supply the light that will reveal individuals.

But the tradition of art cultivated in Europe from the Renaissance onward is pledged to the value of the individual. It is the work of individuals prompted by their own inner compulsions and employing their unique attitudes and talent. European humanist culture recognizes the personality of the artist and has nearly worshiped him for his eminence. It is accepted that some artists profit from their work, but it is assumed by the culture that that does not interfere with the integrity of the author. "To thine own self be true" is the expected dedication of the artist, and if the result is *Pale Fire, Don Giovanni,* or the ceilings of Tiepolo, then surely that proves how far the artist is unlike other men, not created equal? He has more imagination, more skill or facility, more application or selfishness; he may be less tolerant of ordinariness than other men. The artist belongs to an elite, and that privileged position holds even today when elitism is more mistrusted in Europe than ever before. Not all artists feel comfortable to be put in an elite, and the attitude may be a gross fallacy, but still the distinction operates and runs counter to equality. We so revere the artist that we are vulnerable to any opportunist grabbing the title.

Similarly, the person exposed to art is made aware of a response that is his alone. Appreciation of art is taught to enhance an individual's responsibility to his own faculties and intellectual processes. When we read *Dombey and Son* we are meant to have our own reaction, and the value of reading is to guide us deeper into ourselves and into the particular moral sensibility that literature is deemed to foster. A well-read man should be firm but moderate in his own convictions, not easily swayed, but sensitive to others and their opinions. Such a man might still qualify as "philosopher-king." But we expect him to be put off by the jungle of politics, and thus he is excused exposing his fine sensibility to the ultimate test. The good man lives with his books, and virtue hibernates.

It was predictable that art designed to pick out individuals should become rarefied. At the very moment when art began to escape earlier social and economic privilege, it became more complex and less accessible, as if shy of a large audience. The period of "popular" fiction is short and might not be as clear without the prominence of Dickens. As the reading public became larger, literature went deeper than narrative. Of course, our experience intensified and as novelists faced such novelties as electricity, flying, and cinema it is no wonder that prose fiction moved from Dickens to Henry James, Joyce, and Faulkner. We disparage the authors left with the large public—be they Harold Robbins or Mary Stewart—but we should not forget that high art took a course that kept it the treasure of a few, and thus still the means of showing that some people are not like others.

In the halcyon age of Hollywood, Scott Fitzgerald treasured art for "conveying thought and emotion from one being to another," and in this century it has sometimes been presented as a lively but endangered resistance movement fighting drabness. That disappoints the wishful notion of art being the ultimate defense of an enlightened world. For if the artist speaks to the individual in the crowd, that reminds him of the communicative potential in art. Then, its hold on truths —passing or absolute—becomes so much more of a burden. European culture revolves around the idea that if the world paid more attention to artists it would be less barbarous. Some artists doubt that, but not many are spared the occasional lust to be delivering a sermon on the mount that could set human history on a fresh, benevolent course.

America in general has not followed the European cult of the artist. One cannot simply defend that independence: There is an awesome philistinism in America, unaffected by education, even if the imaginative life of the country is more exercised by open space, the supermarket, sports, and the car than professors of art appreciate. Still, America's characteristic artists are not the retiring, meticulous creators esteemed in Europe, but flamboyant performers—Hemingway, Charles Ives, Frank Lloyd Wright, Jackson Pollock, and

Norman Mailer—and those habitual unsettlers of our response, Andy Warhol and Muhammad Ali. American jazz introduced the threat of improvisation to enduring arts, while movies confront the question of whether art is for the people and of the people, or merely by a few people. The most useful way of looking at film in America is as a modern phenomenon, and not as the story of an art form.

It helps that approach that film was not actually invented in America. The unique American thrust to moving images is in the commercial practice that has overridden the form, and which affects our eyes and attitudes even now that some individuals dwell over film in a way that austere poets are supposed to work.

This commercialism was not immediate or crudely devoid of imagination. The film industry would not have been as successful without talented employees—whether craftsmen, artists, or accountants—or without the impulse to make money, messages, and emotion at the same time. There was an instinct in Hollywood that the new form was reaching deep into millions of people. I'm sure that D. W. Griffith and Louis B. Mayer both responded to that bracing opportunity, and both were made more conservative by the fear of alarming customers. We can call Hollywood a factory to suggest how automatic its operations were. But the factory is a deadly place in our culture, where people get a living in return for boredom, alienation, and withered self-respect. No one seems to have been bored by the Hollywood factory. Sensation was the product, melodrama its instrument, and excitement the mood in which people worked. Not everyone liked it, but not many could resist the fun in making pictures and seeing Valentino sit in the sun while the lights were arranged. Outsiders detected that extra zest and took it as one more proof—along with extravagance, mediocrities made wealthy, and indulged self-dramatization—that Hollywood people were crazy. But as Hollywood shrunk, these ways of life spread in California. A sociologist would need volumes to assess the extent, but I may wonder how far expenditure as a form of identity, the gap between merit and rewards, and the unrestrained outpouring of inner life are now modes in California. That golden state is often attacked for crass materialism. But the facile turning of dreams into possessed things shows allegiance to the imagination. That is California's inheritance from Hollywood, and it ought to make us cautious of treating the movies as a business like any other, or even as a businesslike business.

For nearly twenty years in America, the trade in movies was dense and frenzied. Even the film enthusiast's notion of American cinema begins around 1914 with Chaplin and Griffith. Before then, movies were short, hurried, and perishable. But there were many of them, and a pack of small companies making and marketing them and fighting over the multiplicity of outlets where film was shown. There were not many cinemas, as I used the term in Chapter I. Before the Great War, films were shown in any available dark, and that was provided in variety shows, fairgrounds, seaside piers, amusement arcades, nickelodeon parlors, in traveling tents, saloons, brothels, or living rooms, as well as purpose-built theaters.

The product was usually between ten and fifteen minutes long—the amount of film on one reel. Its place as a novelty in a bill of vaudeville acts was a sign of audiences' limited stamina. Only very slowly did narrative supersede the sheer amazement of seeing lifelike illusions. The most inventive film-maker of the first decade of cinema was a Frenchman, Georges Méliès, a stage magician who used movies as an extension of make-believe. The stories in Méliès's films are slight and naïve; the charm of the pictures is in the lyrical combination of the real and the fake. Without Hollywood's pursuit of narrative, film might have developed as a visual form in which illusion and pure graphic impact were paramount. This tradition lasted in France, but in America the visual was directed toward the ostensible realism of stories. That has often served to explain the unadventurousness of Hollywood movies. But they may have gone further into the mystery of cinema to cater so much to plausibility. The long-term disorientation brought about by Hollywood is in obscuring the boundary between life and the lifelike.

The early American movie was made in a rush and sold frantically. The companies were more concerned with patent rights, equipment, and outlets than with creative decisions. The director was an on-set manager, responsible for getting something shot on time. He might have less to do with the work being made than the actors, the cameraman, even the writer or the company boss. D. W. Griffith accepted a position as director with Biograph only when that company could not use him as actor or writer. The creative functions in theater were taken for granted in cinema, and early films are seldom more than discreetly photographed theater. Méliès actually screwed his camera to the floor so that it would not be knocked over in the hurly-burly.

The transition from short impersonal films and small companies competing for outlets to longer films constructed around identifiable personalities and made and sold by a few large corporations occurred between 1915 and 1925. It is not an easy period to understand, despite the cut-and-dried legends that adorn it. One makes Griffith the father figure of cinema, whereas he may be only a man shaped by popular Victorian theater who discovered, along with several others, some of the devices of narrative fluidity. Historically, I do not think he matches some contemporaries—Louis Feuillade in France and Victor Sjöström in Sweden. The ingredients of Griffith's advance hardly amount to a personal style: They are ways of telling stories visually—the close-up, the moving camera, angled points of view, crosscutting, acceleration toward a climax, the edited whole. It is fanciful to claim that

Griffith invented any of these ploys, though possibly no one else organized them to such commercial effect.

Griffith was a lordly man who dominated the making of his films and clarified the role of an assertive director. As important as the refinement of film technique was his wish to control a project from scripting to the final editing. The greater the variety of shots he employed, the greater the nicety of arranging and trimming them. Consequently, Griffith's day continued after dark in the cutting rooms. He also began to tame the actors. The vigor of stage acting would itself have kept the film camera at a respectful distance. Griffith brought it closer and told players to be restrained. The best moments in his films are those with his actresses—the Gish sisters, Mae Marsh, Miriam Cooper, and Blanche Sweet—where we some-times feel that he has asked them simply (but daringly) to imagine what the character is feeling while he films them. The technique is repressive, but the effect is enlarging. There was room for the spectator now in the minds of those dis-traught ladies. He rehearsed his cast and he liked a regular crew who knew his methods and treated him as a commander —even as a genius.

Griffith is on an American stamp—it is a name everyone knows. In photographs he looks a sad, introspective man; he died a wreck in the city he had helped found, neglected by it and deploring its lost grace. But those are not reasons to elevate an innovator into a heroic artist, much less the first genius trampled upon by a callous system. Instead, we should notice how far *innovator, artist, great director, pioneer,* and *success* are terms forever in an involved dance in Hollywood. Griffith's films are often insufferable and could not have survived without the erotic undertone that comes from in-specting ladies in distress. His stories are flagrant melodrama, while the morality and philosophy behind them are anti-quated and threadbare. Although deeply reactionary, Grif-fith played on every fear of disruption—whether to law and order, chivalry and homestead, or the delicacy of the ladies. Cinema's lip-smacking hypocrisy over showing threats to middle-class calm has its start in Griffith, and his melodrama distances social and human realities. The "intolerance" he lamented was so vague that no one now values *Intolerance* as a commentary on human nature. *The Birth of a Nation* has a picture-book view of history, unquestioning endorsement of bourgeois homilies, distaste for blacks, and, worst of all, more respect for sensationalism than history, ideas, or adult characters.

The sentimental suggestions that *The Birth of a Nation* also inaugurated an art do not bear scrutiny; but Griffith's film was a turning point in the development of an entertainment industry. Rather than simply offer spectacle, wonders, and the crammed activity afraid of losing our attention, Griffith involved the viewer through length, sequence, modulation of pace, and the attachment of real people in the dark to human images in the transient arrangements of light on a screen. Griffith left the Biograph studio determined to make longer films, and in 1914 shot the three-and-a-half-hour movie, *The Birth of a Nation,* which was released in 1915.

It was seven times longer than the longest film that had been available in America: It meant the end of watching movies for instant gratification and the beginning of cinema as a reflective experience. There is an analogous difference between anecdotes and novels, but it is dangerous to believe that neoliterary narrative eclipsed wonderment. Hollywood soon saw itself as a storytelling business and sought what it called "realism" to underpin the stories. But it was not long before the system became known as a dream factory, and that indicates something deeper than realism still functioning. It may be that Hollywood took flight on a technology that assisted daydreaming; fantasies could be realized; the lazy fantasist could relax in the warmth and provided manifestations of a movie house.

In those first riotous years the pattern was mock-industrial: Film footage was a raw material and finished films were commodities to be sold, hired, or exchanged. It is as if no one in the business had time to look at what was on the film. Equipment was often unreliable, every invention was in danger of being pirated, and film-makers were beset by the inefficiency or unavailability of resources and materials. Méliès first realized the trickery possible with movies when film jammed in his camera and was exposed several times over. In New York, the tumult of small companies was rationalized by the Motion Picture Patents Company. This was an outwardly respectable protection racket prepared to employ strong-arm men to smash the premises and equipment of rogue exhibitors. For the figures around whom the industry grew were not makers of films, but men who owned or leased outlets and who had to find fresh feet of film to push into them.

The Patents Company was formed in 1908 by the amalgamation of several companies, including Biograph. They had an exclusive contract with Kodak for film stock and they took it upon themselves to license projectors and charge ten cents for every foot of film that went through the gate for public showing. It anticipated the way organized crime would later thrive on illicit liquor and protection money from the places where it was sold or consumed. The movie business attracted gangsters, lawyers to steer corporations in and out of statute, and accountants who could legally misrepresent their clients' affairs. One way of exercising the "wild one" in America was to put him to work at street level for a profitable corporation. Organized crime in America is popularly traced to Chicago and the trade in booze, but the system was pioneered in New York with movies. Although the Patents Company was overthrown, the struggle for freedom taught the founding fathers every necessary wriggle of enterprise. They soon evolved a far more comprehensive monopoly with less need of the muscle and conniving that made New York so lively in the early years.

Before the First World War, California was four days' train ride from New York—another continent, and a safer refuge than the Florida Jack Lemmon and Tony Curtis go to from Chicago in *Some Like It Hot*. That was not its only attraction. New York State—where Griffith learned to make fifteen-minute film tales—had mixed weather. In winter it was hardly passable and best suited to polar fictions, or the ice-floe climax of *Way Down East*. In California there was a bounty of sunshine and, within a reasonable distance, seashore, gentle countryside, mountains, and desert, as well as a budding metropolis, Los Angeles, with streets wide and empty enough for Keystone car chases. For film-makers light is a raw material like stock, and California was awash with light. The glowing appearance of Hollywood movies is the luster you see on an orange, the twinkle in surf, and the glamorous dappling of suntan. In California, luxury and bliss seep into the American movie, and that light beckoned people westward until California became the most populous state in the union, and a name that makes us think of sunniness. That motif in humanist art, of light being the instrument of enlightenment, turns to parody in California where light is also the illumination of great cities holding back the night, the light coloring fruit in supermarkets, the light of the spotlight that says some people are lovelier, and the light that carries the myth of feeling flesh to a blank screen.

Some film-making had been going on in California since 1907 when Francis Boggs and Thomas Persons made a version of *The Count of Monte Cristo*, cramming Dumas's novel into less than fifteen minutes of flickering light. Griffith went there in 1910, and in 1911 the Nestor Company built the first studio in Hollywood. The place was then only thirty years old and had no more than four thousand inhabitants. Struggling to keep distinct from Los Angeles, it was obliged to become a district of the metropolis in 1910 in return for an ensured water supply. (Roman Polanski's *Chinatown* alludes to the sinuous part of water in the local politics of southern California.)

It was in 1913 that Hollywood had destiny dumped upon it when Cecil B. De Mille went there to make *The Squaw Man*. De Mille liked to walk with history and it is appropriate that the director of Moses' descent from the mountain with the tablets should have attached himself to the founding of the industry's home. Because he belonged to the grouping that would become Paramount, *The Squaw Man* ensured Hollywood's future. Within half a dozen years, the majority of American films were made from a base near Los Angeles. Griffith took his crew and repertory company there to make *The Birth of a Nation* and it was the first of his films that actually opened in California, in January 1915.

By then the Patents Company had been broken by antitrust laws, and a new order was borne by men who had opposed the company. They were rarely film-makers, but immigrant businessmen, many from lowly origins. Their beginnings in America are still shrouded in the vagueness that descends on the early hardships of tycoons—and on the hardships they inflicted on others. In a Hollywood movie on the life of Adolph Zukor or Louis Mayer, a montage would blur those robust years with cheerfulness. For business was one of several subjects simplified by Hollywood on the assumption that it was too prosaic or unintelligible for the audience. This does not mean that the Hollywood major studios had skeletons in their cupboards. But when the bosses became some of the most famous businessmen in America, it was not easy for the onlooker to see where they had come from. Sophisticated amusement at the crudity of a Goldwyn or a Mayer hinted that disreputable tycoons had not entirely forsaken the gutter. This suspicion encouraged a superior look westward from eastern intellectuals. They had a picture of Hollywood—correct in most details—run by foreigners, Jews, people who spoke dreadful English, had little evident education or "culture," yet "got at" the minds of the people. Even enterprising Americans were taken aback by such influence falling to archetypal immigrants. To this day, there persists the notion of movies hanging on the whim of cigar-chewing slobs who talk like Akim Tamiroff. The irony is that the tycoons are portrayed in terms of their own creation.

Two of them began in partnership: Marcus Loew, a New Yorker, son of an Austrian, and Adolph Zukor, born in Hungary in 1873. Loew left school at age nine, in 1879, and ten years later Zukor sailed to America to escape poverty. Both men were in the fur business in New York, and in 1903 Zukor diversified, buying a few amusement arcades in East Coast cities. A year later, Loew joined him and Loew's Consolidated had interests in vaudeville as well as arcades. Zukor fought the Patents Company and in 1912 he set up on his own in a company called Engadine. Independence left Zukor with too few films for his arcades and so he imported a movie from Europe—*Queen Elizabeth,* with Sarah Bernhardt—and then formed a subsidiary to make his own films. These were a way of keeping his selling enterprise supplied, and not an end in themselves. Here we can appreciate the looming effect on film-makers of men who had learned the business in small cinemas taking the public's money. Zukor's company was called Famous Players and its plan was to film Broadway actors in snippets from plays and circulate these records to all the parts of America from which Broadway was geographically and socially remote. Four years later, Famous Players merged with Jesse Lasky Feature Plays, a company of similar intent, founded by Lasky, De Mille, and Samuel Goldfish, a Polish glove merchant. Famous Players-Lasky had a distribution company called Paramount, a name that was soon judged more impressive than any other.

Loew stayed in exhibition and distribution, and it was

not until 1920 that he purchased the Metro Company to manufacture films. Four years later there occurred the most significant merger in Hollywood's history when Metro picked up two hyphens, the Goldwyn and Mayer companies, and found a cowardly lion who would roar on cue. The Goldwyn Company was the result of a brief alliance between Goldfish —edged out of Paramount by the domineering Zukor—and the Selwyn brothers. By 1924, Goldfish had become Goldwyn and moved on to splendid independence. The Mayer Company was the creation of Louis B. Mayer, born in Russia in 1885 and another humble immigrant. He had a junk and garbage business in Massachusetts and in 1907 he bought a cinema at Haverhill that was the beginning of a New England chain. Mayer made a killing on the local distribution rights for *The Birth of a Nation,* and he started production himself in 1917.

The other major companies grew up in similar ways. William Fox was born in Hungary in 1879 and shipped to America before he could walk. He too started in the garment business and set up a film exchange in New York, a glorified swapshop where he took a cut on every transaction. He began to make films in 1912 and three years later he formed the Fox Film Corporation, with Theda Bara as a principal asset. Fox himself was later pushed out of his own business and he watched, from bankruptcy, as Fox merged with Twentieth Century, established in 1933 by Joseph Schenck and Darryl F. Zanuck. Zanuck, an American born in 1902, had been a writer, a producer, and then head of production at Warner Brothers. These four brothers—Harry, Albert, Sam, and Jack —were the sons of a Polish shoe-repairer. Harry was born in Poland, the others in various parts of North America as the family roamed after trade. In 1904, the brothers ran a traveling movie show, and separately or in company they were in distribution, exhibition, production, and exchanges until they congregated after the war. They had hard times and might have foundered but for the gamble with sound-on-film, rewarded in 1927 with *The Jazz Singer* and a new public sensation that intensified the naturalism of the movies. The last major was Universal, founded by Carl Laemmle, a German who emigrated to America in his teens and worked in clothing and jewelry. He went into nickel-odeons and cinemas and his Independent Motion Picture Company led the fight against the Patents Company. It became Universal in 1912, opening its California studio—Universal City—in 1915.

These were men of unblunted energy and egotism, and most of them lived on after the glory of their industry, surviving even their own mistakes. The movie business was theirs, yet "art of film" courses usually ignore them. It is vital, however, to understand the role of unequivocal businessmen in the history of Hollywood, a city-state run by side-street traders. Loew died in 1927, and Sam Warner went the same year, exhausted by the problems of early sound. But Goldwyn lived till 1974 with a proud studio that produced, among others, two versions of *Stella Dallas, Arrowsmith, Roman Scandals, Wuthering Heights, The Best Years of Our Lives, The Secret Life of Walter Mitty, Guys and Dolls,* and *Porgy and Bess.* Mayer stayed at MGM until 1951, and died six years later. Zukor died while this book was being written, and Zanuck is still alive, proud no doubt of a son who produced *Jaws.*

In the twenties and early thirties, Zukor's name had been on most Paramount films, and he rode out changes in ownership and control until he was so old that he was made chairman emeritus. Never as interested in pictures as Goldwyn, never identified with particular films, Zukor shows the aptitude for power in American cinema. He was instrumental in setting up one of the great majors—creatively perhaps the most interesting, what with Lubitsch, Von Sternberg, and Mitchell Leisen—and, not much bigger than a dwarf, he lasted longer than most of the stars his studio made. In *The Last Tycoon*, written by Scott Fitzgerald in 1940–41, when Zukor was in his late sixties, there is a portrait of a wizened tycoon, named Marcus, who is lifted out of his chair by a personal waiter but dances every night with a girl a third his age. That careful allocation of energy must have been shared by Marcus and Zukor, and this hardened business shell is not unlike the laconic self-sufficiency of the "cool" movie hero—Gary Cooper, Bogart, or even Clint Eastwood:

> Old Marcus still managed to function with disquieting resilience. Some nerve-atrophying instinct warned him of danger, of gangings up against him—he was never so dangerous himself as when others considered him surrounded. His gray face had attained such immobility that even those who were accustomed to watch the reflex of the inner corner of his eye could no longer see it. Nature had grown a little white whisker there to conceal it; his armor was complete.

Fitzgerald's unfinished novel is often read as a critique of Hollywood or, in the words of his young narrator, a book to dispel the myths about the movie city:

> My father was in the picture business as another man might be in cotton or steel, and I took it tranquilly. At the worst I accepted Hollywood with the resignation of a ghost assigned to a haunted house. I knew what you were supposed to think about it but I was obstinately unhorrified.

But what we have of the novel is enchanted with Hollywood, no matter that Fitzgerald was a failure there as a scriptwriter, pained that he could not lay hands on the fame or money that Hollywood offered. The idealization of a shallow gangster turned wistful richie in *The Great Gatsby* is repeated in Fitzgerald's Hollywood hero, Monroe Stahr.

Fitzgerald would have allowed no other old man in a novel to be as impregnable as Marcus. That studied detachment is movie armor, and both Gatsby and Stahr have the self-regarding romanticism typical of the star in close-up.

Stahr is derived from Irving Thalberg, the man responsible for production at Metro-Goldwyn-Mayer from the time of the merger to his death in 1936. There are many points in common: Both were diminutive, cultivated, and physically exhausted. Fitzgerald's account of a day in Stahr's life—mollifying hurt actors, regenerating dead scripts, lifting a director from the set, as if the man were his own jacket, scrutinizing the rushes, and tempering the coarse profiteering of the other executives—may do justice to Thalberg's command of scattered details. But the portrait is gilded in a way Hollywood would have admired. Stahr melts into Franchot Tone or Fredric March once he embarks on a soulful love affair—like Gatsby's, the reincarnation of an earlier, lost love —no matter that his schedules are already too crowded. He defends the making of some films that will lose money—though he has little thought of what those films might be—he is disturbed by a black he meets on the beach who dismisses the movies as irrelevant. Overall, he fulfills the liberal intellectual's hope for a cultured commercial genius who will make Hollywood respectable, still reach the millions—and employ that liberal intellectual writer.

Thalberg was out of the ordinary chiefly in style and bearing. His films are prestigious, glossy, and unadventurous; the MGM product now looks conservative and dilute beside pictures from Paramount and Warners. What impressed everyone who worked for Thalberg was his courtesy and the patina of taste, so rare in other executives, especially Louis Mayer, who hired Thalberg and to whom the "boy genius" was always responsible. Mayer was unabashedly most comfortable with Andy Hardy, but Thalberg's territory was not much more sophisticated and was often far from America—

in European costume films and the pseudo-China of *The Good Earth*.

Nothing so proved Thalberg in the eyes of Mayer as his decisive dismissal of Erich von Stroheim when that self-destructive but grandiose director made *Greed* to run ten hours. This story is so legendary that it is hard to trust details. A few years earlier, at Universal, Thalberg had already removed Stroheim from one project in a clash that signaled the humbling of the "great" director by the studio control system. Stroheim moved on to Metro in advance of the merger, and the extravagant *Greed* lay waiting as an early opportunity for Thalberg to assert himself. It was a grotesque confrontation of tidiness and creativity, and even now the reduced film opens with this war cry from Frank Norris's *McTeague* (the basis of *Greed*), which Stroheim surely identified with, and had too much vanity and too little wisdom to moderate. No doubt, Stroheim thought fatal uncompromise proved an artist; yet not many artists today would share this certainty of what the truth is:

> I never truckled; I never took off the hat to Fashion and held it out for pennies. By God, I told them the truth. They liked it or they didn't like it. What had that to do with me? I told them the truth. I knew it for the truth then and I know it for the truth now.

The battle was ridiculously theatrical and depended on two men courting their own image. Stroheim was "the man you love to hate," living on the legend of having been an officer in the Prussian army. He was emphatic and brutally handsome; he wore riding boots and a monocle and his hair was cropped short. At the end of the war he played ruthless German officers, and this authority stayed with him on set. I think it was tongue in cheek: Stroheim is an early example of the solemn fake; but, if challenged, his humor hardened and he began to insist on his own grandeur.

Thalberg was dapper, he dressed like an accountant, and his charm was as forceful as the power behind his decisions. *Greed* at ten hours was willfully perverse, but it was also a movie set against the grain of pleasing, digestible romance. It is about shaggy, intractable people, so caught in their own obsessions that they are incapable of a smooth front. The manner of the film is wonderfully naturalistic—it is the first American film that has not dated—and its subject is the acquisitiveness of ordinary people and the way security based on ownership warps the emotions. Despite melodrama and neurotic care with tiny detail—itself a sort of greed—*Greed* is a panorama of capitalist unhappiness and too robust for Hollywood's protective care of the audience. The aggressive honesty of treatment left no character with whom the audience could identify. Thus the bleak structure of relationships becomes inescapable. That is the strength of the movie, and a power Thalberg had to neutralize.

The "system" evident in Fitzgerald's tycoon is the unwitting influence of Hollywood styles and attitudes. Stahr is a more contradictory character than the studios would ever have employed, and so inconsistent that a finished *The Last Tycoon* would have had to reconcile Fitzgerald's observations of Hollywood with his unconscious debt to its imagery. But nothing makes the disharmony more vibrant than Fitzgerald's feeling that the movies are important and exciting for America. Still, here are some of the several Stahrs in the firmament Fitzgerald called Monroe (thereby laying an unwitting trail for another luminary):

"That's a question of merchandise," said Stahr. "I'm a merchant. I want to buy what's in your mind."

Though Stahr's education was founded on nothing more than a night-school course in stenography, he had a long time ago run ahead through trackless wastes of perception where very few men were able to follow him.

He had flown up very high to see, on strong wings, when he was young. And while he was up there he had looked on all the kingdoms, with the kind of eyes that can stare straight into the sun. Beating his wings tenaciously—finally frantically—and keeping on beating them, he had stayed up there longer than most of us, and then, remembering all he had seen from his great height of how things were, he had settled gradually to earth.

He was a marker in industry like Edison and Lumière and Griffith and Chaplin. He led pictures way up past the range and power of the theater, reaching a sort of golden age, before the censorship.

The mixture of common sense, wise sensibility, theatrical ingenuity, and a certain half-naïve conception of the common weal which Stahr had just stated aloud, inspired him to do his part, to get his block of stone in place, even if the effort were foredoomed, the result as dull as a pyramid.

The oracle had spoken. There was nothing to question or argue. Stahr must be right always, not most of the time, but always—or the structure would melt down like gradual butter.

Stahr is a luminous American hero, wonderful but intangible. Perhaps Fitzgerald could not bear to entrust the movies to anyone with as little sensitivity to their potential as a real executive possessed. The wishful thinking in the characterization overrides the caustic view of a hollow charmer operating a self-perpetuating system and furnishing a pap product for the minds of millions. That shows the attraction of the idea of the movies, even for people whose cultural roots were far from California. Movies were not the biggest business in America, though in the twenties and thirties they were among the largest. But no other corporation system received a fraction of the publicity that the movies swam in. Movie people were underwater creatures—exaggeratedly slow and splendid, like swimmers—in a thick liquid of publicity, gossip, and merchandised lie that a secondary industry poured over them.

For many Americans, their most vivid tycoon, the colossus of industry, was a movie mogul—Mayer, perhaps, who was reputed to be the highest paid man in America, or Thalberg, extravagantly mourned by the industry when he died young. Such men were not especially sensitive or talented. But in their own lifetimes they found themselves at the center of a legend composed of a semimagical power over reality, arbitrary authority toward others, and the fabulous use of wealth. They were made to seem dauntingly more than human, and big business was colored by Hollywood's parade in its own spotlight. Think of stories of these moguls, and think how often they are concerned with an almost Roman power. There could not be so many stories unless people "needed" such momentous figures. Charles Foster Kane derives not only from William Randolph Hearst—a Californian institution, and a member of the movie colony, whose house, San Simeon, was evidence of the Hollywood art department invading domesticity—but also from public belief in attractive ruthlessness directing the businesses of entertainment and communication. The clearest example of this response to the tycoon—and of the tycoon's wish to be remote, unreal, and immaterial—is Howard Hughes, a man who made and liked movies for much of his life, and whose very existence was problematic for his last fifteen years.

Kane finishes his wife's sentence, "The people will think—what I tell them to think"; it is a line that Welles veils in ambiguity. For only in America are there such mixed feelings about that tyranny; only there is the ideological fear of corruptive power offset by the glow of charm—call it glamour, star appeal, or charisma—that comes from the powerful.

There is a film about Hollywood, made at MGM and directed by Vincente Minnelli, about a ruthless but compelling producer. The film is told in flashback, by a writer, an actress, and a director, all of whom he has betrayed professionally or personally. Yet after his sins have been retold, this trio cannot resist him, and they crowd to a telephone intrigued by his new project on which they will work together again. Hollywood is admitting its flaws, but in a way that romanticizes them. This equivocation is in the title of the film, which implies that exploitation is attractive: *The Bad and the Beautiful.*

As Hollywood grew, and its systematic speaking to the American public became more extensive, so there was disapproval and opposition from several quarters. Censorship was the result of fears over what the people might think and do if shown libertinism—but it only barred common cursing, semiundress, unpunished criminals, and happy adulterers. As to suggestiveness—the nerve system of movies—censors had no way of knowing how to operate. But these are the petty worries that obscure greater anxieties. There is an argument that Hollywood steadily trivialized the American mind. Thus, adjudicating whether a woman could or could not be seen in her slip curtailed the nature of a woman and made her less a person than a dummy waiting to be dressed. Real care might have questioned her whole life-style on celluloid and the way she was put on show.

The regular provision of palatable fantasies may even have persuaded people not to test tastes. When viewers were encouraged to imagine themselves as Valentino, Mary Pickford, or Clara Bow, then that pleasure could divert them from sensible thinking about their own lives. The Hollywood system was a way of making films—keeping the factory turning over—of distributing and selling them. It also provided attitudes and a manner of thinking, and the white lie that all things could be made as orderly, pleasant, and untroubling as the happy ending. Above all, cinema initiated the comfortable but erroneous thought that the mass could understand and manage its experiences. Compared with the arts, it simplified life and transmitted a graspable scheme for dealing with it. Unhappily, this coincided with the complication of our experience and lent itself to the tranquilizing smoothness of the merchants who wanted stability.

That stability is political as much as commercial. If America was once populated with malcontents, then how much care must have been taken to keep them pacified? And though America offered individualism, equality, life, liberty, and the pursuit of happiness, it did not quickly appreciate how far such ideals were contradictory. But that delay leads to the preservation of a docile mass.

Hollywood has often told stories about itself, and one of these is a fascinating commentary on democracy and public entertainment. The film is *Sullivan's Travels,* written and directed by Preston Sturges. It concerns a successful movie director who wakes up one morning, unhappy with his diet of inane comedies. Suddenly, he wants to show real people and suffering on the screen. His studio is skeptical, but Sullivan elects to dress up as a hobo and go off in search of unhappiness, so that he may understand it. Hitherto, his swimming pool has sheltered him. He travels and, in due course, ends up in a wretched rural prison. His spirits sink there and are only lifted by the odd chance the prisoners have to watch, and laugh at, a Laurel and Hardy comedy. When fate and an agile plot free him, he goes back to Hollywood, his faith in the system restored. Unhappiness is bad enough, he agrees, to leave well alone: The best thing the movies can do is give the miserable and unfortunate a chance to forget their troubles.

But when people for so long neglect their troubles, the

perplexity can be all the greater since they no longer know what is troubling them. Sullivan is permitted the blitheness of a child; the studio system seems parental—allowing him an outing so that he may discover the "truth" for himself; and America is made into the garden of the factory.

III

THE ARTISTS

*Life Achievement Award, founded by
the American Film Institute*

AMERICA HAS DONE WHAT IT COULD TO NEUTRALIZE THE ARTIST
and guessed that patronage might be more devastating than
neglect. That grows out of the fear that an isolated artist is
a dangerous heretic because of the affront he gives to comfortable understanding. He denies the orthodoxy that American idealism can be translated into material goods, comfort,
and security. In the democratic tradition, everyone is now
ushered into the society of artists and no one is excluded
from the salvation of a "God-given creative talent." Education has encouraged the dull and the lazy with the thought
that they are artists, or artistlike. Some sort of compromise
is then reached in school in which the system believes that a
kid is "fulfilling" himself with absentminded and occasional
paintings, no matter that he reads or writes haltingly. Ameri-

can academia is a large patron of art, artists, and the complacency that helps individuals to regard themselves as artists, through the practical but silly process of paying them to instruct those kids. When everyone is "creative," what need is there for anyone to be an artist?

That is a disenchanted account, but in America no idealist is unable to do the handstand that makes him an entertaining cynic: Groucho Marx ridiculed money and sex with the rabid deadpan of someone needing to hide his real absorption in *l'argent et l'amour fou.* The horrible jokiness of the dedicated does not conceal their own disarray; it only denotes men split apart, still having to button up their appearances. Hollywood has its version of the broken man. He is the writer in movies, lamenting the way he has to watch his finely wrought works ironed into unwrinkled smoothness, suffer the interference of vain actors and actresses, be respectful of stupid executives who treat him like dirt, live in the scorching Philistia of Los Angeles, sit in the sun and pretend to enjoy it, submit to having his own name on trash, and for what? A small fortune.

At the very least, the movies have undermined our confidence in art. Some of the most provocative creator/critics of established attitudes to art—Duchamp, Cage, Warhol—have been stimulated by the bogus nature of the artist, his confessed lack of integrity, and the masquerade that encourages—all of which are recurring issues in the American imagination. They owe some of their playfulness to the state of mind stirred by the "dramatics" of art when it is Cornel Wilde as Chopin, Paul Muni as Zola, or Kirk Douglas as Van Gogh. We enjoy the comedy of those who have not read *Anna Karenina* but who are partisans of Garbo or Vivien Leigh in the "role"; or of those who no longer need to see Van Gogh's paintings, having witnessed the CinemaScope gallery of images, prints, and copies in *Lust for Life.*

Lust for Life moves me to tears, despite Parker Tyler's resounding charge that it cheats:

> The "point" of *Lust for Life* is dismayingly simple: van Gogh failed in everything but painting, and the fact that he even seemed, during his lifetime, to fail in that is supposed to reinitiate mortally self-satisfied audiences into the sublime irony that some champions, either in bed or with their boots on, die before their enviable prowess is recognized for what it is.

I think that the movie—whether it belongs to Kirk Douglas, Vincente Minnelli, or MGM—provides the materials for an appreciation of Van Gogh's paintings, while describing him as a wretched and self-destructive man. Douglas's performance is serious and uncomfortably identified with the pain in creativity; it goes far beyond the effete moodiness of Wilde's Chopin. I doubt that the mortally self-satisfied are reassured by the film. And yet . . . the turbulence is clothed in the sumptuousness of a big studio film. Tyler's sly confusion of Kirk and Vincent is inherent in the system, and the film does musicalize the heroic melodrama of Irving Stone's novel. Furthermore, my fondness for it would not stop the film serving as a convenient facade for "culture": like the hollow spines of Henry James that slide back to disclose bottles of liquor.

Hollywood has bowdlerized the artist, just as it has God, the businessman, and the politician: The religious epic is as sententious as biopics about "Great Dead Artists/Presidents/ Benefactors of the World." And it is disconcerting that films, which move and excite many of us, have reduced the seriousness possible in art by mimicking its chief thrust—arousing the imagination—only to leave it unsatisfied and insecure. Hollywood always wanted the influence over minds exercised by art, and the credit with posterity. But it would not risk failure, the intensity of work, or the solitariness of creativity.

It is an obvious point, but one often overlooked in these days when Hawks, Fuller, and Sirk are written and talked about as if they were fully fledged artists, that virtually no film made in Hollywood has been initiated by an individual. We think, as a matter of course—no doubt influenced by the scenes of "revelation" some films copy from the Bible—that Beethoven was inspired to compose the Ninth Symphony and, over a long, difficult, and montagelike agony, arrived at notes on paper that an audience could hear performed. *Paradise Lost,* Goya's paintings, or *Middlemarch* are all presumed to have germinated in such a way.

But that scheme is too easy. Beethoven would not have turned to the symphony had he not lived in a time of the symphonic form. Artists are directed by the state of their art. Nor is any "finished," "performed," or "published" work of art an assured triumphing over all difficulty. Joyce's *Ulysses* has preserved printer's errors, and scrutiny of his proofs shows how restlessly he changed his mind. We honor the legend of an insatiable search for resolution in artworks. But if that is so, we should abide by some imperfection in "finished" works. And since no artist has yet found a lasting way of working without eating, then he cannot be as indifferent to money as he would like, or as some of his characters manage to be—in literature itself there are perpetual pensions, but writers are as bare as free lances. Many artists were successful in their own lifetimes; they enjoyed that success and incorporated it in their work: Dickens, Stravinsky, and Picasso were comfortably off for much of their working lives. Their popular acceptance may indicate some larger failure—though that is a dangerously precious dogma. It may equally force us to weigh labeled popular artists more carefully—say, Dashiell Hammett, Cole Porter, or Vincente Minnelli.

Nevertheless, the urge to create faces daunting obstacles for a young Minnelli—far easier to be a performer. The writer "needs" only pen and paper, and so on. Whereas, a would-be director will want equipment, film stock, money to process that stock, a studio, and others to help him. He cannot raise funds without a reliable prospect of selling the product: Thus, immediately, creative inspiration is infused with commercial reckoning. Today it is possible for an individual to make a film on his own, buying a super-8mm camera and having to satisfy no outside requirements. That facility has reassessed "underground" or "experimental" cinema, and it may yet leave the bulk of film-making underground, private, and unseen. But still a majority of aspiring film students would like to make big films that are technically sweet enough for large audiences.

The costs of such a venture are often criticized on the grounds of the money paid to stars. But the companies making big films have not inflated their costs artificially; on the contrary, they have struggled to keep them down. Expensiveness derives not only from the salaries of skilled or unique contributors. It was always a fruit of the huge success of films, a way of controlling and sharing the prodigious take. Salaries were the result of the early boom in movies. Only later, as the audience retracted, did that scale become a burden to add to rising costs of production. The equipment involved—for shooting, recording, and editing—is refined and delicate; the manufacturing effort is intense and perfectionist, and the product wears out slowly. Films require costumes, furnishings, and buildings; they call for the construction of rooms, streets, and the plausible outlines of castles or skyscrapers.

The "extravagance" of such items is very questionable. Those stars paid the highest salaries only lasted if their films recouped the investment, and audiences in the cinema have always responded to the visible shell of a winning personality. Reservations about what stars were paid did not obstruct star appeal: It may simply be that envy and a puritanical disdain go hand in hand with fantasizing.

Furthermore, Hollywood always put riches and luxury among its most appealing offerings. Audiences have luxuriated in movie rooms, clothes, and life-styles remote from their own; they have often rejected worlds as shabby or uneventful as those they inhabit—once it was almost a definition of popular film that it had sensation and glamour, and that something was always happening. The construction of buildings or the purchase of ships and planes often allows the audience the vicarious pleasure of breaking up these things: This is the release provided for every man mortified by a scratch on his own car. Suppressed destructiveness in anxious property-owners shows in movie car chases. The expense of movies is not incidental or decorative: It has to do with the liberating nature of the form. Prodigality with money and the unhindered destruction of precious or costly things are elements of movie entertainment and of the most penetrating fantasies. *The Towering Inferno,* for instance, encourages our trust in secure buildings, our fear that they are dangerous, and the glee that witnesses lavish destruction.

But a realization of that was rare within the system; perhaps it could not have flourished honestly with it. Outsiders alleged that idiots led the movies, but they misunderstood the scope for people who stopped short of philosophical dilemma, and who would act instead; successful presidents may require the same reliance on momentum. What brought about a system was, simply, the way in which investment and speculation were too great for any individual, let alone a self-conscious and halfway egotistical artist-director. Thus, Hollywood films were "made by" the most memorable part of the credits: at MGM, the lion; at Paramount, the snow-topped mountain; at RKO, the radio beacon; at Columbia, a rather glamorous Statue of Liberty—liberty of the red-light district.

Irving Thalberg required that his name not appear on films and won the humbug luster of modesty by intimating that credits were a child's game played at his feet. Directors were invariably named last and given responsibility in reviews, but the exaggeration of their power is one of the more serious fallacies misleading the study of Hollywood today. In part, it is the old humanist urge to celebrate an author; but it is also the pretense that the system is not supreme. If a critic says movies belong to directors it sustains his discriminating eye for style and meaning.

In the previous chapter, I referred to directors like Griffith and Stroheim inaugurating a narrative fluency that was the chief impetus for the movie industry becoming the monopoly of a handful of large corporations: MGM, Paramount, Universal, Warners, and Fox. These companies were involved in production and distribution. They had factory studios where staff and machines had to be kept in work to justify the overheads; and they had an East Coast operation that marketed the films all over the world and dictated orders to the productive base—more Joan Crawford, less Garbo, cut costs by 7½ percent this year in view of raised interest rates on Wall Street. The control center of the industry remained in New York, and the accountants there mistrusted the West Coast practitioners every bit as much as did the American intelligentsia, the writers, actors, and critics who were torn between the acid put-down of Hollywood's vulgarity and envy of the salaries paid there. In turn, Hollywood actors resented this superiority, while the Californian system was irritated by remote control. The rift contributes to the East-West polarity that has gradually overtaken the old difference between North and South.

It is neither harsh nor whimsical to compare the West Coast factory with the process that produced automobiles: For much of this century, movies and cars have mingled utility and an unconscious appeal to fantasy for many Americans. A new car has the sheer and functional smoothness of a movie; it is the vehicle that physically transports us, while movies shift us without need of energy to overcome friction. It is fitting that America should have brought the two together in the drive-in movie theater, where the technologies confront one another: The image is exaggeratedly fake because of the open air, and the audience is further isolated in their capsules.

The movie factory depended on certain raw materials: an acceptable working script; a chosen cast of players; studio space and the proper sets, costumes, and props; cameras loaded with film and served by a competent crew; the various other necessary technicians; and a director.

These people did not gather by chance; the system organized them, and in so doing often overshadowed the duties of a nominal "director." We have foreseen this in the clash between Thalberg and Stroheim. Griffith had defined the power of the director over the finished product, and his generation of directors had a facility that changed the form commercially. But the system wanted the facility without yielding control to the director. Not every director was as self-indulgent as Stroheim, but a creator is always tempted to do a scene over again until it is "right," and he is victim of the fresh thoughts for another scene that strike him as he sees an expression on his heroine's face. That way in which novelists admit that a novel starts to "write itself" is impossible in making a film when the studio space is held until Friday and Widmark has to be on location in Arizona on Monday. Anna Karenina could have lingered in Tolstoi's mind forever, but a successful star has other assignments and may already be jaded from having to bend to so many fantasies. Not many writers can read their own novels, for fear of seeing mistakes or missed opportunities; imagine, then, the frustration of a film director with his "signed" works. No wonder many directors learned a protective indifference to their product; this is only the alienation of the assembly worker from the automobiles that pass him by.

I am not suggesting that a Griffith was ever free to film whatever he wanted, or that subsequent directors meekly did as they were told. Nevertheless, the task in film-making that is now studied and celebrated was restricted by the studio policy that men like Thalberg instituted. In *The Last Tycoon,* Stahr plays with a story conference, making the writers, director, and producer dance to his tune. At one point, the director reflects:

> Broaca put his hand up to his half-closed eyes—he could remember "when a director was something out here," when writers were gag-men or eager and ashamed young reporters full of whiskey—a director was all there was then. No supervisor—no Stahr.

Thalberg had only acted on the way; before metal reached the assembly worker, someone had to decide what sort of car was being made, or for whom it would be a "vehicle." The initiating impulse, at MGM say, was twofold: to maintain the momentum of activity and to provide subjects for the star personalities who were the selling point for the public. MGM boasted, with daft hyperbole, of more stars than there were in heaven. Among actresses it had Garbo, Joan Crawford, Norma Shearer, and Jean Harlow. Four distinct women: an aristocrat, a working girl, a lady, and a broad. Those are cramping stereotypes that the actresses often resented, but the studio seldom departed from a successful role for one of its stars. As that role was repeated over the years, it could become very mannered or very simplified. It might weary the star to dullness but it gave the audience an unearned and unrequited familiarity with the star.

This "intimacy" could be hypocritical and grotesque, and several human beings were crushed in the embrace of star personalities and their following. Fatty Arbuckle was ruined by a scandal suggesting he might be as scapegrace as "Fatty." The romantic solitude of Garbo in films eventually carried her away from the public altogether. John Barrymore ended his life unsure whether he was drunk or playing a drunk, and there is a famous wound in Marilyn Monroe's life when her director Laurence Olivier told her firmly but kindly to be sexy.

Commercially, the imprisonment of the star seemed astute, yet it was nervously protective. One can argue that there was only one generation of stars: the people who made their names between 1920 and the early 1940s. A few bloomed later, but never with the same intensity. Stars could not compete with themselves, allowing only one age of absolute monarchs. The Hollywood film does not reproduce life's conflict and interaction, because the star was always dwelt upon by a treatment that promoted self-centeredness. Stars hold firm like citadels and glare out at one another. Thus, the generation of stars could not handle competition, and in the 1950s one had the unhappy spectacle of aging stars appearing in romantic situations with ever younger supports. By then, of course, the cinema was not the sole source of stars: The fifties had some in the movies—Elizabeth Taylor, James Dean, Audrey Hepburn, and Monroe—but their competitors were from other fields: Lucille Ball (on TV), Elvis, and a little later, the Kennedys, Che, Mao, the Beatles, Muhammad Ali, and Farrah.

Stage actors were stuffy about the movies: They disapproved of the way film required no acting or training and did not confine its stars to genteel affluence. You had only to stand there and bank it! They claimed that Gary Cooper or John Wayne on stage would be embarrassing. Cooper himself lived with the fan magazine legend of someone bewildered at getting away with doing so little. Yet on film he was riveting and dignified, whereas many theater actors seemed fussy and self-important. No one invented the star, but the realization of an exploitable constancy in a screen personality came from the studio bosses and producers. It was part of their conservatism to cling on to anything that worked. Probably none of them had the wit to put the insight into words, but in the cinema it is the spectator who pretends he might be someone else. The star therefore has to be a hollow receptacle into which millions can believe they are pouring themselves.

The star system was a denial of film's aptitude for change, but it catered to the private metamorphoses going on amid the audience. So it was that the studios hunted for subjects or properties that suited the persona of one of their stars. The larger stars might scout for their own vehicles, and there were some novels written with this or that star in the author's mind. The stars themselves were slaves or freemen, depending on how they chose to handle their own working status. They were under contract to a studio, usually for seven-year stretches. That ensured them a huge income, but obliged them to make whatever film the studio decided on, or even consent to being loaned out temporarily in some deal between companies in which the studio gained far more than the star.

An uneasy relationship could exist between moguls and stars. On the one hand, there was a band of proprietors, fat little men, faces pinched from counting and shy of the limelight; on the other, a coterie renowned for beauty, glamour, and the preposterous equation that looks meant character. Some of the stars would have been stretched to find other work; they had few skills and little education. Yet looks, the studio's decision to promote them, and the star's willingness to be used could make him a household name and suddenly wealthy. Thrift or meanness in a mogul did not admire extravagance in an impetuous star, and they often regarded their own creations as spoiled brats whose widely reported indulgence put social stability at risk.

For the star there could be indignity. Your face might be lifted and amended, a new name invented for you, your life story revised, your private affairs dictated. Awkward spouses were paid off, inconvenient pregnancies were aborted, unwholesome histories were smothered—and held in reserve by the studio against the star's pliant behavior. But after sound, actors were hired from the legitimate theater. Many of them had been well educated and carefully trained, and felt uncomfortable with the pressure of public adulation deliberately stimulated by the studio in press leaks, contrived scandals, and the dizzy fabrications of the fan magazine. It may be that only an unambitious or slow-witted actor could endure the monotony of screen performances. Those more versatile and imaginative—Bette Davis, Spencer Tracy, Katharine Hepburn—might be distressed by the swelling of a "persona" that did not remind them of themselves. Some stars had had to submit to the ramifications of civilized slavery. They were owned, trained, and used by the bosses, and yet when they looked in the surrounding mirror—the public—they could not recognize themselves.

How long could the insignificant admire loveliness before resentment crept in? The sexual possessiveness of the movies —for both the tycoon and the person in the dark—turns on the aphrodisiac of power, and makes love and sexuality into warped expressions of ownership. In *The Deer Park*, Norman Mailer describes a boss, Herman Teppis, who maneuvers and manipulates the "image" of two young stars, both shockingly dissolute and mercenary compared with the ingenue parts they play, and visits his disgust on a studio starlet ready to provide for him. The girl comes into his office by a private door, hopelessly in quest of a big break, but "Her mouth was painted in the form of broad bowed lips to hide the thin mouth beneath the lipstick":

Tentatively, she reached out a hand to finger his hair,

and at that moment Herman Teppis opened his legs and let Bobby fall to the floor. At the expression of surprise on her face, he began to laugh. "Don't you worry, sweetie," he said, and down he looked at that frightened female mouth, facsimile of all those smiling lips he had seen so ready to serve at the thumb of power, and with a cough, he started to talk. "That's a good girlie, that's a good girlie, that's a good girlie," he said in a mild little voice, "you're an angel darling, and I like you, you're my darling darling, oh that's the ticket," said Teppis.

Not two minutes later, he showed Bobby genially to the door. "I'll call you when to see me again, sweetheart," he said.

Alone in his office, he lit a cigar, and pressed the buzzer. "What time is the conference on *Song of the Heart*?" he asked.

"In half an hour, sir."

"Tell Nevins I want to see his rushes before then. I'll be right down."

Teppis ground out the cigar. "There's a monster in the human heart," he said aloud to the empty room. And to himself he whispered, like a bitter old woman, close to tears, "They deserve it, they deserve every last thing that they get."

I do not intend to catalog the humiliations of great stars, and I am not suggesting that such exploitation was suffered by many screen actresses. But the possibility existed, as in any slave situation, and Mailer's gallant rescue of Marilyn Monroe's life from chaos shows the interlocking of whore and goddess in the career of the female star. Unstable people were broken: Judy Garland was so valuable to MGM that, while she was still an adolescent, the studio fostered the hysterical activity and depression, and its dependence on drugs, that killed her so early and meant that she made only four films in the twenty years after MGM discarded her. Yet other stars have come through as intact as anyone can hope to be. Fred Astaire, James Stewart, Barbara Stanwyck, Cary Grant, Myrna Loy, James Cagney, Mae West are all, as this is written, alive, prosperous, and revered. I cannot say they are happy: That is as problematic as infamous beginnings.

Film stars once upon a time could hardly move without being reported, and many reacted by becoming recluses or show-offs. It was alleged, often, that they were overpaid, irresponsible, and "ruined" by their magnified reputations. But much of this is the envy of the very people who used them in their own fantasies. An impossible burden was thrust upon the stars. If so many remained recognizably human, that may be a sign of special stamina and resilience. Actors are not commonplace people. In groups they can be aggressively mannered and keen for admiration. They take open risks in the calculated make-believe that everyone else indulges more secretly.

Nor should we underestimate the remorseless pressure of being photographed. Even today, 130 or so years after the first photographs, many people are reluctant to have their picture taken and share the superstition of some "primitive" peoples that photography steals the soul. Perhaps it does, or makes the soul a more rubbery thing than we credited before photography. Movie stars are the most photographed creatures in the world, living in a reflecting labyrinth where they are always faced with a version of themselves. Ask yourself how comfortable you are with many mirrors. Have you ever despaired at the sight of yourself in home movies? Is it any wonder that the Hollywood picture has often dealt with the splitting of identity that can follow such massive celebration of appearance? Or that the mirror is a regular instrument of social and personal contempt in the American movie?

Stardom is so diffuse that it seems academic to wonder

whether stars were the creative or artistic force in their films. It is a twentieth-century phenomenon transmitting personality to the masses: Politicians are starry today, cultivating show-biz looks and styles and even training for higher things in the movies. Stardom may be the most significant consequence of Hollywood, inseparable from the political history of the century, so that the artistic impact is dwarfed in comparison. The advances of civilization, and of political structures to accommodate them, have in some ways left us more primitive than we were. The need for stars is the religious propensity of an unbelieving people, and it requires an attitude to character that is submissive and uncritical.

The analysis of character in the nineteenth-century novel achieves a subtle balance of the moralistic, the psychological, and the social. By contrast, stardom in the movies projects a monolithic but shallow version of personality. In the larger cultural sense, stardom diminishes the worth of people and heralds the media power by which a few dominate the many. A democracy with a compelling leader and a state of crisis is not far from a willing tyranny. Roosevelt is the first clear instance of the benevolent and inspiring populist dictator, and it cannot be chance that *Citizen Kane* was made during his administration. Stardom's effect is awesome: It is that coherent, marketed personalities can be bought by a mass of people, and that the coherence overrides our knowing that real personalities are unresolved. The confidence of actors has tempted us into acting: We need to present ourselves and can no longer simply be. Stardom is one more condition of knowing duplicity.

It goes without saying that the cinema audience went to see certain stars—or does it? Some stars were more popular than others; the audience, asked where they were going, would reply, "To the new Loretta Young," or whatever. They had no awareness of the director, the writer, or even the studio—which irked those parties and soured their attitudes to stars. But at the height of the movies, people went to see stars, and to be in the cinema. The lack of discrimination may be more important than any choice. Few spectators were faithful to one star; most, I suspect, enjoyed the idea of stardom and could stretch it to cover Lassie, King Kong, or even Jaws.

We flinch from calling stars artists, yet think how deep they lodged in our imaginations. Stories were conceived with them in mind, special scenes and dialogue catered to their strengths, and every studio had a proven way of photographing its house stars. Examine Hollywood in the thirties, and you will find Gable always a no-nonsense adventurer; Garbo had a vein of slow, enigmatic talk, as if she were speaking to someone unseen by the people on screen with her; and Dietrich was so habitually photographed with set lighting positions that she learned the arrangement herself and advised lighting cameramen on their own job. Our conception of a star is in terms of those cinematic devices. Bogart would not be as sardonic anywhere but at Warner Brothers. Claudette Colbert hardly ever allowed a right-side profile of herself—she had a faint scar—so that she is always looking one way, like a pilgrim. Equally, Roosevelt was photographed by the press so as not to expose his disability.

Not that everything was camouflage. The personality of stars does come through and, over a number of films, can be intriguing and creative. Gary Cooper never played a bad man, yet he managed that without sanctimoniousness and with such honesty that his integrity seemed the result of exhausting effort. Cary Grant did not hide a tetchy, intelligent, private man in his screen parts, and his romantic appeal rarely disowned a darker, disturbing character. Both of these men are triumphant, and that is essential in a star. Stars sometimes die, but they are not overcome; death is a sanctuary for their special energy. The audience identification is not betrayed. The stars are superhuman demonstrations of the efficacy of prominence, enterprise, honor, wit, and the dynamic of their bulging self: That is their sweetest lie.

Actresses are less dominant, as if women's duty to suffer was being forecast in movies. But their suffering does not diminish or crush them; it is their glory, the experience that displays them. Garbo's fated yearning is disappointed, but her passion sustains her and leaves us brooding over what might have been. Joan Crawford is let down by cads, cheats, and weaklings, but she only becomes more resolute. Happy, she might be deprived and ineffectual. The lovely frailty of Margaret Sullavan often perishes, but she is a martyr to romance and sensitivity; the illnesses that take her away are brought on by her own exposure to feeling. Bette Davis dies, goes crazy, or is found out, but all these fates clarify her masochistic identity. The natures of the stars are celebrated by the motion of their vehicles. They are not put to an unexpected test, and they do not encourage the spectator into responsibility for their decisions. I do not mean to suggest that art must always be didactic. But there is a shaping effect when any message to the people so regularly endorses escape from choice. In fantasy all choices are open, and no decisions need be made. The evanescence of moving images matches this dangerous freedom.

There is something disconcerting in stars having such great effect yet being so powerless: Manet's painting of the French prostitute, Olympe, catches the implacable gaze of the woman while she is tethered for inspection. Bette Davis once fled to England to escape the harsh contract system. But Warners pursued her to the London courts and, like a headstrong heiress in one of her own films, Davis was required to go back in disgrace and do as she was told. She was thwarted but glorified; her public understood the impulsive gesture and the studio found better parts for her. How often the stars seemed driven to behave in reality as if still in a scenario, and how imperceptibly that turned life into a screenplay.

The system devised by Thalberg was for a stream of properties to be bought or optioned for the stars. In the way of big business, Thalberg decided to delegate, and so he introduced a new breed—the supervisor or producer—responsible to him for every project in hand. A producer saw the property through the various stages of scripting, he had a budget and a schedule made, he assigned a director to the film and cast the remaining parts. It was also his duty to see that sets were built and costumes made ready. He supervised the shooting —so that neither the budget nor the schedule was overstepped —and he then had charge of the editing. At all stages, a Thalberg was likely to intervene, and many producers were only agents of the management, bent on speed, economy, and smoothing out the awkward independence of anyone along the line.

The producer is often the villain of Hollywood stories. He could be an opportunist, a place-seeker, a yes-man, a stealer of credit, a double-crosser, despised by the film-makers for ignorance of their craft and indifference to anything but the boss's whim. He is a brownnose in *The Last Tycoon*:

> Originally a man of some character, he was being daily forced by his anomalous position into devious ways of acting and thinking. He was a bad man now, as men go. At thirty he had none of the virtues which either gentile Americans or Jews are taught to think admirable. But he got his pictures out in time, and by manifesting an almost homosexual fixation on Stahr, seemed to have dulled Stahr's usual acuteness.

The producer has few advocates and fewer still who measure his achievement. That may be because the Thalbergs preferred nonentities and obedient instruments, or because anyone with more character soon looked for independence. And producers did achieve a latitude denied directors that could benefit from a broad grounding in most departments of film-making. David Selznick, I think, is the greatest of producers, not a profound creative intelligence, but a man who loved every facet of the craft, who was true to his own notion of the entertainment movie, and whose organizing enthusiasm kept others so busy that they had little time for creative schemes of their own. His product may or may not last, but it includes remarkable pictures: *A Bill of Divorcement, Little Women, King Kong, Viva Villa!, David Copperfield, The Garden of Allah, A Star Is Born, Nothing Sacred, The Prisoner of Zenda, Intermezzo, Gone With the Wind, Rebecca, Spellbound, Duel in the Sun, Portrait of Jennie.*

There is hardly a book with more flavor of the daily life of Hollywood at work, or which is shot through with such uncomplicated creative-commercial idealism, as *Memo from David O. Selznick.* It portrays a real American hero: the success who does not admit complexity greater than his energy, but revels in accomplishment. Selznick coordinates the network of skills and concerns in any movie; but his thorough matter-of-factness prefers skill to inspiration.

On *Gone With the Wind,* for instance, he fussed over how much to pay for Margaret Mitchell's novel and on the immense and pointless task of transferring it to the screen—without any thought that he should not be as faithful as possible, or that the filming of popular novels was not sensibly based on a direct process of translation. He was exhaustive in casting, testing every conceivable actress for Scarlett O'Hara and settling on a relative outsider in a mixture of desperation, self-conscious fatefulness, and quixotic hunch that owed something to every Hollywood movie about show biz. The hunt for Scarlett became a promotional tool for the film so that the discovery had to be heightened: Vivien Leigh's career may never have recovered from starting at such a fevered pitch. Selznick took great pains over sets and costumes, interested equally in authenticity and dramatic impact. He nagged Technicolor, his photographers, and every craftsman involved for more quality: Production values were held dear in Hollywood, for their own sake and for what they boasted of investment and taste. A film had texture and feel, like good cloth. Or so it seemed to men reared in the garment industry. Selznick used at least four directors on the film. The obsession that it turn out "great" was such that he traded away much of the eventual profit on the film in distribution agreements with MGM for Gable's reluctant services.

And *Gone With the Wind* did exceed everyone's expectations, partly because it was famous before it was released. It was another daringly long film; it was more expensive than anyone had reckoned—producer-kings could ignore their own budgets; and it had been talked about in the press for two years before the public saw it. Its success remained a Hollywood measure for over twenty years, yet it is an impersonal film, and that points to the inescapable authority of directors and the creative remoteness of producers.

Selznick is as bursting with vitality and invention as Cagney in the thirties, but no one could conscientiously support him as an American artist. Still, those intent on reappraising American cinema as the history of an art form ought to understand the regularity with which a Selznick met the industry's own standards of success. *Success* is a word that means different things in *Variety* and *Film Comment,* and Hollywood always read *Variety.* Selznick was not hostile to directors: He appreciated them, knew good workmen from bad, trusted them more than many producers did, but confused efficiency and vision, and could not tell tastefulness from style. His enthusiasm for movies did not give him the highest understanding of how film worked. If he had had it, he would have directed, and nothing reveals a man's instinct about the medium as much as the job he wants.

The producer and his apparatus could rationalize literary spark and novelty out of existence; they were dedicated to preventing excessive collaboration among their hired talents, lest that engender conspiracy. Their nervousness earned Hollywood a reputation for the unscrupulous sacrifice of quality or controversy to profit. The process helped to separate America's small intellectual class from its masses; the intelligentsia and the movies looked at one another askance in America until the 1960s. Reputable novels were bought and gutted; sometimes little more than a salable title reached the screen. The celebrated writers shipped to Hollywood were sat in cells to make Dostoevski or Zane Grey concise, decent, and digestible. They were unaware that other writers might be working on the same project. No one was more vulnerable than an author hoping to "write well" for the screen. Novelists did not always find the knack of dexterous construction and pert dialogue. Scott Fitzgerald labored to do his best and was hurt by the rejection of MGM producers. Cynicism was the surest protection, and weary loyalty the long-term response. William Faulkner quietly took his bit of the small fortune back to Mississippi, while Herman Mankiewicz noted the ridiculous ease of writing banal material and signaled his buddies in from New York for plunder in a famous cable to Ben Hecht:

WILL YOU ACCEPT THREE HUNDRED PER WEEK TO WORK PARAMOUNT? ALL EXPENSES PAID. THE THREE HUNDRED IS PEANUTS. MILLIONS ARE TO BE GRABBED OUT HERE AND YOUR ONLY COMPETITION IS IDIOTS. DON'T LET THIS GET AROUND.

Between the purchase of a property and the actual filming, there might be many more writers involved than screen credits announced. Some producers took over the writing themselves, others acted out their ideas at grisly story conferences. Experienced directors learned ways of playing this system, just as some producers allowed that there was an acquired expertise in directors of knowing what worked. There was a legion of writers whose chief employment was for the screen, rather than literature, and who mastered the skill of making stories that fitted together like jigsaws: for instance, June Mathis, Sidney Buchman, Jules Furthman, Dudley Nichols, Jo Swerling, Philip Yordan, Robert Riskin, Nunnally Johnson, the Epstein brothers, Samson Raphaelson, and Lamar Trotti.

The narrative intricacy of Hollywood films owes a lot to the ingenuity of such writers. It amounts to another message, for there are no loose ends, everything contributes to fluency and speed, and the story itself becomes a streamlined machine. The effect is incalculable, but that need not deter us from wondering how far Hollywood's criteria for narrative—that it be immediately comprehensible, resolved, and tidy—affected the audience's expectation of life. All of fiction must take credit and blame here, and fiction is in part an attempt to make redeeming models of order from life's disorder. But the narrative thread of cinema was more influential than any other sort of fiction, and it leaves the audience to reconcile the gap between their own indecision and the charmed conviction on the screen. That created effect may be far more important than the contribution of individual writers.

In other technical-artistic areas, we find the same high skill cultivated by Hollywood but seldom traveling outside that town. Directors of photography had no other field of work before TV—which has hurried their delicacy almost out of existence—and they were seldom still photographers. Yet the craft of making consistent, evocative, and "beautiful" moving images is one of Hollywood's achievements. Theoretically, the cameramen were subordinate to the directors, so that the look of a film married a dramatic conception and a visual treatment. But the naked eye has difficulty foreseeing the photographed "look," and few directors knew enough to be sure that their wishes—not always coherent or technically phrased—were being executed. Sometimes cameramen took advantage of that, and aspired to direct, but with daunting lack of success. Other photographers scorned the script or the action, and concentrated on gorgeous effects of lighting and composition.

The lasting meaning of that gorgeousness is enormous; but, again, it is hardly attributable to individuals. There were outstanding photographers in Hollywood, whose work is often recognizable—Lee Garmes and Gregg Toland are two such individualists. But it is much easier to recognize a Warner Brothers picture or an MGM movie than to make the distinction between, say, Sid Hickox and Ernest Haller, or William Daniels and Joseph Ruttenberg. Studio style could owe itself to particular film stocks and processing methods, as well as ways of lighting perfected over decades. There is an overall characteristic to studio lighting stronger than individual style, and which has since been lost in the rediscovery of natural lighting. That character is of a flawlessly rendered romantic glamour: The image shines, no matter how dowdy the people are meant to be. A subject may deal with squalor or ugliness, but the image is always lovely. This is the consequence of an approach striving for correctness, taste, and pictorial harmony. How rare it is to see a shot in a Hollywood picture that is miscalculated or unresolved. And if we did see it, would not so many years of protection leave us disgruntled at the impropriety? Hollywood stylishness makes conservatives of us all. There is a certainty and serenity in the balance of light and shadow, and an implicit commitment to order and stability in the neatness of every composition.

The eye is directed and pleased by Hollywood imagery, and the same gentle persuasion works in fashion photography and graphic advertising. The perfection of camera angling— reached in the forties—is the climax of meaningful shape being imposed by light and point of view. It does not simply "discover" things in the image, but locks spectator and spectacle together in a process that whispers, "This is insight."

The style of photography insinuates honesty and intimacy, so that millions accepted the premise that an angled close-up conveyed insight. Yet it was a Hollywood axiom to "put the light where the money is": Illuminate the stars and show the public what they wanted. It is a short step from that to see that movie light aroused understanding but was inspired by commerce. The Hollywood message therefore is tacitly commercial, and the text is its own packaging. Shiny paper might not have been invented but for the moist luster in all movies.

To take only one more aspect of the finished film, music, once more the effect is overwhelming and systematic, and the men who excelled in the contortionist rigors of movie composing were little known in the larger world of music. There are instances of "respectable" composers trying their hands with film—Prokofiev, Walton, Copland, and Virgil Thomson—but the movie music with the surest sense of idiom is by Max Steiner, Franz Waxman, Erich Korngold, Alfred Newman, Miklos Rozsa, Dimitri Tiomkin, and Bernard Herrmann. Herrmann also wrote "serious" music, but I doubt if that will last as long as his movie scores for Hitchcock, Welles, and Scorsese. Film composers were shown finished movies and told exactly where and for how long themes were required. That approach grew out of silent cinema, in which anything from a full orchestra to an upright piano accompanied films with themes that were unmistakable indicators of mood and situation.

That way of composing is very extreme, and the music is as much of the nature of melodrama as the pressure put upon the composer. Music in the cinema is a narrative shorthand to codify atmosphere and a melodramatic ground swell, so that the lifelike action is mysteriously accompanied by music that thrills, swoons, or agonizes, as if it were an electronic impulse connecting us with the characters' feelings. Producers, moguls, and even musicians cheerfully proclaimed that if you "heard" the music it was obtrusive; when it was right it entered into you like air. What is that but the scheme for the mood music that holds off unnerving silence in super-markets, jet liners, and that spreading world of lobbies, transit areas, and intervening space? What does that music do but attempt to deny boredom with mood? Film music may not be as wicked as that suggests. But it is important to recognize the way music reinforced the experience. It indicates how far the cinema is not just a visual or dramatic event: We cannot "see" the music, and its source is inexplicable. It arises emotionally, and is as satisfying as opera or the Mass. Sometimes Hollywood looked on films as warm baths that never cool, and this lapping comfort was also musical. Dentists, too, know the reassurance that comes with musical accompaniment, and cows apparently yield more to anodyne melodies.

This can be only an outline sketch of the collaboration or rivalry among creative people on any movie which a producer had to control and a director tolerate. So how much artistry is left to the director? Some had story, script, and actors imposed upon them only shortly before they were to start shooting. Sometimes the script came later still, and the rewriting did not always keep up with shooting, so that a film might have to wait or improvise—this last, the most alien way of working in Hollywood, yet a fruitful possibility else-where. The Hollywood dream owes more to fate than spon-taneity. "Can't I dream?" or "Tomorrow is another day" were mottoes typifying Hollywood—but assent to both only encouraged cultural whimsy. The possibilities in improvised films are much more constructive, as if film's openness to chance took heart at being trusted.

So much of the Hollywood product was anticipated in advance: A Ronald Colman picture would only move in Colman-like directions. Moreover, audiences were astute enough within moments of a film beginning to appreciate the sort of picture it was, the rules operating, and the likely outcome. This is a phenomenon known as genre, the way in which Hollywood pictures were in one clear convention or another: situation comedy, screwball comedy, horror, gangster, women's pic, film *noir,* epic, biblical, western, costume, adventure. The study of genres is not clear-cut. Most films partook of several conventions, and there are more variations than the system named. Stars were their own genres: For instance, "horror" does not adequately contain Boris Karloff films and Bela Lugosi films. But all genres have common conditions; genre is a state of mind rooted in the planned selling of stories: The taste of the market then takes priority over the needs of the story, and all stories resemble one another. Photography, music, and narrative rhythm were also equivalent to genres, and more influential than any of the labeled varieties.

Nevertheless, one pleasure for the audience was familiarity with known forms and ritual being reworked. It is rare for a star to be cast against type or for there to be the conflict between genres that we expect in life. At a practical level, the "rooms" seen in films are only portions of rooms built in advance as sets. Thus a director was restricted in many scenes by the preconception built into design: It is not simply a truism to say that Hollywood films take place in sets rather than rooms, for the word *set* also denotes something prescribed and decided upon.

Still, the director had opportunities. Even preoccupied technicians and egocentric actors look for someone to organize them and take responsibility. Some directors bullied, some wheedled, others charmed, and a few had every manner and the instinct to know which actor to overawe and which to wait for. One of the things that deflates young people excited by the wish to direct films is that talent is not enough. It must be armed with the will to be in charge, to coax here and endure there, to wrangle with financiers, to shout down electricians and still be capable of going up to flustered players and saying the useful words that will conjure an extra conviction in the few seconds of a movie climax. If there is an imaginative conception at stake, only huge energy can protect it, and fine judgment must tell when to compromise and when to play the tyrant. Not even sincerity is left as an escape. The director is surrounded by fakes, hams, and try-ons, and he must act out both kindness and implacability. At the end of the day, he may have nothing real left. The hermit artist, the shy, retiring creator, the artist locked without humor or ambiguity in the intensity of his own work may or may not be a reality. But the film director cannot hope to work in that fashion. He is ringmaster in a rowdy circus.

The rowdiness meant that there was often no chance of dignity in the Hollywood circus. Intelligent or feeling men were forced into Herman Mankiewicz's scathing contempt— for the system and for themselves going along with it. It suits some young critics to build elaborate interpretations of films that may have been made by men aghast at the silliness of their material and the obtuseness of their colleagues. I cannot explore this in detail here, but Hollywood films are sometimes self-mocking: *Dark Victory, Jet Pilot,* and *Sign of the Pagan,* for instance, can be taken at face value or as surging oceans of hokum bearing a survival raft and an S. J. Perelman-like author waving to his friends.

But the director's greatest asset is the awareness that film is about moving images, rather than stories, transferred novels, or supercharged theater. Before a screenplay is filmed, it is converted into a shooting script: a detailed plan of action as seen from precise points of view. It is as inscrutable as an engineer's blueprint. You may exclude a director from story construction and dialogue, but he has to be allowed the shooting script and the decision on how to film every speech or moment. The textual choice in cinema is of what to do with the camera. This is not simply a functional decision; the camera in every shot is like the locus of God to a religion.

Not just point of view hangs upon the camera, but visibility itself; what the camera does not see does not exist; everything it does see is significant. The same event can be travestied or fixed forever by the manner in which it is seen. Cinema is the business of seeing and being seen, not telling and being told. The literary subtext is of marginal importance. That is why a novel is only a pretext for a film and why it is wasteful to trace links between the two forms. Director Nicholas Ray once pierced that vacuity with a story about frustrated writers deploring the way their work was spoiled in the filming. "It was all in the script!" they cried. "But if it was all in the script," replied Ray, "why make the film?"

The restrictions of schedule, budget, casting, and scenario could not eliminate cinematic inventiveness. Thus there are brilliant directors—Hawks, Hitchcock, Von Sternberg, Minnelli, Sirk, Mann, Ray himself—who may even deserve to be called artists, who certainly give us pleasures like those offered by less hindered artists. But the richness possible in that narrow liberty was still inhibited. The commercial, melodramatic, and glamorizing conditions of cinema were far more intractable than a dense producer and too little money. It is in the nature of this directorial freedom that invention is cut off from purpose and a larger reflection upon life.

In *The Last Tycoon* there is a fascinating encounter between Stahr and an English writer hired by the studio and fretful at not grasping the movies' secret. It explains the vital creative capacity in seeing things, but, unwittingly, it underlines how isolated that opportunity was. At first, Stahr gently rebukes the writer's tendency to patronize the hectic activity of the film he is struggling with:

"Would you write that in a book of your own, Mr. Boxley?"
"What? Naturally not."
"You'd consider it too cheap."

"Movie standards are different," said Boxley, hedging.
"Do you ever go to them?"

"No—almost never."

"Isn't it because people are always dueling and falling down wells?"

"Yes—and wearing strained facial expressions and talking incredible and unnatural dialogue."

"Skip the dialogue for a minute," said Stahr. "Granted your dialogue is more graceful than what these hacks can write—that's why we brought you out here. But let's imagine something that isn't either bad dialogue or jumping down a well. Has your office got a stove in it that lights with a match?"

"I think it has," said Boxley stiffly, "—but I never use it."

"Suppose you're in your office. You've been fighting duels or writing all day and you're too tired to fight or write anymore. You're sitting there staring—dull, like we all get sometimes. A pretty stenographer that you've seen before comes into the room and you watch her—idly. She doesn't see you, though you're very close to her. She takes off her gloves, opens her purse and dumps it out on a table—"

Stahr stood up, tossing his key-ring on his desk.

"She has two dimes and a nickel—and a cardboard match box. She leaves the nickel on the desk, puts the two dimes back into her purse and takes her black gloves to the stove, opens it and puts them inside. There is one match in the match box and she starts to light it kneeling by the stove. You notice that there's a stiff wind blowing in the window—but just then your telephone rings. The girl picks it up, says hello—listens—and says deliberately into the phone, 'I've never owned a pair of black gloves in my life.' She hangs up, kneels by the stove again, and just as she lights the match, you glance around very suddenly and see that there's another man in the office, watching every move the girl makes—"

Stahr paused. He picked up his keys and put them in his pocket.

"Go on," said Boxley, smiling. "What happens?"

"I don't know," said Stahr. "I was just making pictures."

Boxley felt he was being put in the wrong.

"It's just melodrama," he said.

"Not necessarily," said Stahr. "In any case, nobody has moved violently or talked cheap dialogue or had any facial expression at all. There was only one bad line, and a writer like you could improve it. But you were interested."

Fitzgerald is convinced by Stahr's argument, yet Boxley's hesitation is sensible. The event Stahr dreams up is melodrama because of the rhetorical gulf between aroused curiosity and any useful consequence. This "art" is desperate to hold our attention, and while it is working to do that it neglects more testing needs. The multilayered voyeurism in Stahr's story is melodramatic in exactly the way of cinema itself—the furtive, privileged inspection of people under stress. And it is melodrama because of its very virtue: It is "only making pictures." Furthermore, the hook of suspense carries the assurance of resolution: This girl is already a heroine, forced to lie by circumstances—Sylvia Sidney, perhaps. She will be vindicated and we are right to begin to support her. Already, the film is a thriller.

Alone among the arts, film sees self-contained crises occurring and being worked out within the confines of the work, before returning to some sleeping happy-ever-after. In art, life itself is a crisis. The movies may have lied fatally in portraying crises as blooms growing on life. Film is concerned with making pictures and imprinting them on the viewer's soul. Stahr's scene is intriguing but forgettable: It has no substance. Consider instead Ingmar Bergman's admission that *Cries and Whispers* began in his mind with an image of women in white in a dark red room. The gravity of that film surely grows out of the way Bergman struggled to explain that image to himself. In *Cries and Whispers* there is compatibility of visual interest and consequence. And its agony would disturb and bore millions—even if millions have accepted *The Exorcist*.

IV

THE AUDIENCE

I'll bet you that nine out of ten people, if they see a woman across the courtyard undressing for bed, or even a man puttering around in his room, will stay and look.
— ALFRED HITCHCOCK

THE AUDIENCE IN THE CINEMA IS PLURAL: IT IS ALL THE children of Chapter I, each attentive to his or her secret garden, from which intimate memories are carried away, like cuttings, to bloom in that narrow plot given to all of us—a portion of the dark before sleep. In that plurality, each child buys a ticket for the pleasure and privilege. At the same time, the audience is singular: It is the impacted solidarity of so many individuals congregated to give up or escape their uniqueness; and the system calls them the "box office" or the "take." Only a mass as hardened as a fighting unit could endure the implacability of a screen pretending to be an animated wall, but actually an inert surface. The insult in cinema is as great as that suffered by the millions regarding a leader who is a grinning fish without sight in that fevered aquarium in the corner. In both situations, the imitation of human contact is humiliating for the viewer.

Today, the contrast with theater may seem obvious. But when cinema began it was persistently confused with theater, by audiences and practitioners alike. Because the confusion now looks simpleminded should not disguise lasting misunderstanding of the transformation that had occurred. For the change is not simply a matter of technical differences between two media; it involves a redefinition of the audience that affects art and society. The cinema is not quite art, and it is a disconcerting version of religion or politics. It is the beginnings of a great blur in our experience in which many once-distinct ideas are lost.

Here is one way to make the contrast believable: Suppose that you are alive in 1895, and expecting to go to the theater tonight; you have arranged to meet friends there. You are dressing specially and will dine afterward at a restaurant— the evening is anticipated as a pleasant mixture of entertainment, the chance to see actors, and a convivial gathering of friends. You reach the theater to find a notice saying that no actors will perform that night. Instead, a white screen will block out the proscenium and images of the actors will wind across it.

Arranged in that way, the collision is absurd. But that one night took only a few years in reality, and the capacity of the human species for change was expected to digest the hurtful desertion of real performers. Would you sit in the theater knowing no actors would appear on stage? or dress as carefully for that? Would you have such expectations of a cheerful occasion with friends?

Of course, the theater has had the reputation of appealing

to a higher-class audience than the cinema. But that may only be because the movies rapidly embraced a far larger crowd than had ever been to the theater, thereby turning the fraction that adhered to the theater into an elite. It behooves that elite to pay more for the privilege, to dress, mix, and entertain themselves afterward ostentatiously; they may also defend their pleasure in terms of the greater immediacy of "live" theater. All manner of snobbery has been dragged into the matter. But it still leaves cinema as "dead" theater, and no movie enthusiast should simply laugh that cold thought away.

Stepping as carefully as possible between the twin distractions of snobbery and real class differences, some things about the cinema can be discerned. There is an air of indifference hovering around it. It is common and permitted that people wander in and out during a performance. Whereas in the theater, latecomers are often excluded until the first interval, and it is regarded as uncivilized for people to leave while the actors are speaking. The distraction and the interference to audibility are resented by the audience, for their own sake and on behalf of the actors. There are anecdotes of plays resuming after an interval, having to compete with the din of stragglers so that a frustrated actor stops in midspeech, comes to the edge of the stage, asks everyone to blow his nose, fidget as necessary, cough and scrape, and only then will he begin again. It produces delighted awe, and may be the most "theatrical" moment of the evening. Even if done in bad temper, it endears the actor to the audience, increases their respect for him, and strengthens the personal bond that exists in theater. This bond is more vital and complex in any form of theater where the actors do talk to the audience—vaudeville, music hall, and nightclubs. But in the cinema we are not addressed directly: It is a safe place for the mute and shy, and for those wanting to be secret.

I have not carried out experiments to prove it, but may

I suggest that people in the theater and the cinema do not sit in the same way? The theater requires attentiveness, and people must sit up alertly to see what is often a small area of concentration. Whereas in the cinema, the screen looms above us, and many people sink into reclining positions to watch. Some luxurious movie houses have seats that slide back to allow this posture. In the cinema we sometimes put our feet on the back of the row in front, loll across two seats, and damage the upholstery. Would this happen with a lively and commanding presence on the stage, or is it the result of a sort of loneliness in cinemas? There is less pressure to dress up for films. Movie houses—warm in winter, cool in summer —invite the elderly today in a way sensitive to their limited means and correspondingly tactful and anonymous. At the theater, people often dress so that they may be "seen"; but cinema has evolved a subform—the dirty-mac* trade—where that shabby garment covers surreptitiousness. Only a very moralizing society could have invented that label (or the condition it describes), insisting on the urban insect voyeur as the ultimate, forlorn moviegoer. It is a clinging stereotype because we all recognize something unsociable about cinema and unwittingly struggle with the contradiction of a medium concerned with "being seen" where we are encouraged to think ourselves protected spies.

Let me propose some larger implications in this situation. Filmgoing is a form in which the individual is simultaneously allotted no distinct, individual merit and ushered in to fantasies that belong to him alone. The hurt and the reward go hand in hand, and they represent the frightening pact that has been contrived in our democracies between personal liberty and alienation. The audience in the movies typifies the modern crowd, that shambling mass of humanity, so large that it is measured in statistics, a herd that authority tends,

---

* mac = mackintosh = raincoat—Ed.

feeds, pacifies, and regulates: This is the crowd that goes to the factory, the supermarket, and the bank, the material of armies and mobs. It is the populace turning into concrete affirmation for Hitler at Nuremberg, the line filing past Valentino's open coffin, the audience going each week to the movies, and the horde shuffling through the Ellis Island obstacle race.

Ellis Island was a prototype for cinemas, despite the lack of screen, projector, or film. There was a large, awe-inspiring and physically separate institution, a place unlike others, to which the crowd came. They were apprehensive and excited at this threshold, for having overcome the difficulties of a voyage and escaped from their original land, they now faced a test that all heeded as the first gesture of the new land they longed for. America was notional freedom, but it met them with an initiation test. Picture lines of men and women, waiting to be tested (or "screened"), all facing forward, at the future and possibility, hoping that their bodies will negotiate this last barrier and join the imaginations already on the other side, roaming the wide spaces: It is like a cinema—a screen could easily slip into place at the end of the transit hall. The test formalized the drastic alteration in their lives and the impossible loveliness of what they hoped to attain. But, most important of all, Ellis Island indicates the separation of body and imagination that America will require of them, and which the movies ceaselessly enacted.

The immigrants who dispersed all over America gathered again in the cinemas. No cinema could hold them all, but in the 1920s and thirties there were twenty thousand in America and as many as one hundred million tickets sold every week. The cinema was the fifth largest business in America, and only clothing and food had more basic appeal. The cinemas were built in the most crowded parts of cities; they fitted into a pattern of life that included tenements and factories. The industry fastened on a profitable duty to bring relief, adventure, and hope to people tired and sometimes near to despair with the hard grind. The everyday monotony and the real obstacles to hopes were offset by this nocturnal expansiveness.

The two preeminent stars of early cinema—Chaplin and Douglas Fairbanks—observe that duty. Chaplin actually made a film called *The Immigrant,* replaying for laughs some of the hardships of Atlantic passage that Charlie had remotely shared with many Americans. He came on a cattle boat with a variety company, and within three years of reaching America he had raised his salary from seventy-five dollars to ten thousand a week. He was not a typical immigrant, therefore, but a boon to all those who wanted to think of being out of the ordinary.

He played a charming failure, a tramp or hobo, the sentimentalized little man, so Italian-looking that he might have traveled steerage with expectant godfathers. For some, the clutching at pathos in Chaplin amounts to self-pity, and his soulful idealization of failure does lead to a world split between victimized barbers and tyrants—who happen to be twins. But who can doubt that Chaplin was loved by people grateful for his inventive and wistful response to disappointment, who felt their own dismay a little less as they watched?

Chaplin's films do show poverty—albeit as something picturesque—and he does poke fun at the rich. In time, he was challenged by an America that solemnly found links between his naïve populism and its own bogey concoction, communism. No one ever noticed the more intriguing paradox of Chaplin's great success from playing pauper: In that sense, his self-righteous artistry has always been at odds with itself, as he helplessly gathered the rewards of enterprise. If Charlie had had less need to be an artist, and less wish to preach to the crowd, he might not have ended up in Switzerland, sterile tax haven of the lost, exiled, or contradictory.

Enterprise was also the scroll legend beneath the leaping

stride of Douglas Fairbanks, a man who celebrated success in acrobatics, stunts, and twinkling swordplay. Doug cheerfully promoted himself as the model of young American success: He was neither handsome nor intelligent, but humorously good-looking, shrewd, and hyperactive. For some years, on and off screen, he was the epitome of immigrant dreams: lucky. He converted America to suntan (another Californian by-product), stretched his face around a huge grin, and adapted the talent of a flashy athlete to displays of physical daring that seem fanciful, no matter that Doug did without stuntmen or tricks. He moves with the spirit of the viewer: He cloaks difficulty in naturalness, so that he vaults, leaps, and somersaults as easily as the mind's eye. Magazines stressed that Doug performed every feat of agility, but this verification missed his appeal, which was the flying mixture of fact and fantasy. His talent was to do things in a way that made them seem magical.

That swashbuckling overcame all the exotic villains who confronted D'Artagnan, Robin Hood, the Thief of Bagdad, Zorro, or the Black Pirate, but Doug's real-life image was founded on more practical achievements. Whereas Chaplin was a private man offscreen, Fairbanks loved to play himself and sport in the sun. He wolfed down his own celebrity like a schoolboy eating hot dogs. He wrote books and articles on how application, hard work, and enterprise could pay off. He married America's sweetheart, Mary Pickford, and took on the panoply of international fame in world tours, his house with Mary, Pickfair, the setting up of United Artists to safeguard the interests of the practicing "artist" who made films, and always continued his lighthearted cartwheel through the twenties.

Every aspect of his career failed eventually, and disappointment killed him off, even if he had lightened that shadow for millions. He had been daunted by the coming of sound, and, like Chaplin, resisted it longer than most stars. Enterprise then turned to reaction and cold feet. Doug's fear, that what he had others might take, went so far as to impede his son's career. Middle age was stripped too bare by two Dougs, the younger better looking.

The hostility to sound proved how far Charlie and Doug depended on mime and movement. Perhaps their "art" required silence as a respectful frame. The universality of the tramp was reassessed when he gave forth in elocution-lesson English, and Doug's being like a flag in the breeze was humbled by a pedestrian voice and the need to talk and explain. No one who talked could move like that: The combination was at odds. Sound coincided with Fairbanks's decline and a serious reduction in Chaplin's output.

Furthermore, the pattern of feature-length movies may have misled Chaplin from his natural vehicle, the twenty-minute picture, derived from variety routines and geared to a short span of attention. Chaplin seems uncomfortable with prolonged form and, Griffith's advance notwithstanding, one wonders whether early audiences were not often happier with short films. Silent cinema united a diverse America and gave those without English a chance to learn from simple titles. Again, sound coincides with the depression, and talking pictures lost the poorest part of the audience just when capital reinvestment drained the studios and left them vulnerable all through the thirties. The audience may naturally have taken on a higher level of sophistication. Equally, perhaps the slow English of some immigrants retreated from the rapid eloquence of Edward G. Robinson and Katharine Hepburn.

But remind yourself of that screen on Ellis Island and think how appropriate the films of Chaplin and Fairbanks would have been in the eyes of immigration authorities. Not only are they entertaining for people waiting and depressed by their own insignificance, but they also encourage a belief in unreality that will divert the watcher from his present misfortunes. However harsh those circumstances, a movie dilutes them with a pleasant alternative or a comfortable interpretation. Slightly but significantly, that intrusion suggests that reality in America is not only circumstantial, but also extends to imagined possibility. This amounts to a romantic materialism in which objects and possessions are tinged with the glamour of indistinct identity. It is the state of waking dream so often attributed to watching films. For anyone going through Ellis Island, it would make America not just a physical continent, but a realm of promise and expectation. It is an idea and a reality at the same time, and thus it has stolen dreaming from its proper abode, sleep.

That seems a more useful point than to pretend that the movies re-create the state of sleep. They do not mimic sleep: You will know that if you have ever dozed off watching a film. But they may betray wakefulness, concede the elusiveness of reality, and yield to the vagueness with which fantasy clouds critical objectivity. Indeed, it is a joke today to lay claim to critical objectivity; we are all cynics, allowing that subjectivity says I am right while objectivity is other people telling me I am wrong. The possibility of graspable truths has been lost in the estrangement of the individual and the crowd. Observation of the world seems a private practice, cut off from the hope of describing what you have seen, and the rarer hope of your view being useful to the world. If you see only what you see, and if understanding is isolated by subjectivity, then you become a voyeur rather than a participant. You may even wonder if you are dead—if the dead could observe us, they would be as cut off as we are from the life in films.

The comparison of the movies and dreaming is far-reaching and suggestive, and the details are worth examining, even if less striking than the conspiracy that has mounted the comparison, at every level from cinema management to academic film studies. It is dark, warm, and secure in cinema, this hypothesis goes. The first two points are generally accurate, but the third is questionable. Cinemas are so out of the normal run of life, and so associated with the sensational that it is surely not security that beckons us. But, of course, neither is dreaming safe: Part of its fascination comes from our helplessness as the story unfolds—and that powerlessness is very like feelings in a cinema. Anyone who has been tempted to walk out of a "disturbing" movie must have been reminded of the dreamer's wish that he could wake.

There might also be an affinity between the "flicker" form of images on a screen and the rapid eye movements that accompany dreaming. When we watch a movie, we are seeing the suggestion of lifelike motion, but we are subconsciously aware of the subsidiary effect of twenty-four separate images replacing one another. A shutter accomplishes this, interrupting the light for fractions of a second, which the eye cannot detect. I do not underestimate this mechanical process: I have already urged the absence of human involvement as a part of the cinematic experience, and any stress on automatic processes will add to that.

We do feel subjected to a machine, and there must be connections between the flicker and neurological reactions. A few people have had epileptic fits while watching films because of the flicker, and similar fits might be triggered in others by finding the rhythm that unhinges them. There is a possibility that something less violent than a fit, but still of nervous significance, occurs while watching films. And that is something we cannot avoid; as long as we watch the film we must submit to it—though "submit" suggests that it is painful, whereas the effect could be pleasant or soothing.

The comparison with rapid eye movements is beyond proof or disproof, but the movement in question is of the eyeball, and not a shutterlike flickering of the eyelid. Still, the mystics of the body can reply that dreaming needs a generating motion. I cannot deal with that scientifically, but movement is often restful and pleasing: Children in prams or cradles are calmed by it, and people of all ages can occupy themselves with gazing from a moving vehicle. To look at a painting is to concentrate, absorb, and be absorbed: Art galleries, for that reason, and because we have to walk around and see too many pictures, are very tiring. But the movie seems to relieve us of the burden of concentration. Images succeed one another so that we have only to "keep up." Furthermore, it is movement that carries on regardless of us, and without our assistance. There is usually more satisfaction in being driven than in driving, and cinema reminds us of the intellectual fascination of perpetual motion. Not just the laws of physics seem set aside, but larger human limitations and even the weight of mortality. Those frustrating moments when a film breaks, or a projector grinds to a halt, are like an interrupted journey or a missed heartbeat.

Perhaps study of the art of film has bypassed inherent movement too quickly. Motion is both form and content in cinema, and as form it has an intrinsic delight that can confuse Astaire's legs dancing and the death tumbles in a Sam Peckinpah film: If both are artificial and abstract, then the realities to which they refer may be less clear-cut.

The more important consequence of rapid eye movements is that vision is implicated in dreaming. Here, the comparison suggests how "literary" the bulk of film criticism has been. Is the eye as impassioned as a bird that cannot land or rest? How poetic that, as soon as the shutters come down, the eyes begin a night life. Not everyone dreams in the same manner, but for most of us the dream is a thing seen, or an experience rendered through simulated witness. "Our dreams think essentially in images," wrote Freud, though "think" may be as misleading as the idea that films are photographed literature.

Very often we have a stronger sense of dreadful inertia in

dreaming: We are not conjuring up the imagery of the dream, but are trapped onlookers. The most penetrating compatibility of dreaming and watching film lies in that loss of volition in the viewer. This is sustained by an autonomy in the stream of images that allows it to run on, without our consent and free from our interference.

In the theater, the actors cannot ignore us: They time their lines to the mood of an audience, and wait for laughter to subside. Hurl a missile at Hamlet and the prince may be jolted out of his introspection. When John Wilkes Booth leaped down on the stage, staggered up on a broken leg, and uttered his cry, the play was submerged in drama. Yet in the cinema, we behave like exhausted people in an airport lounge because we feel we are unobserved. Damage the screen, and the faces are oblivious of their sudden acne. Rip away half the white and the image falls back, stippled and dull, on the bare wall behind. We ache with the inability to reach movies—poor reward for those first viewers who had such faith in the Lumières (or so little readiness for deception) that, when a train came toward them, they rushed out of the cinema screaming.

Trains in dreams are as alarming as that because the imagery seems loaded with a significance or intent for which we are the available victims. The experience of dreaming is of being tied down beside an automatically unwinding roll of images—the manifest train of thought. We can no more escape than could Pearl White; we are apprehensive of the imagery involving us in a life-and-death struggle. Yet the locomotive force never crashes into the auditorium; it is forever hurtling past like an arrested express. The impact does not occur, but we flinch and tremble. We are rescued, or our fate is averted, because we are not alive or the train is a phantom, and because of the trick that makes the performance so fearsome—its ability to change itself in a split second.

In film-making, that effect is called a cut. For the film-maker it is a routine working device, often taken as a measure of style or intention. It is something teachers call "a basic grammatical tool." In that sense cutting punctuates cinematic narratives. Film-makers and viewers alike become accustomed to cuts, so that a long shot of a man going to a window leads to a close-up of his face looking out and thence to a shot of whatever he sees. We know that syntax so well that it is easy to regard the cut as a means of fluency, a cement solidifying the "story." Yet that type of cinema may be the most restrained. The cut is also antigrammatical and as violent as the word sounds: It is a sign of the irrationality and unliterary power generated in cinema. When a close-up of a woman's face changes to any other shot, she is cut off at the throat. We are too sophisticated to feel her pain, but "primitive" peoples have often been distressed by cinema severing parts of the body so murderously while keeping the faces talking.

The cut can wound us more deeply than a head-on train. In 1928, in *Un Chien Andalou*, Luis Buñuel begins the film standing on a balcony at night. He looks up, sees a cloud spearing across the moon, and goes into a room. We see a girl's face in a close-up; a hand draws back the eyelid and a razor slices through the eyeball.

The sequence has always been shocking, and no warning nullifies the fusion of cruelty and humor. Buñuel is teasing us: It may be the first film to exploit our readiness to be victims. Our feelings are exposed to whatever enters through our eyes, and we are at the mercy of every cut whereby, in about a fiftieth of a second, and too suddenly for us to avoid it, any image can be replaced. Some juxtapositions may be emphatically violent: a girl taking a shower—an intruder with a knife. But all are inherently shocking. Our knowledge that a cut can come at any time and bring any threat ensures

apprehension. Some forms—the thriller and horror movie—
employ that power methodically: *Jaws* is a tormenting exercise in cutting, and those teeth are the more acute because
of the stylish appropriateness. But all movies must cut, and
tidiness or storytelling do not smother the threat of breakdown in cutting.

In dreams, transitions can be sudden and inexplicable, but
the momentum of the form keeps us amenable, even if near
panic. Therefore, mystery or inexplicability is the function
of the form, not meaning. From Joseph to Freud, dreams
have been open to interpretation: We awake with a dread or
curiosity clinging to the strangeness of our dream. The peril
just escaped does not stop our anxiety at not understanding
its riddle. Evidently, for centuries, the dreamer has searched
for people who will explain the dream—astrologers, priests,
analysts—for we hate lack of meaning or the denial of explanation. But there is a passive explanation of dreams that
says they are unordered play, a medley of images and events
that mean no more than randomly selected numbers. This is
an upsetting answer, even if it is meant to allay fears, for our
greatest anxiety is that we may be without purpose or meaning. We have proposed God, Art, the Law, Knowledge, Progress, and even Death to fill that void.

Yet the cinema may point us at such emptiness chiefly in
the manner in which it evades choice, something fundamental to all those structures of meaning we have invented. You
may recall how far the first makers and watchers of film were
impressed by the sheer wonder of imagery. We still respond
to the medium's self-contained authority: Our right to choose
is undermined by its assurance. Therefore it is important to
see how far the cinema promotes order or disorder. Hollywood's influence on the history of the new medium insists
that it tells stories, and that those stories can be sold. Thus
(the makers claim) the stories have to be acceptable or in-

offensive. But this faith in storytelling might yet be revealed as a passing aberration; it is certain that the audiences see more than stories.

In describing the opening of *Un Chien Andalou,* I found myself converting the images into a story. Yet the power of that sequence—and it is a power central to a short, surrealist film that resists understanding, but remains endlessly viewable—is the variety of possible sequences or antisequences. Consider the elements shown in the film, in the order in which they appear, and with as little added cohesion as possible:

> hands sharpening a razor
> the face of a man, a window behind him
> hands testing the razor blade
> a man standing in front of a window;
>   he opens it and goes out onto a
>   balcony; he looks up
> a moon approached by a cloud
> a woman's face; a hand opens her eye
> a moon traversed by a cloud
> a razor cutting through an eyeball

We readily construct a spatial and temporal continuum for these separate elements so that the film becomes a story in which one man (*he*) carries out this odd assault on one woman (*she*). They are all in the same place (*there*): a room, a balcony outside it and in the sky above a moon with cloud. As such, it is as gripping as the start of a thriller. But *Un Chien Andalou* is far more creatively mysterious. The hands sharpening a razor need not be the hands of the man. The man who looks up might be in Madagascar, the moon in Menilmontant—the moon, anyway, is bogus, not a heavenly body but a bright disk. The man could be any man, and the film has players taking more than one part each as evidence of the universality of male and female. The girl may be in the room he came from; she may be somewhere else alto-gether—it is possible that they never met or knew of one another. It may be other hands than his that open the eye. Admittedly, we see in that shot glimpses of a shirt and tie like those worn by the man. But such pointed clues warn us to be doubtful—plot so easily becomes intrigue. And in *True Grit,* in several long shots we are seeing not John Wayne, but a man resembling Wayne and wearing his clothes. Or are they Rooster Cogburn's clothes, or clothes belonging to Paramount or to a costume hire company?

Is the sliced eye the girl's eye? Or is "sliced" too suggestive of personal violence? How can I describe the thing seen—itself a sensation—without adding inflections unavoidable in language, which tells? We shudder to think it could be a girl's eye cut apart, yet the reliability of imagery is funda-mental to cinema's appeal. We like to think—in the way of scandalmongers and gossips—that we saw Clark Gable kissing Jean Harlow, that Marlon Brando really screwed in *Last Tango in Paris*, and that Bette Davis shook hands with her-self in *A Stolen Life.*

The fan magazine and the innuendo of the gossip column identified the devious pleasure of mistaking actual and fic-tional identity, and picked out our unwholesome peeping curiosity about these immense celebrities. I have not seen any of them, but apparently films are now emerging from South America in which people are "actually" killed. What wondrous pornography, what obscene depravity, that actual-ity should be pursued so far when the form is in its nature open to doubt.

How can we be sure that a wretched prostitute from Buenos Aires has indeed been killed, merely on film's evi-dence of broken flesh, blood and the choreography of assault, death throes and final stillness? The movies do not deal in proof, but in mingled precision and speculation. The eye Buñuel cuts might be a corpse's, might be that girl's, might be a sheep's, might be ours. "Might" is the vital spark, and the cinema is always in the subjunctive. Thus the opening of *Un Chien Andalou* concerns the interplay of real acts and the imagining of them. The man we see may be an eye-slicer, or a man contemplating slicing an eye: In that way, he is like us, for as we watch the film we imagine the same things. Here is the sweet intercourse of the cinema: not in involving ourselves with people doing things, but with people thinking of doing things. The "text" in cinema is not factual, but fictional. In eighty years, I wonder what discredit that has done to the status of facts and reality?

The celluloid strip is real, even if unseen in cinemas: It is the end product of immense industry. But who would pay to look at that? We go to see its enlarged image, an evident illusion. Our culture, on Hollywood's advice, has taught us to look for stories, to smooth away possibility with the starching iron of plot. Plot, here, means not only recountable story line: Significance is a plot, too. At film school one afternoon, I made a film, cheaply and easily. In the cutting room, I sat beside the wastebin that received the trimmed ends and throwaways of every film being made at the school. It was a large bin, emptied rarely, and there may have been fragments of a hundred films in it. I had only to dip in my hand—like a child at a big store's Christmas grotto—pull out one shot, or length of celluloid, then another and splice them together. I did not select. I did not even look at the material on the lengths of film. When I decided I was finished—for, clearly, such a film could go on forever—I went to the viewing theater and showed the accumulation to a group of students who had been trapped there with the doctrinaire *Battleship Potemkin*. They watched the cohered chaos and began to perplex me with what it meant.

I am not advocating the mockery of film studies, analysis, and criticism. But I am urging that it recognize the power of the automatic and unchosen in film. It does have more dada in it than other forms—the helpless witness of sensation. It is not only a medium that means something, but also a medium that *is*. And at that sedimentary level, we are playing with the mutability of reality, the unsoundness of facts, and the undermining of observation with dreaming. We are awake in cinemas; we may be unusually wide-awake. If, therefore, we are reminded of dreaming, that only illuminates the uncertainty of wakefulness and the suspicion that life is a reverie.

Some of the unliterary aspects of film have been considered already: the underlying inferiority we feel toward the mechanical medium; the size and radiance of the image, with all that represents in terms of domination; the inconstant potential of the stream of images as an unsettler of calm and concentration. As with sensational events of other kinds—accidents, moments of fear, great joys—we may be very alert, but too on edge for the intense "dwelling in" a work that we hope to attain when listening to music or reading.

But the uniqueness of the sensation in cinema is in the antagonism between realism and abstraction. Although cinema is a popular spectacle, this sophisticated tension brings it close to the hopes of the surrealists. That enables a film to be appreciated on different levels, but it sets off an unresolved struggle between commercialism and esoteric formal dilemmas. In short, the activity of sitting in the dark and "believing in" the images is complex and delicate and demands a philosophical agility that few filmgoers could articulate. That does not mean that they have not acquired it, or that reactions do not show the scattering of an agile sensibility. It takes remarkable organizing power of disparate data to drive in a city—and any fool can drive. It may mean that the conscious understanding and unconscious effect of film have often wandered apart.

There is a pervasive disorientation in watching film. Photographic naturalism is the persuasive text of a movie. A photograph is accepted as an accurate record of its subject's appearance. One rejects that only if accuracy seems too generous a term for mere verisimilitude. But a photograph is only *like* a thing—thus a metaphor—so like it as to be confusing and to make us think of literalism rather than poetry. Even then, the photo does not evoke a thing, but stands for or replaces it, making the actuality less necessary. We abide by the limitations of a photographic record, but we have agreed that the world and the photograph look alike—the inviolability of optics is involved, and the passport picture testifies to its documentary fidelity.

Such naturalism can be altered by slow motion, silence, or any of the lenses added to a camera when filming—these are truly poetic devices. Nevertheless, the camera does not have the wit to lie or cheat, only artists and craftsmen do that. The apparatus records whatever is in front of its particular refinements. Despite such discrepancies as a lens not seeing perspective in the same way as the eye, or Technicolor being more pronounced than life's color, we have adjusted our comprehension so that the photograph is regarded as an imprint of life's surface. The first impact of a film is not that it is funny, sad, exciting, or touching, but that it is lifelike. And as soon as anything is lifelike, then life loses something of its uniqueness and integrity.

It is still the sensation of moving pictures that life's transience can be captured and reproduced. Not only appearance, gesture, and spatial relationship are hobbled. We also seem to repossess past time. The identical, but repeatable, rendering of duration is one of the most beguiling and baffling of film's capacities. When all these opportunities are combined, as they usually are now—lifelike imagery, color, sound, and an equivalent passage of time—the viewer concedes that he is looking at something so lifelike as to be deceptive. From television, he knows that feature films can look like newsreels, except that the fiction is probably more accomplished and therefore more plausible.

Against that, the lifelike is deathly and cold-bloodedly manipulated. There is no warmth, breath, or impulsiveness; chance never obtrudes. The screen is sterile and the mechanism heartless. The lifelike is cut off from real life. People are employed in mounting the performance, but they are not seen. The people on the screen may be dead. The loss of Gary Cooper does not alleviate his pensiveness in *Man of the West;* nor is Carole Lombard less lively now that she has been dead for longer than she lived. This is disconcerting, and movie fans were incredulous that Valentino, Lombard, or James Dean were dead beyond recall. But even when actors are still alive, the recorded images of them come to us as if from the dead, over an abyss, representations from a spirit world so that the naturalistic seems magical too. Norman Mailer has touched on this:

> *Film is a phenomenon whose resemblance to death has been ignored for too long.* An emotion produced from the churn of the flesh is delivered to a machine, and the machine and its connections manage to produce a flow of images which will arouse some related sentiment in those who watch. The living emotion has passed through a burial ground—and has been resurrected. The living emotion survives as a psychological reality; it continues to exist as a set of images in one's memory which are not too different, as the years go by, from the images we keep of a relative who is dead. Think of a favorite uncle who is gone. Does the apparatus of the mind which flashes his pictures before us act in another fashion if we ask for a flash of Humphrey Bogart next? Perhaps it does not. Film seems part of the mechanism of memory, or at the least, a most peculiar annex to memory. For in film we

remember events as if they had taken place and we were there.

Mailer reveals his humanism in stressing the "living emotion" carried by film. It is hardly that, since an actor pretends to it and employs a set of presentation signals that communicate such an emotion, but are not "living" parts of it. It is, rather, a ghost of emotion that comes on the journey, or an invented sentiment, and we may remember that translucent appearance is associated with ghosts in literature and graphic art—the ghostly thing glows, has lifelike appearance, but no substance. We can "see through it": an enigmatic phrase suggesting transparency, blatant fakery, and the spirit as a source of enlightenment.

How much difference is there between photographs of the dead and the living? As I write this, I can look up and see photographs of relatives, some dead, some alive, but none with me. I know the differences, but the photographs do not convey them, for the photograph does not evoke presence so much as absence. In watching films, the thorough evocation of, say, Robert Mitchum, does not give us Mitchum to play with as if he were dressing-up clothes, but gives and takes away. It is like saying: "This is Mitchum. You cannot have him. Imagine him."

Thus, as Mailer says, memory is copied by film; we are having to begin to remember as we see. The most satisfactory movie experiences lead to one going home, half-recollecting, half-reinventing that face and those moments from the film. If anyone doubts this weird interacting of film and memory, they should see *Celine and Julie Go Boating*, a film that goes back and forth in time, and where several moments are shown more than once. Better still, they should attend the editing of a film and watch every shot over and over again. Then, the reiteration loses sense and turns the "facts" into hallucination. The outward monotony does not bore. It gives us different sensations of time: Repetition is only one. Reversal is equally stunning, as witness the eerie wonder of action shown backward, a diver rising feet first from a lake, his splash retreating and forming a placid surface and the diver vaulting backward to land, with perfect poise, on a rocky ledge and there subside. That charm comes from the medium agitating the conventions of memory. Film, famously, has a constant present tense, but as we watch it we seem to exist in both the past and the present.

It cannot be chance that film discovered the flashback: It is the medium of appearance through hindsight, like looking at images of man from deep space that have taken minutes or years to fall to earth. Film ridicules the present by preparing it in advance and giving us the feeling that it has happened before and will happen again. Our loss of confidence in the linear, forward movement of time, the occult interest in *déjà vu,* and the fashion for circular motions of time coincide with the existence of cinema. It may have been very discerning of cinema managers to admit viewers at any place in a film, for nothing so clarified its resemblance to a wheel slowly revolving, or the way in which all sections of a wheel are alike.

Not the least subterfuge in the movies affecting an audience is the pretense that there is no audience. This too is deathly: A stage actor is alive to us; the movie actor who reflects on his thoughts is only proof that millions of people in the world will never meet one another. This contrast brims with irony. The stage actor adjusts himself to unconcealed performance: He speaks and gestures broadly enough to be seen from the farthest seats. But the movie actor's efforts are attuned to narcissistic detail: Some stage actors fail in the movies because they lack that finesse. A film is so much more calculated, being broken into fragments seen from carefully selected angles. The most touching moments of films are when the camera shows us a human face "lost" in thought and feeling. That is often accomplished by the camera coming so close to the face that we would back away in consternation if a person came that near. But the movie actor pretends the camera is not there, and looks studiously past it. If you doubt the significance of this, study films and notice the uniformity of the lie in close-ups. It is a trick that allows us to believe we have a privileged insight. At the same time we are made into spies, or peeping toms: A habitual furtiveness accompanies the act of seeing.

The effect of this can be felt in a comparison of the Hollywood movie with Rembrandt's portraits. The concentration and compassion of Rembrandt's work is held together by the way one eye, at least, is looking directly at us. The experience of the painted person confronts us. The journey of age, compromise, and pain cannot be shirked: The portrait knows it will be seen and brings a candor to that ordeal that the viewer must match or turn away from, overwhelmed by its force. It is unusual in movies for anyone to look directly into the camera—indeed, it was warned against in Hollywood as a violation of some superstitious imperative—and the look away, compared with Rembrandt, is fantasizing and self-pitying. This is not to mention the emphasis on beauty, cosmetics, and glamour in the Hollywood face, and "ordinariness" in Rembrandt's faces. Stardom easily accepted the idea that the stars were gods; by contrast, Rembrandt's people are mortals—a race we hardly meet in Hollywood films, either because film faces are rarefied or because they are already dead, or only lifelike.

If the audience in movies represents the crowd of this century, it is worth asking how the crowd figures in Hollywood films. The huddled masses were offered life, liberty, and the pursuit of happiness; in the cinema, the audience enveloped by darkness are provided with the lifelike, loneliness, and the tantalizing freedom of fantasy. With rather solemn disapproval, in *1984,* George Orwell foresaw television being turned against the viewers so that the television sets not only broadcast Big Brother's message but also served as domestic surveillance systems. That shows his own taste for the thriller. The actual development of television has been less melodramatic and sinister, and all the more sapping. It is not a conspiracy, but the choice of society. Today, in America—and in other countries—the same instrument carries information about the world, time-killing entertainment and promotion of values and valuables that sustain the economy. And, as if the system appreciated the dangers of an aroused or morose audience turning into a mob or concerted opposition, television has regularized the loneliness of every one of the huddled masses. We watch television in the barren security of our own homes: Alienation has been made concrete, domesticity has diminished the chance of community.

How easily Cassandra guides my pen; how painfully the child who loved the garden sees betrayal. How necessary it is to spell out the cultural implications of Hollywood without sounding alarmist, doctrinaire, or bitter. The predicament is too dangerous for alarm, too complex for solutions, and too sad for hurt feelings. The question remains: What has the mass appeal of Hollywood done to individualism?

Look above you in the cinema and there is a geometrical diagram of the experience: A beam of light widens as far as the screen. Alternatively, light from the screen converges upon one tiny nexus. That arrowhead indicates all the sensation pouring into one mind. Every member of the audience can look up and see the model of his or her experience. Art, too, prides itself on the private revelation. It is not that art always has an educative duty, but still the insight is reckoned to be applicable to life, even if only as consolation or delight. The individual accepts some responsibility to himself and to his world in that he will not endure sham consolation or hollow delight. The means of consolation and delight in art is that, however agonizing the situation, art can express it with formal grace. That grace is not frivolous. It is the noblest human handling of tragedy or difficulty without evasion or morbidity. Its accomplishment sometimes encourages us so that we can live with the difficulty.

In the minds of many more men than Monroe Stahr (admittedly a ghost, but one striving to be real), Hollywood was once an imperiled fount of idealism. Just as America sought to nourish deprived millions with Eden-like rights, so Hollywood anticipated a universal appeal to the imagination in which every anxiety about art being the preserve of a minority founded on money, class, or education might be dispelled. This hope still grips every film-maker: To speak to the people, to unite the world—that has beckoned ever since the end of the First World War when, amid so much confused hope and fear, the most universal and comforting image was the brave but pessimistic Charlie.

But the system that made and transmitted those images could only function in terms of industry, organized marketing, and the alteration in Chaplin's income. This is not an attack on capitalism. The means of broadcasting Mao's image are essentially the same: Profit obsesses one, propaganda the other—and both are destructive of truth. Idealism cannot confront the masses without method, and in Hollywood that has produced inescapable brutalities that do not necessarily signal brutal men. Listen to Mervyn Le Roy on Hollywood practice, and remember that he has an honorable record as an entertainer, and consider how far the toughness of his voice is as assumed as the belligerence of James Cagney in Le Roy's own small masterpiece of the confidence trickster, *Hard to Handle:*

> As for movies just for the intelligentsia, these so-called critics' pictures rarely make money, and I'll tell you why. Anyone who makes a picture for a critic is out of his

mind. A critic isn't representative. I have never found a bad picture any critic could help and I've never found a good one any critic could hurt. *Another Part of the Forest,* for instance, was a critic's picture. It was beautifully done, *but it was not a picture most people wanted to see.*

If you saw *Francis,* the movie about the talking mule, you saw a really enjoyable picture. The people in it were great and the people who made it were great, *and it was a picture everyone wanted to see.* They needed a talking mule in *Another Part of the Forest.* Because it's this way: *The Blue Boy* is a beautiful picture, but comparatively few people have seen it. The *Mona Lisa* is one of the greatest pictures the world has ever known, but more people have seen Lana Turner. My answer to that is: People want entertainment. If the Blue Boy sang like Jolson, they'd go to see him. Or if Mona Lisa looked like Hedy Lamarr, more people would go to the Louvre.

The coarseness of this is boastful and suggests how often Hollywood sounded like itself. (One thing contributing to that could be the secluded life Hollywood people led. Their community was inward-looking, incestuous, and a self-parody.) The argument is flimsy, the style reckless. "A critic isn't representative," Le Roy protests; but neither is a banker, an executive, or a stockholder, whose interests money-makers presumably hold dear. No one is representative of anyone except himself. The whole notion of anyone being representative refers back to the sense of huddled masses, the amorphous body that has swamped discrimination with what Hollywood called box office. Le Roy's argument can easily persuade its own adherents that they are responding to popular taste: that they know what the people want and manufacture it. That is the theory of the tycoon as commercial mastermind—and it is claptrap.

The system did not give the audience what it wanted, and it took little trouble to find out what those wants were. It provided something the public would buy, and which the system could comfortably produce. The anxious emphasis was always on the danger of losing the audience: Proved successes were repeated, failures shunned like lepers, stars turned into statues of themselves, the diversity of material ranked into genres. The underlying approach to the audience was cautious and fearful: Do not disturb. Le Roy, like *Sullivan's Travels,* summed this up as "the majority of people who go to movies go because they want to forget their worries for a while." Notice that those going to the movies are described in collective terms, even if it is actually individuals who go. Irving Thalberg's version of this process is more tactful than Le Roy's, but just as specious: Its shallow populism sounds like Adolphe Menjou and Edward Arnold as chairmen gulling the stockholders and believing their own rhetoric:

> . . . entertainment engages the attention of people, and . . . brings about a pleasing response in them. Entertainment is the objective of the photoplay and we must keep in mind that as entertainment it must appeal to the varied tastes of all people. Other arts generally appeal to a selected group, but the motion picture art, and it is an art, must have universal appeal. This is fundamental, for the motion picture industry, with its investment of hundreds of millions of dollars, is based on the hope that it will appeal to the people of a nation and of a world, and if it did not have this appeal, it could not have reached its present state of development.

That was written in 1929, but Thalberg is still thinking of films as "photoplays" and trying to have the best of commerce, art, and mass satisfaction. Only a politician wants prosperity, approval, and high-minded nondisturbance in the same complacent stew. And the "universal appeal" Thalberg yearned for was centered on a set of personalities as looming as the faces in Mount Rushmore. The industry organized itself around the stars it possessed; they were the abiding draw for the spectators; and it was through these phantoms of glamour that the masses inhabited a world of fantasy. The entertainment took root in the spectator's wish to imagine himself a little different from his real self; and the warm comfort of the form ensured that he would never resort to actions that could make the desired state a reality. The concentration on a life of unreality, especially allied to the conditions of indifference and loneliness produced by cinema, took away responsibility and the thought of involvement. Art fosters the whole person, but the movies have fragmented the whole and dulled the desire for integration.

The world presented by the movies was gently insisted upon as visible, but inaccessible: Voyeurism is not as delicious if we can actually walk into the world seen. The comprehensive perfection of the people in films forbade ordinary human trespass. The people in movies are so good-looking that they constitute a species apart. This is not just cosmetic beauty, but typecasting so that people in movies look as they are. The stooge supporting characters are graven stereotypes, appearances in whom there can be no doubt of identity: for example, Edward Everett Horton, Thomas Mitchell, Butterfly McQueen, John Carradine, Margaret Dumont, Spring Byington, William Demarest, Walter Brennan, Ward Bond, Thelma Ritter—names that instantly communicate capsule personalities. That is the alien grace of movie people: the utter confidence in knowing who they are; doubts are burned away by the lights and sharp focus that pick them out from the background. And if we are dowdier than Joan Fontaine or Tyrone Power, how can it not depress us further when the atmosphere of Hollywood movies is implicitly certain that meaning lies in appearance?

"Other people" or "the crowd" in movies are treated with

almost totalitarian severity. More often than not, they do not even exist. No one is in a film except for a purpose: the hero's uncle, a double-crossing sidekick, the boss, the man he asks the time of as he hurries to meet Ann Sheridan, the plain-faced dullard he sits beside on the bus as he dodges the police, so that even that contrast of agitation and stolidness gets a laugh and contributes to the smartness of the film—all of these are furnishings in his room, splashes where he breaks the surface of events. No *one* is truly unexpected, a chance bystander, an unplanned encounter, the man on the street. No crowd bristles with the unpredictability of real crowds. All these "others" are counted and paid for. They are called extras and hired in bulk from Central Casting, another Ellis Island congregation. They stand where they are told and move like a team. No one of them wants to be noticed: Familiar extras, faces picked out, were not hired again. The crowd had to be anonymous, and it was unlit and out of focus, as much in the background as the music.

There are two ways of suggesting the effect this had upon the crowd in the cinema. The first is to point to the alienation of so many millions unable to tear themselves away from television but by now dispirited by the news, unwarmed by the heartless entertainment, and incredulous of the advertisements. What destruction of self-respect has this induced? Where will that contempt go but into furious outrage or perpetual self-deception?

The second suggestion is a livid etching of that outrage: Nathanael West's *The Day of the Locust,* a book about Hollywood with hardly any stars, producers, or film-set scenes, but on the loose like a lost dog in the suburbs of Los Angeles, amid people drawn to California but unable to attain the inner church of the film kingdom. The hero of West's book is Tod Hackett, an artist hired to do designs for films: As such, he stands for the way West, one of America's most mordant satirists, himself wrote trash for the movies. But the book is West's revenge and warning. Tod sees this crowd of failures and detects its resentment. He plans a large painting—*The Burning of Los Angeles*—which will show this abused energy running amok. The riot he anticipates occurs at a movie premiere when the adulation and worship veer toward hysteria. But before then, Tod and West have analyzed this frustrated power, and this is the rancor of stagnant idealism among the huddled masses:

All their lives they had slaved at some kind of dull, heavy labor, behind desks and counters, in the fields and at tedious machines of all sorts, saving their pennies and dreaming of the leisure that would be theirs when they had enough. Finally that day came. They could draw a weekly income of ten or fifteen dollars. Where else should they go but California, the land of sunshine and oranges?

Once there, they discover that sunshine isn't enough. They get tired of oranges, even of avocado pears and passion fruit. Nothing happens. They don't know what to do with their time. They haven't the mental equipment for pleasure. Did they slave so long just to go to an occasional Iowa picnic? What else is there? They watch the waves come in at Venice. There wasn't any ocean where most of them come from, but after you've seen one wave, you've seen them all. The same is true of the aeroplanes at Glendale. If only a plane would crash once in a while so that they could watch the passengers being consumed in a "holocaust of flame," as the newspapers put it. But the planes never crash.

Their boredom becomes more and more terrible. They realize that they've been tricked and burn with resentment. Every day of their lives they read the newspapers and went to the movies. Both fed them on lynchings, murder, sex crimes, explosions, wrecks, love-nests, fires, miracles, revolutions, war. This daily diet made sophisti cates of them. The sun is a joke. Oranges can't titillate their jaded palates. Nothing can ever be violent enough to make taut their slack minds and bodies. They have been cheated and betrayed. They have slaved and saved for nothing.

West's warning vision sees no hope in populism or politics. It dreads the angry crowd and only thinks of ways of occupying or diverting them. The next chapter examines a film for all times, but one that observes a hope of the thirties—that the crowd might stay cheerful. Citizen Kane is a man who dreams of applause, votes, and popularity—the happy manifestation of national energy.

V

ORSON WELLES
AND *CITIZEN KANE*

> *He was disappointed in the world, so he built one of his own, an absolute monarchy.*
>
> —LELAND of Kane

Citizen Kane GROWS WITH EVERY YEAR AS AMERICA COMES to resemble it. Kane is the willful success who tries to transcend external standards, and many plain Americans know his pent-up fury at lonely liberty. The film absorbs praise and criticism, unabashed by being voted the best ever made or by Pauline Kael's skillful reassessment of its rather nasty cleverness. Perhaps both those claims are valid. The greatest film may be cunning, slick, and meretricious. If that is so, it could help us abandon an important part of the legend attached to *Kane*—that it is valiantly independent and ambitious, and made with an integrity no other Hollywood film has known, before or since.

Welles himself has always encouraged the assumption that he is not a Hollywood person. He allows that he may be a great and noble artist, that he knows a commitment to honesty indecently abused in Hollywood, that he burst in upon the jittery Babylon when very young, and adroitly turned it to his own high purposes. But in so doing he attracted the hostility of a mean system so that ever afterward he has been a wandering genius, sometimes a voice in the wilderness announcing projects yet only occasionally finishing or releasing films, but sometimes the voice on commercials for beer, sherry, mashed potato, and shredded wheat (a diet that could account for his bulk), and sometimes the guest seer on the *Tonight* show, Falstaff to Johnny Carson's emaciated Hal, the great wobbling jelly of humanity beside that lean eminence of sunnyCal's drikoolade.

Kane is too pungent a picture to be wrapped up as a masterpiece, and Welles has done and said enough to make us wary of accepting him on his own terms. The film and the man are intensely American. *Kane* reeks of Hollywood, and Welles is addicted to show biz. I am not enlisting the film to cut across my study of Hollywood with a glimpse of some alternative way; nor am I seeking to clip the film's billowing wings. The working title for *Kane* was "American," and I see no reason to be skeptical of that. *Citizen Kane* epitomizes every method and attitude in Hollywood—albeit at the behest of a man opposed to any system. It is a working model of the tragic alienation of film as a form; it is a movie about the idealism that longs to communicate, and is spoiled by the fatal intrusion of personal pride. "The people will think" is the determined hope for social enlightenment; but the addition, "what I tell them to think," is the disappointed brutality of pained experience. *Kane* is also the key work of the first American director to identify comprehensive fraud as a topic central to his culture. Nothing is as intriguing as the film's fascination with unsoundness, or as indebted to the early influence of films. But the intricacy lies in Kane's manipulation of his world being inextricably tangled with Welles's own finesse. It would be less absorbing a film if it was simply a satire on American success. In addition, it shows a romantic and idealistic passion for power, style, impact, meaning, and success, everything a true American might desire—be he Charles Foster Kane or George Orson Welles.

Kane and Welles are children who converge as they grow older, even if they meet in shadowland, with Welles playing Kane at the age of twenty-five, one young man domineering newspapers, the other bullying and charming his way through Hollywood. "It might be fun to run a newspaper," the script has Kane say, with the flippant deprecation of real enthusiasm that does not hide the man's lust to run things and people. One can hear a similar worldly claim coming from Welles's sensual mouth (rosebud lips): Indeed, there's a quote attributed to him, on the young virtuoso first seeing the kingdom of Hollywood, and it has Kane's taunting superiority: "This is the greatest train set a boy ever had."

The boy Kane grows up in an isolation like an illustration from a story book: a cramped log cabin in the middle of the prairie. Its place in the American imagination is as a wishful hideaway or the origin of presidents. We only see it in winter, covered with a mantle of snow that bestows an enchanted resonance on every sound—the boy shouting "The Union forever" as he plays in the snow, and his mother's anguished cry, "Charles!" when she calls him to go away with Mr. Thatcher to wealth, education, and his cold future. Nothing in *Kane* is natural, everything is manufactured and contrived: The studio method of making a film becomes symptomatic of a tycoon's America where everything can be controlled, made, or owned, and reality is a stage setting for the individual. The prairie is a set: The sky is gray backdrop from the horizon up to the rafters where props men are sprinkling "snow" down upon the characters. This adds to the feeling of the cabin being as much a place of mind as the miniature house in a glass snowball that fell from Kane's hand when he died.

Everything in *Kane* is emotionally expressive: The film aches with loss, and that prairie outpost is a Christmas card memory as well as the last felt possession of a man who owns so much but connects with so little. Kane dies as wealthy as his mother meant him to be, and, schematically, the film is a commentary on material deadweight in America. Kane is the son of a feckless father and a commanding mother: We know very little about them; they might be immigrants— Kane could be the Ellis Island simplification of Canino, Kalinowski, Kael, Kahn, or Keohane; they are living in the remoteness of Colorado until a sort of barroom good luck descends on them: "How, to boardinghouse-keeper, Mary Kane, by a defaulting boarder, in 1868, was left the supposedly worthless deed to an abandoned mine shaft, the Colorado Lode."

It remains unclear why Mary Kane enters into the peculiar agreement that sacrifices her son for financial security. Our one scene at the little house on the prairie has Thatcher, from "the bank," reading the terms of the agreement to the parents and preparing to go off with young Charles. The filming idealizes the mother: She dominates the interior, her movements monopolize the camera, she overrides her hovering husband, and she is as beautiful as drawn-back hair, plain garb, and the severe oval of Agnes Moorehead's face allow. We feel her torment, and the scene ends on a camera movement that unites the mother and son in a Madonna and Child image. Yet the mother is sending her son away, and she says, "I've got his trunk all packed. I've had it packed for a week now."

The script is too meticulous for that to be an oversight; and if few notice it on first viewing of the film, that indicates the extent to which *Kane* was packed so full that it required more than one viewing. The paradox of anguish and calculation is intended, and it remains an awkward enigma. Why is it that this mother, who seems businesslike, should for fifty thousand dollars a year consign her only son to a bank that will shape his life and act as trustee to the mining fortune that will become his at the age of twenty-five? Could the mother not have gone to Chicago with him, ditching the husband who tries to explain the oddity away:

> You're gonna live with Mr. Thatcher from now on, Charlie. You're gonna be rich. Your Ma figures—well that is me and her decided this ain't the place for you to grow up in. You'll probably be the richest man in America someday, and you ought to get an education.

The scene is a wound based on the contrariness of the cinematic adoration of a mother who severs bonds with her son. Emotionally, it is central to Kane's lifelong perplexity at the way feelings and money were equated and he was rejected. I said that this treatment was schematic; the notion that power and possessions cannot compensate for severed feelings is taken for granted and offered as an easy platitude to those (the audience) who are not rich, but who (always in the cinema) are assumed to be vessels of correct sentiment. Creatively, the scene barely works, and on analysis the "mystery" becomes downright implausible.

The subsequent survey of the pursuit of money and power growing out of the early loss of love, and the implication that people and affection are commodities, is presented as starkly as a controversy in a Kane paper. The dramatic emphasis discourages considered debate. Far better is the somber lament for past time and lost ties that rises to an overwhelming climax when "Rosebud"—Kane's dying word—proves to be the name on the sledge that the boy used to fight off Thatcher when the banker gathered him up for the train to Chicago. The film's separation of the cabin scene and its explanation adds to the element of puzzle and to the impression of Kane gazing back at his past. Cinema's backward look is the consistent point of view in *Citizen Kane* and its precision is as emotional as recollection.

A comparison with Welles's early life is not made for neat correspondences. Men so alike can retain their affinity despite great discrepancies. And it is more useful to see the pair as brothers than belabor the not very interesting attempt to imitate William Randolph Hearst. Treating Kane as a portrait of Hearst only illustrates Welles's need to pretend to be other people. Welles was born in Kenosha, Wisconsin, in 1915. His father was an inventor and his mother a concert pianist, but both were dead by the time he was twelve, and Welles became the ward of a Chicago doctor, Dr. Maurice Bernstein. Do not let sympathy smother the young orphan; nor should we quickly ply so clever a man with Freudian excuses; perhaps the loss of parents freed a rampant imagination. Charles Foster Kane would be a braver, more intelligent man if more prepared to live in the present. But he is only clever and rhetorical and thus, when disappointed, he creates and dwells in a past for himself. Still, this may be a shrewd insight in the film: Perhaps tyrants and tycoons step backward into the future, encouraged by such emotive fallacies.

One understands the influence of inventiveness and artistry on Welles, while the experience of a small, spreading Midwest town emerges with feeling in his second film, *The Magnificent Ambersons*. One must also wonder about the loss of his parents, the need of a guardian, and the role of Chicago as *the* nearby center of civilization for the growing boy. All these things are touched on in Herman Mankiewicz's ingenious script for *Kane,* a work quite happy to exploit a friendship with Hearst and to implicate Welles himself.

Kane's chief aide in the film is named Bernstein, and there may be more private teasing than anyone has yet annotated.

There is no reason to sentimentalize the loss of parents to Welles; perhaps the elderly Kane wallows in the loss of his mother, but actually feels little. Certainly, the arrogant, self-sufficient hardness of Kane has a passing resemblance to Welles. Kane is a young man made superhuman by the capricious use of wealth. Welles was known as the "boy wonder" because of precocious talent and his unwillingness to moderate it with older, duller men. Nevertheless, the legend of wonderfulness is stronger than the factual detail supporting it, and Welles's life is a blend of real achievement, publicizing accounts of it, and sweet lies—white, cream, and purple. Matter-of-fact honesty is not in his repertoire; he is hardly able to be dry or self-effacing. Which is not to call him dishonest. But he is borne upon clouds of self-romance; he is his own hero, inspired by the challenge of playing himself for the rest of the world. Kane is preoccupied with a similar projection of himself, in which the needs of inflated self-importance and a massive audience meet in the larger-than-life image. The tycoon is the sum of all opinions other people have of him, and Welles has courted a similar fragmentation to be everything imagined by his audience or conveyed by his own riot of dedication, teasing, and magic. Like Kane, he has wanted to impress us, to be famous, and there lies another passion of the huddled masses, notionally fulfilled by America's provision that the lowliest newcomer may become a millionaire, a president, or a star.

The young Welles was always a star—perhaps an insufferable one—and temperamentally an actor. As a child he mounted productions of Shakespeare in which he directed, bestrode, and upstaged all his young friends, until they turned into awestruck critics devoted to but disliking him. This flair was encouraged at Todd School in Woodstock, Illinois, where he lorded every dramatic production and cultivated himself as a virtuoso in his abiding vein—sincere ham. To add exoticism he traveled around the world with his widower father and spent some time in China in the early 1920s—this is the outline of experience that easily leads to Welles's "acquiring" no mean role in the struggles of Chiang Kai-shek and Sun Yat-sen. More practically, it furnished his imaginative view of the East as a place of intrigue, mystery, and colorful wickedness: Much of Welles's work is rococo decoration of cliché.

At the age of sixteen, Welles graduated from Todd and found himself with a sufficient inheritance to go traveling on his own. He went to Ireland and bamboozled himself into the Gate Theater in Dublin, one of the more celebrated theaters in the world. He arrived in Dublin and told Hilton Edwards of the Gate that he was already a Broadway success but prepared to assist the Irish theater. Edwards cannot have failed to recognize a sixteen-year-old, for Welles looked like a teen-ager until at least thirty. Nor can he have been deceived by such picturesque boasts. But he hired Welles and said later that he was tickled by the mixture of nerve, theatricality, and conceit: Compelling charlatan is one of Welles's most persuasive roles.

This was the start of a professional career that developed so rapidly that, by 1938, Welles was one of the most conspicuous talents in American theater. He had acted with Katharine Cornell's touring company and began to work regularly for radio. The craving for public reputation in Welles turned to the willful pursuit of dramatic surprise: Impact that distracts us from content is also central to his lifelong hobby and occasional stage performance, magic. In 1936, he managed and produced, in Harlem, a version of *Macbeth* with an all-black cast, set in Haiti and applying the atmospherics of witchcraft to voodoo. No one is any longer sure how good a production of *Macbeth* it was; but it is the

most famous, in which this very white kid juggled Federal
Theater support, a difficult cast, and widespread hostility to
the promotion of black art. Welles produced the play on-
and offstage with indefatigable energy and bravura, and
when one night his Macbeth was unable to appear, the
Welles who had spoken sanctimoniously about the dignity of
black peoples put on blackface and played the part himself.

This heralds a time of furious activity in which colleagues
said Welles worked twenty hours a day; another interpretation is that, by 1945, he was burned out and so weary that he
has procrastinated and been undisciplined ever since. In
1937, with John Houseman, he formed the Mercury Theater
Company and began a series of notorious, flashy, or startling
productions in New York in which novelty made up for depth
or care. *Dr. Faustus* had Welles playing the man who invented fatal compromise; a production of *Julius Caesar* in
modern dress referred Shakespeare's play to the Europe of
fascist dictators and had Welles himself as Brutus. Other
productions included Marc Blitzstein's *The Cradle Will
Rock, The Shoemaker's Holiday* by Dekker, *Heartbreak
House,* with Welles playing Captain Shotover, Büchner's
Danton's Death, in which he took the part of Saint-Just, and
a compilation of scenes involving Falstaff in which Welles
put on false stomachs and played to a Hal, Burgess Meredith,
six years older than himself.

There are scenes in *Kane* of the young owner galvanizing
a sober newspaper into a sensationalist tabloid, and losing
sight of journalistic ethics in the exhilaration of working
every hour and remaking the front page five times in a night.
Surely Mankiewicz wrote those scenes mindful of Welles's
shooting-star prowess with Mercury; and surely Welles caught
the reference to his own career and played the scenes with
that much more relish. In 1937–38, he was not only producing and acting for Mercury, but also helping to manage

a tempestuous company, adapting, writing, directing, and acting for CBS radio and, it seems clear, leading a hectic private life.

Radio converted Welles from a celebrity of the New York stage to an international outrage, and it was the medium that carried him from the traditional, minority appeal of theater to the mass reaching-out of film. The most memorable things in Welles's career involve a large audience and a raising of their expectations. As artist or would-be demagogue, he wanted everyone to know and admire him, or know and shudder at his name: It hardly matters which. He grew up in the age of Hitler, Mussolini, Stalin, and Roosevelt, and only Stalin among those neglected radio. The need of both artist and politician to grab the public is caught in a speech from *Kane,* when Kane tells Bernstein and Jed Leland what he wants his new paper, *The Inquirer,* to be:

> I've changed the front page a little, Mr. Bernstein. That's not enough, no. There's something I've got to get into this paper besides pictures and print. I've got to make the New York *Inquirer* as important to New York as the gas in that light.

At which point, with a dramatic irony that is subtler on film than when recounted, Kane turns out the light. This leaves his face dark with shadow when he reads his pompous "Declaration of Principles." But once he is through with that self-congratulating recitation, he straightens up, his face comes back into the light, and he yells for "Solly!" to remake the front page once more. The ethical *Inquirer* is a humbug; the restless yellow press tycoon is lively and human. The style spreads hyperactivity in which a reasoned, flexible attitude will turn into stubborn prejudice: thus the alternative headlines on election night—"Kane Elected" sorrowfully replaced by "Fraud at the Polls."

Radio enlarged that streak in Welles; or he discerned the

guile in the medium. Although his theater work was prestigious, radio saw an effortless switch to barnstorming melodrama: Again, this is typical of Welles's ease at straddling
Shakespeare, Kafka, and B-picture rubbish, and the creeping
confusion of standards. He had been playing the daft, tele-
pathic detective, Lamont Cranston, in *The Shadow* for some
time before CBS commissioned the Mercury Theater of the
Air in which the company adapted classic novels or films as
radio plays. *The Shadow* is as raw as Méliès and Griffith—
though much more tongue in cheek—and Welles clearly
adored it: Cranston is not just a mastermind, but a figure
of magical authority—"Who knows what evil lurks in the
minds of men? The Shadow knows." That omniscience is
hokum, but power over the minds of men fascinates Welles
and Kane, and it is the immature fantasy realized in movie
houses everywhere.

It is the theme of what still appears to be his most famous
work: the live broadcast of an adaptation of *The War of the
Worlds* on October 30, 1938, an eve that the Shadow would
have appreciated—Halloween. In hindsight, one is reluctant
to allow that anything to do with that broadcast was not
calculated. Some say he merely arrived at the studio to read
the script. But the credits of Mercury productions had as
many Welles as an oil field, and the Shadow, after all,
knew everything. Welles had an America nervously alert to
thoughts of invasion. Even Howard Koch, who wrote the
radio play, awoke next day to hear talk of "panic" and "invasion" and wondered if Hitler had taken some momentous
step. No one can explain how Germany might have invaded
America, but we need not believe that a technologically
sophisticated people do not also imagine the impossible. It
seems unlikely that Welles could have foreseen a lull in the
rival Edgar Bergen-Charlie McCarthy show in which many
listeners switched over to be gripped by the simulated documentary that Koch's adaptation took as its style: Perhaps

that was Welles's luck, just as the Colorado Lode was Kane's. If so, it teaches us to attend to the minute ways in which different media work. But I am sure Orson Welles had noted the likely misunderstanding in the minds of listeners between his own name and that of H. G. Wells, the original author of *The War of the Worlds,* and anticipated an aftermath in which he would pick up extra credit, and blame. Who knows how easily the public misunderstands? The promoter knows. As it was, Welles's concern for authority smoothly appropriated authorship.

The program took Wells's novel and altered it so that an ordinary evening's radio—Ramon Raquello and his orchestra in the Meridian Room of the Hotel Park Plaza in downtown New York—was apparently interrupted and then replaced by "live" coverage of the landing of a spacecraft near Grovers Mill, New Jersey. It was to prove characteristic of Welles that the program switched the styles of fact and fiction. As radio, the program was a cunning trick: Using anxious announcers, ominous pauses, frightening sound effects, and the orchestrated development of "spontaneous" alarm, it mimicked news-reporting radio to misleading ends. If you heard the program from the beginning, you could not have been deceived. But tune in a little late, and you might wonder if this was the end of your world, especially if you lived in New Jersey. The play ended with New York devastated and deserted, by which time some real listeners had taken fright, packed up essential things, and headed for the hills. No doubt the press exaggerated the panic: The cynicism of journals like the *Inquirer* would have gloated over the spectacle of foolishness. Perhaps thousands fled, perhaps only hundreds. It was a milestone evening for radio, and terrible evidence for anyone who feared that the public was a huge weight easily tipped this way or that. It also showed how far the mood of 1938 respected the tone of "documentary" and was unable to distinguish the authority of a medium from the nature of its message. A part of the huddled masses stood as transfixed as rabbits by the shining light pointed at them. And Welles himself wound up the program with this sardonic restoration of normality. Notice how far it fluctuates between the genius and anarchist, the brilliant schoolboy and the blithe manipulator of other people's insecurities:

> This is Orson Welles, ladies and gentlemen, out of character to assure you that the War of the Worlds has no further significance than as the holiday offering it was intended to be. The Mercury Theater's own radio version of dressing up in a sheet and jumping out of a bush and saying Boo! Starting now, we couldn't soap all your windows and steal all your garden gates, by tomorrow night . . . so we did the next best thing. We annihilated the world before your very ears, and utterly destroyed the Columbia Broadcasting System. You will be relieved, I hope, to learn that we didn't mean it, and that both institutions are still open for business. So good-bye everybody, and remember, please, for the next day or so, the terrible lesson you learned tonight. That grinning, glowing, globular invader of your living room is an inhabitant of the pumpkin patch, and if your doorbell rings and nobody's there, that was no Martian . . . it's Halloween.

At press conferences in the following days Welles widened his large eyes, swept the flop of hair back from his brow, and said he had never dreamed such consternation would be caused. Nearly forty years later, the broadcast seems like one of the first modern happenings in America: the absurd exaggeration of impact stemming from the special relationship between the people and the media. As calculated lie or entertaining illusion, the program could have been made by a Kane radio station: It has the personal and political contempt of a brilliant advertiser persuading the public to eat shit.

It was dressed up as show biz, but it was nearly totalitarian: The lights had been commandeered by a conjurer, turned off and on again so that some of the people had shown themselves terrified of the dark. Yet the playfulness resisted any profound reflections; whatever the broadcast indicated about America could be veiled in "entertainment." The educative potential of the movies had always been similarly compromised. The sweeping nature of the trick, the uneasy balance of game, melodrama, and larger effect, and the deliberate duplicity of style pointed Welles toward the movies, and at least one film company heeded the controversy.

The film industry had faltered during the thirties. The investment required by sound coincided with the Depression, and audiences were never again as large as they had been in the late twenties. One company after another faced liquidation or takeover. Censorship and the first serious economic fears together restrained the sort of risk that might have developed in cinema: The novel and the theater took America to task in the thirties, but the movies calmed anxiety with the reliability of genre. Only one company, MGM, stayed out of the red, and its product was gentle, conservative, and inert. That is the broad pattern, but there are other factors that may have contributed to the decline. Perhaps sound dissipated the command of the new medium; perhaps the human dismay of the thirties began to cast doubt on the optimism of movies; perhaps talk separated those wanting sensation from those prepared to listen to arguments.

RKO, despite the profitability of the Astaire-Rogers musicals, lurched from one crisis to another. The great public reaction to *The War of the Worlds* persuaded two key executives at RKO—George Schaefer and Nelson Rockefeller—that Welles might make a sensation to rescue the studio. The legend goes that they invited Welles, persevered after his early refusals, and eventually gave him a free hand to make what he liked, if he would only come.

This part of *Kane*'s history is not properly researched. I doubt that Welles was given the carte blanche that many accounts allege; I cannot see what carte blanche might be in the context of a man making a film for an impoverished but professional company. Nor is it safe to present Welles as a New Yorker, dedicated to theater and radio, and only eventually yielding to importunate offers from a drooling Hollywood. Welles had made two films already: one in 1934, less than five minutes long, on 16mm; the other, in 1938, on 16mm again, forty minutes long and used in a stage production of *Too Much Johnson*. So there had been an early taste for the medium. More important, I suspect Welles saw the cinema as his destiny: He would not have been the only magician and manipulator of reaction to make the move west. Perhaps *The War of the Worlds* was aimed at Hollywood; almost certainly, the first invitations turned down were steps in a campaign to secure better terms. What distinguishes Welles is the extent to which "better" meant creative latitude rather than pecuniary gain; perhaps nothing else shocked the system more.

But those terms should be examined more carefully. For instance, *Kane* is a studio film; it looks better than the average RKO film, but essentially like it, and it was made on sound stages where Astaire's heels had beaten out their cool frenzy. *Kane* cost only $686,000 and is a skillful maximization of resources: The grandeur of the sets is not in huge constructions, but the disguise of models, backdrops, lighting, and lenses; and for a film about the crowd it has a modest cast. *Gone With the Wind,* made at about the same time, cost $4,250,000, and yet it is rather less rich-looking overall. Arguably, it was made with greater liberty, for David Selznick spared nothing and was impeded only by the imaginative limits of his approach. Carte blanche suggests unrestricted means and unrestrained impulses: And if they were not employed on *Kane* it is likely that they were not available. If *Gone With the*

Wind seems, in comparison, circumscribed, that measures two talents and suggests how stimulating limited resources can be: Carte blanche is too bewildering for an artist, who is invariably trying to eliminate excess and grasp the simple. Budget always confines a movie, and some of Welles's proclaimed "freedoms"—for instance, the Mercury company as players—were also a means of economy, newcomers getting less than celebrated stars.

Against that, Welles was given time: He was allowed nearly a year in Hollywood, seeing an array of old films, talking to technicians to learn the craft, and mulling over a subject. It is said that the subject was also of his choosing, but that seems doubtful. RKO wanted a sensation, not philosophy or a monument of art; they hoped to reproduce the shock of *The War of the Worlds* and capitalize on Welles's reputation. His first suggested movie—as respectable as Joseph Conrad's *Heart of Darkness*—was shelved, after tests, because it would have proved too expensive. A Hollywood not kindly disposed to the outsider presold as a genius, or to the studio publicity boasting of unprecedented opportunity, was already mocking Welles's inactivity. A second project, Nicholas Blake's thriller, *The Smiler with a Knife,* foundered on RKO's unwillingness to accept Welles's choice of their own Lucille Ball in a star role.

Carte blanche is a term suited to publicity handouts: It has the sweeping simplicity of a fake panacea or a comprehensive insurance scheme; it is the powder that will get your wash whitest. In practice, Welles seems to have worked within clear boundaries, and it is probably his own manner that provoked the industry's resentment of a youth who had bypassed the exhausting protocol that stood between "artistes" and "freedom." Such blaring liberty was insulting to Hollywood people, and Welles has seldom opted for tact. Still, it is possible that he was daunted by what liberty he had. The search for a viable project found him, for the first time in his career, hesitant and unsure. The eventual decision on what to make owes itself not to the newcomer, but to a sour Hollywood professional. Welles influenced the subject less in terms of idea and development, than as a living model for the central character, which his contract decreed he should play. Without being fanciful or perverse, one can regard *Kane* as one more star vehicle, conceived for the unique spoiled-child energy of Welles the actor, but alluding to the unwholesome mixture of genius and tyrant struggling behind the shy passion of those self-loving eyes. The script was written with Welles—his bearing, voice, and temper—in the writer's mind; and it was written by a man never quite sure what he thought about the fluctuations in Welles.

The writer was Herman Mankiewicz, once a wild success in Hollywood, but so contemptuous of the rewards for inane work that he had slipped into self-loathing, cynicism, alcohol, gambling, and a comic proneness to accidents. He wrote the script in bed after an automobile crash, and with secretaries at hand to make sure he had no liquor—in the screenplay, this is echoed in the geriatric Leland's scrounging for cigars, just as Leland's love-hate for Kane expresses Mankiewicz's shifting attitude toward Welles. Mankiewicz and Welles were impressed with one another, respectful, suspicious, and fearful: two sharp edges on guard. Mankiewicz was a Hollywood man with one craft Welles lacked—the ability to write a movie so that the parts slotted together with intricate precision. On screen, this meticulousness dominated the listless viewer, blinded him to deeper implausibility or human untruths, and kept him happy with the rapid momentum of the engine called plot.

Furthermore, it was Mankiewicz who proposed that they make a film about the life of a famous American, as seen from several different points of view. Pious biopics were not uncommon; searching studies of real celebrities were very unusual; but it was the notion of scattered points of view that surpassed the cinema's taste for simple truths. Dillinger and Aimee Semple McPherson were first targets, but Pauline Kael has established that Mankiewicz had already been working on a story line based on William Randolph Hearst, and this suggestion was eagerly accepted by Welles, and by RKO. For boy genius and studio alike, here was the promise of a best-selling outrage: a film that teasingly referred to a living tycoon. For Mankiewicz and Welles, it was another schoolboy prank and an unkind betrayal of hospitality—for they had both been guests of Hearst. For RKO, it was a stroke of box-office daring to embark on a scandalous satire. Why should Hollywood resist that prospect when it was chronically loyal to scurrilous gossip columns and when salacious rumor glazed every celebrity? Hearst was a Hollywood figure, a real tycoon, but ponderous, vulnerable, and potentially ridiculous. It shows the studio's narrow glee, and the creative potential of gossip, that this "unique" film grew out of a private joke. Perhaps it also exercised the narcissism of the various makers involved: If Hollywood ever thought of itself as a Babylon in decline, then *Kane* and Xanadu are the confessions of a culture gigglingly proud of its excess and sentimentally hopeful of some salvation in significance. The studio could see a pulp meaning in *Kane*—that richies were sad failures at home —and offer it as an appealing reassurance to ordinary failures.

Hearst was phenomenally wealthy and owned an empire of newspapers and magazines. Like Kane, though without Kane's glittering instinct for style, he developed sensationalism, tabloid formats, and what was called "yellow" journalism—the sacrifice of responsibility to entertainment. In America and elsewhere the huddled masses have not been bored by laborious truths or asked to find the stamina to deal with reality. The news media have made their presentation predigested, exciting but undisturbing. In *Kane* the comedy fastens on this compromise in a scene between Kane and the old editor he is harrying toward resignation:

KANE: Look, Mr. Carter, here is a three column headline in the *Chronicle*. Why hasn't the *Inquirer* got a three column headline?

CARTER: The news wasn't big enough.

KANE: Mr. Carter, if the headline is big enough, it makes the news big enough.

BERNSTEIN: That's right, Mr. Kane.

By 1940, Hearst was over seventy, living much of the time in his California mansion, San Simeon, where he had an indiscriminate collection of works of art, wild animals, tame guests, curios, and rubbish. His companion there was the blonde movie actress, Marion Davies, whose career Hearst had tenderly fostered. She was a vivacious girl, a little over-cast by his wish that she be romantic on screen. Still, Marion Davies could only have been hurt by Kane's blatant maneuvering of his second wife, Susan, toward an unmerited and unwanted career as an opera singer. But Kane uses Susan to regain the love of the people for himself, and his stage use of "we" when speaking of Susan's career is psychologically acute, just as his single-minded promotion of her never senses her humiliation.

Hearst was not as clear-cut a tyrant as Kane, nor as melo-dramatic a recluse. He entertained generously at San Simeon, and Mankiewicz had been one of his favored guests. Hearst was elderly, deeply in love with Marion, and real: One con-clusion to be drawn from the enterprise is that Mankiewicz and Welles no longer quite believed that the character in their script need be restrained by the capacity of real indi-viduals for being hurt. Part of the cruelty lies in overlooking others' reality; but that is exactly what makes the film so prescient. We do not easily see Welles as one of the huddled masses, but how far is his selfishness an extension of their alienation? Only a thorough disorientation can explain Welles's glib denial of any reference to Hearst. This was a reprise of the press conferences after Halloween, 1938, and it is an injured innocence to make a politician weep with envy. Here is Welles, in March 1941, declaring principles to the press as *Kane* seemed threatened by Hearst's attempt at boycott:

> I have been advised that strong pressure is being brought to bear in certain quarters to cause the withdrawal of my picture *Citizen Kane* because of an alleged resemblance between incidents in the picture and incidents in the life of Mr. William Randolph Hearst.
>
> Any such attempts at suppression would involve a serious interference with freedom of speech and with the integrity of the moving picture industry as the foremost medium of artistic expression in the country.
>
> There is nothing in the facts to warrant the situation that has arisen. *Citizen Kane* was not intended to have nor has it any reference to Mr. Hearst or to any other living person. No statement to the contrary has ever been authorized by me. *Citizen Kane* is the story of a wholly fictitious character.

That thunderous self-righteousness can be heard in *Citizen Kane,* and it shows us the subject of the film: the loss of objective standards, the surrender of a hope for truth to fantasy and subjectivity. Hearst was lampooned in *Kane*: His remarks were quoted, his national stature and life-style were aped, his mistress was parodied—and in that process, Kane's mania was attributed to Hearst. Kane's manipulation of news for effect—and the eventual confusion of substance and style in his own life—is exactly reflected in the way Welles handled the project. And at this early stage of his life he was himself a tycoon of the imagination: Exceptionally talented, resourceful, and energetic, he wanted to spellbind the people. Welles had no great wealth and no constituency in America, but looking back it is not fanciful to see his surgent rise taking him higher, even into politics. Suppose *Kane* had been not just a great film, but an enormous hit. In the context of war it is easy to see Welles as a sort of roving ambassador before 1945 and a congressman thereafter. Welles might have been President by 1960: On the one hand, that speculation is far-fetched; on the other, so easy that it could have occurred to him. For he had shown how naturally show biz, the media, and the administration of a democracy are related.

Mankiewicz had not spared Welles in the screenplay. His own mixed feelings for the prodigy collaborator emerge in the equivocation as to whether Kane is to be admired, pitied, or condemned. Even his failure is heroic and passionate: The duty of movie characters—to live intensely on behalf of the viewers who lived palely—saves Kane from the most debilitating effects of Xanadu, tedium, senility, and inconsequence. The old man dies as young men hope to die: alone, aware, and dramatically. Nor did Welles bother to hide his own dark temper in the film. One evening a quarrel sprang up in a restaurant as the Mercury company began to stagnate from so much waiting for a film to emerge from carte blanche. Welles's tantrum that evening—a mixture of frustration at breakup, anger over trivial things, and a sense of being betrayed—was reproduced in Kane smashing his second wife's room to pieces after she has left him. Pauline Kael has recounted the intense personal involvement Welles felt in doing that scene, as if the egotist was entranced even by his awfulness.

There is the same tangle of Kane's tyranny and the film's fond endorsement of dictatorship. The script reads as a satire on power, but the film is a celebration of it and a mournful reflection on how the powerful can be lonely and misunderstood. The most important source of authority in the film itself is the way in which it carries to ultimate heights all the elements of Hollywood method. In the making, carte blanche meant not novelty but a more complete resort to the battery of expressive artifice than ever before.

The script is often defended as a structure of elaborate originality: Yet it only marks the baroque period of flashback, crosscutting, and contained discontinuity. If you compare *Kane* to French cinema of that time—with, say, Jean Renoir's *La Règle du Jeu,* made in 1939—there is an evident contrast. Form for Renoir is open, unfinished, natural, and lively: Human behavior is more tangible than formalism itself. But *Kane* conforms to an opposite tradition of stunning cleverness. Indeed, the comprehensive articulation of what is an unexpected sequence probably contributed to the first limited popularity of the film. Chaotic as it seems at first, every loose end turns into an elegant bow. *Kane* confirms the way Hollywood films progress not like life but like a clever toy or a perfect construct—like a movie. *Kane*'s development grows out of cuts, slow dissolves, flashbacks—all of which were common, if not normally put together with such mannered ingenuity. They are also devices of dislocation making for an artificial coherence. Carte blanche meant time to make perfect, and the chance to pull every trick that more routine films had omitted. Like Kane, like Welles, like carte blanche, the plot line draws attention to itself: It is a show-off construction, offset by the emotionalism in the other elements of the movie. Mankiewicz justifiably howled when Welles laid claim to the script—another flagrant instance of conniving—but that does not mean that the film belongs to Mankiewicz. It is far greater than its script; and just because Welles could be spoiled child, ham, and charlatan, does not prevent the perplexing addition, that he was also an artist, intelligently aware of his medium and conscious of some of the implications of his own nature.

Kane drew upon some of the best technicians in Hollywood. Welles had used his time to discover talented men, but he had not gone outside the system, and he asked none of them to work in ways that they had not learned from the system. The only luxury of *Kane,* again—and it shows in the richer texture—was the extra time and indulgence allowed the makers. The editors were young men—Robert Wise and Mark Robson—who went on to be proficient directors, more professionally successful than Welles ever managed. *Kane* is a textbook on editing, from the rapid wipes of the mock newsreel to the very sensuous extended dissolves, not to mention cuts as elastic as Leland swinging around the pole at the *Inquirer* office or as violent as the screeching cockatoo. The array of editing is breathtaking but still conventional; it almost advertises the formidable but everyday task of assembling fragments into a movie. Even the surprise cuts are predictable, and only the consistent loveliness is remarkable in the editing, and that is due to stimulated craftsmen trying to please a tempestuous genius of whom they lived in some awe and to whom they came running like the "Solly!" Kane yells for.

This sort of relationship existed with many of the technicians. Welles could be lavish with charm and unequivocally inspiring, and no one can doubt that for some veterans he meant a new lease on life, novice enough to need help but adroit enough to harness others' skills to his vision. *Kane* employs every resource of the Hollywood art department, even if the product is Germanic in feeling, evidence of Welles's taste for German cinema of the 1920s seen in that year of preparation. Xanadu is a character in the film, and no one could ignore the expressiveness of its shapes, space, and furnishings. The realization of Susan's cramped doll's house room, the fireplace as large as a cottage, or the tableaux of prairie cabin, Dickensian newspaper office, opera house backstage, indeed of every setting, is done with a rich detail and receding perspective that one hardly digests on first viewing. The settings are as fertile as memory trying to regain its past—and that is proper to the impulse of the film.

But the sets are also fixed in their own artificiality, as if the art department, too—RKO regulars like Van Nest Polglase and Darrell Silvera—were saying, "Look what we can do." Not one set is real or lived in, and gradually we notice the contrived quality of everything. Kane is a giant fabricator: He built Xanadu as an escape from reality, and his recollections and feelings have "made" every location in his life. The prairie cabin is a preserved cameo. The great hall where he speaks is a model theater with a cardboard crowd: but so well done that it is less glaringly fake than an expression of the demagogue's need of a pliant crowd. And Xanadu is a sprawling junkyard. It is the mansion of a man who has been reduced to helpless ownership of things. But the last moments of the film make this storehouse of objects resemble first a derelict city and then a studio properties warehouse. That dark building crammed with assorted items is a sign that both ownership and art attempt to erect meanings out of experience, but risk being overwhelmed by the accretion of inert things. All through *Kane,* there is a palpable sense that everything is occurring on sets, and that the set is the isolating arena of lonely experience.

The sets of *Kane* cannot be distinguished from the lighting scheme and the photography. The genetic code of Hollywood cinema—that the thing seen *is* its own meaning—has never been clearer: Shadow and perspective drape these sets, and they indicate how far the film is seen through Kane's eyes. The romantic grandeur and despair of his view of his life is manifest in the look of the film. That involves the far extent of every set being lost in darkness, obscurity, and possibility; there is a lack of finiteness fitting a man who has never known limits. Looking at the film, I think, helps one appreciate the fantastical darkness in cinema. One scene in *Kane* takes place in a newsreel company's viewing cinema, but many others seem to, so consistent is the pattern of a small central light surrounded by darkness. It is a film without daylight, or natural light; that adds to the unreality of the prairie scene, and accumulates gloom and claustrophobia as the film advances. The light, or whiteness, is sometimes the lost past viewed from the oppressive present, and sometimes the prospect of answer glimpsed in the search. But that straightforward interpretation is also undercut: Kane turns out the light and makes a mockery of enlightenment. The light of snowy childhood he looks back at is another artificial light, a conjuring of his imagination in a world cut off from nature and naturalness.

The interiors of the film have a contradictory character, possible in film and achieved by the photographer, Gregg Toland. In the late thirties, Toland had a reputation as the most progressive and arty of Hollywood cameramen. He had been experimenting with the texture of black and white, the massive shadow and the extensive depth of focus that mark *Kane*. Above all, he was capable of very distinct, hallowed skin tones amid lustrous shadow. John Ford's *The Long Voyage Home,* photographed by Toland immediately before *Kane,* looks like a Welles picture, but to no purpose. Ford's is a pretentious, picturesque work in which the very beautiful imagery betrays the director's attempted poetics of "plain men."

On *Kane,* all of Toland's skill and some of his unattempted dreams were adapted to Welles's visual interpretation. Depth and darkness embody the megalomaniac's view of his own plight, trapped at the center of an infinite but crushing space. The optics of the new wide-angle lenses Toland used distort the eye's normal vision. Space is opened out: The middle ground is stretched. Yet the pressure of space remains, and the relationship of the human figure to space—a key cinematic bond—exaggerates his tininess in the distance and his oppressiveness in the foreground. One feels an emotional force in those spatial relationships, and that is one of *Kane*'s glories. It would not have existed without

Toland, but the need for it only arose with Welles. Such eloquent realization of space does not feature in Toland's other films, yet it becomes a motif in Welles's subsequent work. The boy wonder learned fast, perhaps, or he had what Toland lacked: an organizing artistic imagination that fused a way of seeing with a hitherto undetected human experience. That experience was akin to moviegoing. Perspective is a tool of realism; and *Kane*'s turning of perspective to rubber indicates the deforming strength of fantasy when watching film imagery.

What follows is an exegesis of *Kane* and, I trust, an adequate corrective to what may have seemed hostile comments on Welles's ambivalent personality. The film is a masterpiece. Its relevance to this book is in underlining the frailty of our cultural appreciation of ourselves: *Kane* indicates our own isolation and the way in which cinema captures the misunderstanding between the individual and the mass. Art was once thought a connecting spark, a means of social hope; but *Kane* is the song of an enigma, or as Jorge Luis Borges appreciated, a labyrinth without a center. The riddle is posed as a way of distracting us from the awful surrounds of chaos and nothingness.

True to cinema's aptitude for rendering a dreamlike experience that needs explanation, *Citizen Kane* is a haunting mystery that survives its own briefly satisfying answer. We dream to sustain the hope that we have meaning; in which case, the dream must never be rationalized. The film begins outside Xanadu; it is night, the night of artificial light, melancholy, and nightmare. A sign on the outer wall says NO TRESPASSING, but the camera moves inward, carried by a series of dissolves that open-sesame every barrier and float on a sea of apprehensive music. The movie begins like a horror picture, sucking us into the old dark house on the hill. The initial *K* in the wrought-iron gateway is an oblique allusion to Kafka and *The Castle,* vindicated twenty years later when Welles came to film *The Trial.*

We are brought into a room of the house and we see, head on, in orgasmic close-up, lips that open and say "Rosebud." Then we see a hand holding a snowball with its enclosed house. The ball tumbles to the floor, shatters, and, through a distorting fragment, we see a nurse come into the room. We gather that the lips are dead and we see a sheet drawn up over the corpse, a snow-white shroud.

The silence is shattered by a raucous cry, "News on the March," and a fanfare launches a fulsome newsreel obituary for the man who has died, Charles Foster Kane. This imitates and devalues documentary as much as Welles did in *The War of the Worlds,* and the games enjoyed in reproducing the semblances of newsreel should not disguise a further nudge toward the reality of Hearst. The newsreel also provides a useful outline of Kane's life, details of which will be returned to. In addition, it is the dead man's "professional" account of himself, a public obituary in his own invented style—glittering, emphatic journalese, facts not accustomed to being doubted or tested, but asserted with such conviction that the style wearies us to the point of perpetual mistrust.

The newsreel ends and we are in a viewing cinema where several men discuss the obituary. We never see their faces, only the light that falls on the screen from the projection booth. The facelessness of media men extends to Kane himself and is loaded with the dangers of shallow inquiry in such men. Quite implausibly, they are dissatisfied with what is *by their standards* a masterly obituary, crammed with detail, portentous, rapid, and in the hustler rhetoric that passes for history in the popular press. They complain that the obituary does not explain Kane, as if obituaries in the mass-oriented newspapers were ever interested in that. Beneath so much public show, they argue, there must be a secret to the man. They remember "Rosebud" and wonder if that is a clue. One of the group—his name is Thompson, and the child in the garden did hear that, as if spoken to in the dark—is delegated to find out what "Rosebud" meant. "Rosebud dead or alive," the editor tells him. "It will probably turn out to be a very simple thing."

This instigates the form of the movie: interviews conducted by Thompson with people who knew Kane. I do not think the form is believable in terms of an alleged search for something better by a newsreel company. No matter, one may say, it is not a bad peg on which to hang so rich a coat. But *Kane* is too good a film to have that large an excuse in its origins. There is another explanation for the way the film works, which is to see it as Kane's reflection, reverie, or panic in the instant before death. That is not uncommon in movies; the flashback was often a way of delaying and explaining a death. The unwillingness of the newsreelmen to accept their own product is more reasonable if one sees them as figments of Kane's imagination with Kane scanning the outward signs of his own life—the things owned —and saying, "No, there must be more." This seems too ingenious at first, but there is detail to back it. No one heard "Rosebud" except us: The nurse entered the room after the word was spoken. Only we privileged voyeurs, who were ushered in past every barrier, heard and feel the need to explain the as yet unbloomed rosebud. We become accomplices of Kane in the effort to find a redemptive meaning to his own life; he plants his riddle in our minds.

The flashbacks are ostensibly through the eyes of people who knew Kane: Thatcher, Bernstein, Leland, Susan, his second wife, and Raymond, the butler at Xanadu. But though they begin with the words of those people, the flashbacks end pregnant with Kane's feeling of what they described. For instance, the Thatcher flashback starts in the library with Thompson reading Thatcher's diary and the camera tracking in over his shoulder and onto the page where the white paper dissolves into the snowstorm. But that flashback ends on a shot already mentioned: the beatific profile of mother and child, which hardly needs the old man's caption, "But she loved me. . . ." In other words, as Kane imagines colleagues remembering him, so he urges his point of view upon theirs—the people will think what I tell them to think.

The last episode brings Thompson to Xanadu to speak to Raymond, so enigmatic a house servant that we cynics of a later generation wonder whether he was the Mafia or the CIA plant in the household of the great man. (Or could that poker face double as both?) But Raymond has no more explanation of "Rosebud" than any of the other characters. All he will concede is that his outer indifference conceals affection for the sad old man—what more comforting "discovery" could there be for Kane? Thompson and a gang of reporters meet in the great warehouse of Xanadu's junk, and as they leave, workmen begin to burn nonvaluables. The camera stays and, with the will of its own that it had in the first sequence, moves in, drawing us with it, as far as an old sledge. A workman picks it up, and the camera follows it into the furnace where, for an instant, before the heat melts the paint, we see "Rosebud" on the sledge.

Bernard Herrmann's music soars free with answer and released emotion, and we alone have been allowed to learn the answer—just as only we heard the riddle uttered. Thompson and all the others have gone away: Our pact with Kane is complete. We cut away to an exterior view of Xanadu— a backdrop itself likely to be burned soon, or cleaned off for some other film; smoke from the furnace fills the sky and the last NO TRESPASSING is Kane winking to us at what is now our secret.

The delicacy of the film is to reach every individual of the audience as precisely as that, and yet remain the attempt of a man to prove to himself that he commanded the love and understanding of the huddled masses. But the first flush of satisfaction with the "answer" to Rosebud does not last: The film fulfills the fantasist's search for meaning for only a moment. Then we recognize the inadequacy of clues and answers. The mystery story turns into a metaphysical tragedy, and the last wink is on the face of a corpse—a grimace of pain and futility.

The discovery of Rosebud on the sledge is, as Welles admits, middlebrow Freud. It reduces the story to a version of poor little rich boy, which may fit the real travails of wealthy men but ill becomes the bravura of this inquiry. It means only, and baldly, that Kane remained unhappy because his mother rejected him. A more complex answer grows from that and involves the difficulty of a selfish egotist loving anyone but himself. That permits the overall way in which the film makes all other characters Kane's instruments and traces his failure with individuals through to the attempt to win an audience. Thus, the dissatisfied man goes into journalism, politics, and opera, and tyranny shows equally in his boast that the people will think what he tells them to think and in several comments on the way he uses love as a purchasing power:

> LELAND: He married for love. Love . . . that's why he did everything. That's why he went into politics. It seems we weren't enough. He wanted all the voters to love him too. All he really wanted out of life was love.

> LELAND: You don't care about anything except you. You just want to persuade people that you love them so much that they ought to love you back. Only you want love on your own terms.
> KANE: A toast, Jedediah, to love on my terms. Those are the only terms anybody ever knows, his own.

That bleak awareness is the pith of the film, and it applies to the isolation of a wealthy man and to the self-nurtured loneliness of the fantasist. Kane in Xanadu is a version of the grotesque spiral of American success, but it is also a picture of any man trying to transcend himself and reach others. Kane has the idealistic hope of touching the people that we can suppose in Monroe Stahr, Welles himself, any artist, politician, or entertainer. NO TRESPASSING is the reminder of imprisoning subjectivity, no matter how strenuously a man tries to imagine himself as someone else. There is a scene where the young Kane admits the rift in the soul of the imaginative man—though, typically, Kane describes what he thinks is a strength and versatility:

THATCHER: Charles, I think I should remind you of a fact you seem to have forgotten.

KANE: Yes.

THATCHER: You are yourself one of the largest individual stockholders in the Public Transit Company.

KANE: The trouble is, you don't realize you're talking to two people. As Charles Foster Kane, who owns 82,364 shares of Public Transit Preferred—you see, I do have a general idea of my holdings—I sympathize with you. Charles Foster Kane is a scoundrel, his paper should be run out of town, a committee should be formed to boycott him. You may, if you can form such a committee, put me down for a contribution of $1,000—

THATCHER: My time is too valuable for me to waste on such nonsense.

KANE: On the other hand I am also the publisher of the *Inquirer*. As such, it is my duty—I'll let you in on a secret—it is also my pleasure—to see to it that the decent, hard-working people of this community aren't robbed blind by a pack of money mad pirates just because they haven't anybody to look after their interests.

Kane destroys himself on that duality: The boy from a log cabin fails to become President, he loses friends and wives, his attempt to make one wife an opera singer is disastrous despite his insistent applause, all his possessions amount to clutter, and he retreats to a massive prison from which death extracts him. The screenplay is a scathing commentary on America and on the domineering charm of Welles himself. But the film is more poignant and more serious. So much of it reflects upon the nature of cinema and all human endeavor. Kane strives to be meaningful: That is an old humanist impulse and an American Puritan imperative. But Rosebud is only a clue in a thriller, a gesture toward half-baked psychiatry. *Citizen Kane* is a study of the intellectual isolation of an intelligent, sensitive, enterprising man, a man whose career has helped dilute meaning with style and presentation. All rhetoric, he tries desperately to retain substance, and in that attempt Rosebud is merely a pretext.

Perhaps moments before the film begins, an old man, alone, sick, and world-weary, telephoned a library and asked the night staff, courteously, to find him a word—he directed them by numbers that came into his head at random—the third floor, the fifth room, the second stack, the third shelf, the tenth book, the seventh page, the thirteenth line, the second word . . . " 'Rosebud,' sir," came the reply and the man rang off, having something to say and hoping that meaning might gather around it.

VI

MAN AND
THE MEAN STREET

> *On every street in every city there's a*
> *nobody who dreams of being a some-*
> *body.*
> —ADVERTISEMENT for *Taxi Driver*

WITHIN SIGHT OF ELLIS ISLAND AND THE STATUE OF LIBERTY there is a vision so well known that it is a universal mirage. It is potent enough always to be called "New." Yet it is a real city, as well as a mythic backdrop, with eight million inhabitants, diverse neighborhoods, and soaring debt. As with so many American phenomena, its appearance promises to clarify muddied experience. The towers are massive, upright, as assured as glass, concrete, and steel. They house and embody corporations and institutions competing for control of the city. The forms of the buildings daunt the individuals who pass by in the narrow, gloomy streets. The human figure in that city is diminutive and so much the dot of statistics that he feels he is invisible. The sheerness of the buildings ensures that the crowd stays huddled.

In New York today there is apprehensive tension between those anxious not to be noticed—lest notice draw attack or interference—and those committed to the insolent pose that dares anyone to look back. New York sometimes resembles a contest of drab masses and monstrous leading actors—the scheme of Fritz Lang's *Metropolis*. It is a place where violent crimes are frequent, and where passersby sometimes watch them with a bereft detachment they have acquired in the cinema.

Yet one can live in New York without being a victim of crime; the victimization not avoided is of the imagination— no one lives in New York without a dread of being unlucky. To outsiders, the city bristles with stories of disorder, the staid majority infected by the lurid minority. Proud natives defend the truth of the myth. Martin Scorsese, a New Yorker and director of *Taxi Driver,* rebutted attacks on that film's violence with the assurance that, while filming, they saw far worse, yet far more casual incidents. That is an important distinction: The cinema heightens violence, which may be as mundane as any other human activity. Thus violence affects the imagination more than it does the parts of the body. Actors with broken limbs or raging ulcers can move smoothly on stage in a part, yet collapse in the wings. So, too, real violence and insoluble problems are sometimes more bearable if dealt with in an arena of the imagination.

The stage-set city has turned crime into a staple melodrama. The streets are so concentrating that police sirens howl exaggeratedly, while steam billows from manhole covers as in the stage presentation of a sorcerer's cavern. Perhaps New York still resists wasting complexity by being the "wonderful town" of *On the Town* or the teeming metropolis of the future where protagonists know the elation of watched performance and where onlookers are desperate not to be identified. The subway commuter who witnesses a holdup or a rape will turn inside out to deny his existence, presence, and eyes. In the city, some people chart their day to avoid those crippling moments of seeing or being seen.

The need to be hidden, though alive, hardly sustains responsible participation in life, but it is not too far from the state of watching movies. How often hoodlums on the run in films seek refuge in dark movie houses. Often enough for that eerie concurrence of fact and fiction when Dillinger was shot dead by G-men as he emerged from a Chicago theater that had been showing . . . *Manhattan Melodrama.*

The urban crime film begins just after the coming of sound and economic crash. Is that coincidence? Is it ever coincidence when genres perpetuate a real world, or is it fanciful to put great burdens on such links? There is no way of securing evidence; no science can be wrought from the intangibility of the movies. The cinema itself conjures, and one can only speculate over genres and ask the reader to judge the value of an attempt to describe the interplay of fantastic meaning and historical circumstances. Social science lumbers along behind films, while imaginative sympathy with a movie may serve the purpose attributed in folklore to the readers of dreams.

What is the urban crime film? I mean those films that relate the careers of criminals to the life of cities. The films deal in violence, pursuit and hiding, criminal operations, betrayals, investigations, and death—all the active surface of police work. Cinema's criminal code requires that the criminal should not succeed; but the safeguard meant to dull glorification allows the gangster to be a tragic hero or a cheerful exponent of self-destruction. If the movie criminal had flourished with the commonplace prosperity he has found in life, the form would be very different—but so might America be.

In American cinema, the cities are believable versions of the urban gatherings where audiences live. Today, and for some years, New York and Los Angeles have been used as locations; but until well into the 1950s, the "city" was usually a series of authentic-looking but geometrically tidy sets. In either case, the city is a social organization that works at two levels. Mundane life goes on: People live, work, and amuse themselves—there is variety and turbulence, but it presents a natural and easygoing surface, like the sea seen from an aircraft. This is the city of the men in the street, the life and times of Extraville. Above it there rages a battle of gods and devils: The gray city is at stake in a struggle between cops and gangsters. They know one another and they accept the terms of outright war. On both sides men act with the zeal of wild animals true to their species and the mood of the jungle.

As a generalization, that can be questioned. There are some films more subtle than my scheme allows. But I present it to discredit the defense Hollywood itself claimed in the 1930s—that the gangster was the unhappy result of convulsive social conditions, and that the films wished to remind society of its running sores. That is a high-minded way of making money out of our imaginative curiosity over crime: From 1930 to the present day, we have faced the paradox of movie-makers crying all the way to the bank with the proceeds of works that depict the breaking open of banks. At Warner Brothers, especially, the first home of the gangster, there was a veneer of social responsibility. There is a complacent diagnosis in Warners' films that criminals were the regrettable outcome of slums, broken homes, and bad breaks. *Public Enemy*, therefore, was the consequence of high-spirited youth being badly brought up.

But *Public Enemy* was also James Cagney, a respectable

young man acting as wild as a demon. The gangsters of the early thirties were saturnine star figures, removed from context or roots. Their talk, their wisecracks; their clothes and routines; their life-or-death animation were the racy pulse of movies, along with the flagrant availability of Busby Berkeley's girls. When Cagney smacked Mae Clarke in the face with a grapefruit, the audience gasped, laughed, and expanded at the unrebuked infraction—like children watching a teacher tolerate lack of discipline. Violence enlists our imaginations because we are fearful of its damage and the frustration it admits. Yet again, cinema freed the impossible or repressed urges in us. The frenzied shoot-outs of the gangster film—unthinkable without the sound track staccato of firing—were reveled in as the abandonment of taboos traded on the absence of pain. For the movies describe action without hurt, behavior without consequences. The gangsters were heroes of dynamic gesture: Cagney's strut and Edward G. Robinson's snarl were soon imitated—just as some of their screen mannerisms were picked up from the real gangsters who were tickled to be presented on screen and who often moved in the same circles as Hollywood people.

The story lines of gangster films played with social parable, but the appeal of the films was blatant, fantastic, and anarchist. The hypocrisy lay in solemn accounts of how crime arose that condoned the paying spectator's enjoyment of its lively enactment. The analysis—whether or not it was accurate—always stopped short of salutary thoroughness. Crime was deplorable, but poverty natural. Individuals were the public enemies, not institutions or ways of governance. The form claimed that some people were criminals, while others were immune; and it suggested that the ministrations of Father Pat O'Brien or a wholesome girl ought to be enough to put a miscreant back on the straight and narrow. If not, the electric chair or the cops must eliminate the bad seed.

Incorrigible gangsters perished so regularly that the credulous viewer must have wondered how real crime flourished. The films stood back from any suggestion that Extraville is itself intrinsically unequal, that our democratic and libertarian society generates powers bound to struggle with one another, that the individual nurses aggressive impulses. Although the crime film exploited the law-abider's delight in outlawry, it was rarely sophisticated or courageous enough to examine the flawed nature of man, let alone a free enterprise, puritan society producing conflicts of greed and guilt. Above all, the urban crime movie hints at something scarcely appreciated by its makers—that the city needed crime. This is not another way of endorsing Warners' half-hearted social attitudinizing. Instead, it is the feeling evident in cities that human society no longer conforms with the rules (law) or the available system (politics). Thus, gradually, simulated crime took on an existential significance in which our identification with gangsters acknowledged frustration at human failure and social and cultural confusion.

That helps justify the relevance of the early 1930s. By then, America had come nearer its modern urban and industrial self—whereas before 1920 it had not known failure. It had observed the humorless idealism of Prohibition and suffered from the clash of doctrinaire optimism and popular pragmatism. Prohibition also provided a model for businesslike crime that will industrialize "taboo" or restricted commodities in a "free" society. Booze, gambling, and prostitution were staples of organized crime. They met common wants that only the wish to be immaculate had suppressed—with all the advantages of a fresh start that America offered. America had also to remedy the obtrusive differences of very rich and very poor (of Xanadus and log cabins) and of federal and local authority. New evidence was emerging of a tacit liaison between professional criminals and lawmen, despite the myth's insistence on their impervious opposition.

The twenties was also a time of disillusion and nervy

abandon as social and religious values crumbled, and the homilies about human purpose were doubted. They may never have worked in practice, but they had satisfied the wish for polite slogans and temperate behavior. Now, people had less and less to hold on to, so they resorted to what money could buy and to pipe dreams of a happier past. *The Great Gatsby* is a bootlegger trying to be a Long Island host, but anxiously elevating himself socially with money and attempting to re-create a past love affair. The end of that novel is a nostalgic panorama of lost confidence and the wistful admission, "So we beat on, boats against the current, borne back ceaselessly into the past."

Then, in 1929, the money system collapsed and banks broke like cups hitting a stone floor. Securities proved no more than pieces of paper. Howard Hawks's movie *Scarface,* plainly based on Al Capone, was subtitled *Shame of a Nation,* as if to say that the gangsters exposed America. But that is only a fraction of an unmentionable truth. The real shame was the growing fear in an invented country that the system did not work. The gangster film pandered to the poor, the dispossessed, and the outcasts, allowing them to enjoy a vengeful destructiveness turned on the system that had rejected them.

The twenties had enjoyed films of unashamed frivolity. The harsh thirties sobered that youthful cheerfulness: Cynicism and fatalism became more idiomatic—the films of Lubitsch, Mae West, and Von Sternberg treated love with varying degrees of acid. Marlene Dietrich's cold heat expelled airy protestations of romance and acknowledged the determinism of sex.

There was, at the same time, a hopeful endorsement of the common-man hero, a determined reaction in favor of plain roots to find the decent American. It unearthed Gary Cooper as Mr. Deeds and Henry Fonda as Tom Joad and Abraham Lincoln. Frank Capra and John Ford were sentimental populists, and I doubt that history will admire their sententious heroes. Still, their movies speak for Hollywood's wish to cling to provincial virtues, and present the weird antic of glamour deglamorizing itself. A more robust and fatalistic response was the gangster, a loner who rode the contradictions of the urban system and took greedy pleasure in life. Cagney, above all, loved the thirties, and his exuberance was so gratuitous that it was the more creative and unsettling. He knows life is for living and rejects the soulful protesting of the tall, upright "ombudsman" heroes of the time. One can imagine Cagney's sneer on hearing the trite comfort at the end of *The Grapes of Wrath*—inserted there by Darryl Zanuck—"We're the people, and we go on forever."

Zanuck's line is the tycoon as ventriloquist and suits his hopes for the unquestioning commercial allegiance of the huddled masses. The industry liked predictable, appreciative audiences who accepted what was put before them and maintained business stability. But in times of unprecedented commercial risk, they discovered a widespread appeal in films glorifying cynical, antisocial, and sometimes criminal enterprise. Were stability and the vicarious dallying with law and order compatible? The spiral was like that of a gun manufacturer who guesses that his product will one day come back to the store to command the contents of his own safe. The unpredictability of Cagney on screen could shake the viewer from habitual nonparticipation. Cagney is the most politicizing of American actors, engaging us in his schemes and actions nearly to the point of activating us. On seeing his films, it is possible that someone might leave the cinema and imitate him, but more likely that the viewer will carry away the mocking curse on his own society.

Cagney was small, not cultivated, hardly ever blessed with anything except energy and snappy answers. Yet he would not lie down humbly—as Chaplin did. He is an insurgent, bursting to be visible and recognized. His ambition is not comfortably directed at job, pension, family, and respectability; he is ready to "make it" in any way possible, for he knows that recognition is more important than the way it is won. He is the first American who reacts to the dread of anonymity with "Come on—we're going to make them take notice." Cagney charts the part of a man's life omitted from *Citizen Kane*—the stages by which a poor kid gets attention. As with Kane, the power to impress people is more psychically rewarding than the wish to impress in any particular direction. His walk, his sly gaze, and his endless playing with intonation are always arresting. It was the nervous indecision of Warners that put him on this side or that of the indistinct boundary between the law and stylish crime. In a time more conscious of large-scale, bureaucratic racketeering, Cagney clung to the free-lance spirit of the ordinary American refusing to be smothered. In that sense, he is the "author" of most of his films of the thirties, and it is worth a survey of the progress he made in them.

In *Public Enemy,* he is Tom Powers, a slum kid fulfilled by gangsterdom. His family serves as a positive alternative in *Public Enemy;* in general, the gangster was a man with no more domestic attachment than a doting but unsentimental moll. Still, those crime pictures that include a family are of special social interest, and in *Public Enemy* Tom Powers faces the disapproval of mother and brother. Indeed, it is only when Tom takes on enemy gangsters to avenge a friend's death that he is himself killed. Tom is a doomed character, but the damned—as never before on the screen— have a license for killing, savagery, a domineering attitude to women and a celebrated and prolonged death as he staggers down a studio street in pouring rain. The dance-throes of agony parody death and the headlong motion is as coordinated as Gene Kelly's dance in *Singin' in the Rain.* The street is empty for this tribute to dynamism: The movies always display whatever moves, and Cagney's genius was not literary or actorly but against stillness.

In *Smart Money*, he is assistant barber to Edward G. Robinson, a country boy enjoying the city, but a dramatic stooge disposed of to focus attention on the other star. *Blonde Crazy* has Cagney and Joan Blondell as traveling confidence-tricksters—the "intellectual" aspect of gangsterdom, where violence turns into ingenuity and a critique of the blunt code that honesty pays. The confidence man in American art reveals structural hypocrisy and failure; he is an imp taunting a muddled system. In *Taxi,* he plays Matt Nolan, who leads privateer cabbies against a taxi trust and avenges the murder of his kid brother. One might see this as a metaphor for unionism and the oppressive system, but the radical implications of Cagney's attitudes are softened by the sentimental direction of his energies toward psychotic personal pride. The activist never joins an external group or heeds larger ideas.

Hard to Handle was a title calculated to exploit Cagney's own battles with Warners. He was fighting low salary and typecasting and, like one of his own characters, bucking the system but merrily adding to his effectiveness as part of it. Cagney plays Lefty Merrill, an engaging fraud, and in seventy-five minutes the picture moves across America and through a series of swindles, each grosser than the one before it. But they all deceive the public and, finally, Lefty contrives a national craze for grapefruit with the aplomb of a pool player sorting out the balls. Few films are so successful as genre pieces, or so teasingly aimed at the follies of the movies themselves. The vein of confidence-trickery is Hollywood's narcissism, and the reference to grapefruit is as direct a blow to the audience as anything Mae Clarke suffered. At one point, Merrill says the public is like a full cow bellowing to be milked, and that could be the irritation of Hollywood people with the exploitations of entertainment. It is a film poised not far from the giveaway of self-destruction and abuse of its own audience.

Danny Kean in *Picture Snatcher* is an ex-hoodlum hired to take candid camera shots for sensational newspapers— another contemporary sharp practice, and a further nod at the film world's own methods. *The Mayor of Hell* is a turning point, and a title that predicts the ordeals of Daley, Stokes, and Beame. Cagney plays a benevolent ex-gangster who takes charge of a reform school. This marks Warners' tender wish to make amends by deflecting the energy they had aroused in a more worthy direction. The intentions are ridiculous, and the gangster as teacher proved a booby trap, leading to the intuition that outlaws might operate on the proper side of the law. In time, that enhanced the American respect for energy taking precedence over a sense of direction. *The Mayor of Hell* is not a good picture, but it is instructive evidence of the system entangled in the effort to insure against its own impact.

In *Lady Killer,* the interplay of gangster, practicing deceiver, and movie star is more intriguing than ever. Cagney plays Dan Quigley, who rises from usher in a cinema to confidence man to movie star. Hollywood's self-scorn is accentuated when Quigley fakes his own popularity by forging fan letters to the studio—a jab that could have made several established stars wince. The commercialization of violence, and the disorientation of experience it induces, culminates in Cagney dragging Mae Clarke by her hair and throwing her out of the door—the whole routine being played for laughs. In passing, one might note that this is the heyday of surrealism, a mood appreciative of such absurd violence barely veiling antisocial instincts. The gangster film allows us covert glee at outrage and slaughter, delight at the inner unreality of the world, and satisfaction with disorder: Stated so baldly, it sounds like a surrealist manifesto.

Jimmy the Gent is Jimmy Corrigan, the unscrupulous "finder" of lost heirs to begging fortunes—the long-lost sons of Kane, perhaps, product of a country of surplus wealth and hiding people. (The hobo who proves to be a millionaire is a common figure in thirties cinema and lies behind the director's masquerade in *Sullivan's Travels*.) In *He Was Her Man,* Cagney is Flicker Hayes, a fleeing gangster who falls in love with Joan Blondell, a tart on her way to an arranged marriage. Their love is extinguished when Cagney is killed, and the transient condition of the couple reflects an age of people moving on from doubt, failure, and the past, looking for the pipe dream of a second chance. It is the decade in which many Americans relived the experience of immigrant ancestors, and in which West's brooding crowd gravitated to California.

G-Men, in 1935, is another exercise in reversal, in which Cagney plays an attorney who joins the FBI to avenge the killing of a friend by gangsters. The belligerence and scant illusion in Cagney were transferred to the lawman role. Did the public notice how difficult it was to tell the character or purpose of a vigorous little charmer with a gun when the movies could put him in either corner? In retrospect, this warning is clear, but only because we are sadly aware of law agencies acting illegally. Still, genre must be given some credit for half-grasping that the hoodlum and the cop might be the same person and that splashes of gunfire looked and sounded exciting, whatever the gunman's motive.

That film set Cagney in a new direction. Rarely, thereafter, was he as open a conniver or troublemaker as he had been. The gangster genre was in retreat, because of staleness and qualms in Hollywood about the possibly harmful influence on young people. As American prosperity slowly returned, so the public taste moved toward conservatism and reassessed its own disenchantment. There was vocal opposition to the uninhibited violence of the films, and, though that case has always been beyond proof, Hollywood did not like to be thought offensive or dangerous. Cagney accordingly moved into "adventure"—a much safer use of his energy—and became a wholesome hero. Within the decade, he would be impelled to impersonate George M. Cohan, superpatriot, to convince a mistrustful America that he was sound. Yet his Cohan is a Mr. Punch hoodlum who steals the flag and finds fame and fortune in waving it: Cagney's trembling energy makes patriotism seem like another way of milking the public.

However, at the end of the thirties, he returned to gangsterdom in a movie made from the stance of a reinstated middle class: *Angels with Dirty Faces.* Cagney plays Rocky Sullivan, a career criminal still friendly with a boyhood buddy, now a priest (Pat O'Brien), who is fearful of Rocky's influence on a new generation of kids. This relationship is indulged to the point where Cagney, on his way to the electric chair, is persuaded to act the coward in order to disabuse the kids who take him for a hero. Thus, the audience, the studio, and any sanctimonious censors have it both ways: Cagney revels as the gangster and engages us in violence, but then redeems himself and satisfies the need for a prim example. The society capable of responding in both ways is nearly demented, and it is revealing that the film resorts to an approximation of cinema itself in the acted-out performance that dampens the kids' hero-worship. *Angels* is an accomplished and persuasive film, but the genre is in contortions that indicate the deep impressions left by the entertainment film and its makers' woeful efforts to domesticate their product.

One draws back from *Angels* aghast at the compulsiveness of such unreality: Everyone in the film is so much more vivid than life, not least the kids, who are the genesis of the Bowery Boys, a weird band of commercial adolescents. The taste for sensation and the dependence on action to exercise energy has led to a distortion of motive and behavior, all geared to the idea of "image"—what people will deduce from appearances. The stereotypes of genre have long since suppressed human nature, and relations between people have turned into a code of presented signs. Within that form, identity has been irretrievably mislaid. Cagney is hero and villain simultaneously, and the suspended metamorphosis denies our hope for wholeness. Those mean streets lead toward the abstraction of Xanadu; rather than verifiable urban locations, they are the narrows of meanness and instability, the labyrinth of our selfhood.

The films Cagney made at Warners are quick, blithe, and smart: Stylishness disarms the signs of social disarray. There are crime films from the thirties of greater gravity, more conscious of their own subject. In picking out a few, we may note that all of them see the disillusion of an individual faced by social obligation. The mean street is beset by grim prospects and the indifference of strangers. Streets once were supposedly paved with gold, but in the thirties they saw dole queues, relief lines, derelicts, pickets, and strikebreakers. It was now an unfriendly location, pitiless and dangerous. That is not far from the psychological bleakness of the street in German cinema of the 1920s, and we shall find traces of German anxiety in the American urban thriller.

I Am a Fugitive from a Chain Gang is an uncompromising juxtaposition of the "jailbird" and the hapless victim of economic distress in the thirties. Directed by Mervyn Le Roy—who had made *Little Caesar* and *Hard to Handle*—it stars Paul Muni as a man wrongfully convicted of a crime. So many cases of mistaken arrest hint at the slipperiness of identity and the blurring of individuality in the anonymous masses. A malicious fate sends Muni to a chain gang with a soul-destroying sentence. Hopelessness leaves him only anger and resentment, and he escapes from the prison. With a changed name he gets a job and begins to work his way upward again, still abiding by the ethic of work and reward. But his past catches up with him and he is forced to flee into the "underworld." The film ends with a brief meeting with an old friend horrified at Muni's haggard condition. "What do you do?" the friend wonders, and Muni replies with fierce despair, "I steal," before vanishing into the night.

The curt denial of comfort in the ending is matched by the absence of romantic involvement for his character and the unrelieved hopelessness of his plight. We sympathize with a man who seems an outcast, not just from a chain gang but from the concept of lawful and straight society. Innocence has been pushed into ingrained crime. It is a film that gives a property owner nagging cause for fearing every hobo; it makes us look away from desperate faces on the corner. The directness of the title asks every spectator to measure his own precarious safety.

The disturbing relationship between outlaw and citizen is the lesson of Fritz Lang's American debut, *Fury*, a film that seems to have slipped out of MGM by mistake. Lang was a refugee himself. Once a leading director in German cinema, he had left Germany with abrupt haste after Goebbels offered him the post of head of the Nazi film industry. The legend is that, naturally and properly, Lang declined the invitation and abandoned success for righteousness. But Goebbels had made the invitation only because something in Lang's work appealed to dictators. It could have been the fatuous social contract drawn hastily across the awesome rift in *Metropolis*. It could have been the inventive enthusiasm for the master criminal, Dr. Mabuse, surely not possible without some sense of lassitude in society yearning for his sweeping nihilism. It might have been Lang's mechanical concentration on good and evil, without belief in either, so that life is reduced to a lethal chess. Lang follows melodrama to its logical emptiness. Good and evil become counters only—elements of the pattern. What fearful appeal lay there for Nazis?

Lang's greatest German film is *M*, and it is central to the topic of this chapter. Based on a real-life Düsseldorf child-murderer, it has Peter Lorre as the killer, quarry of both the police and the criminal establishment, equally alarmed that a pervert has jolted the public from its acceptance of "normal" crime. Two things impress in the film and emerge in the American crime movie. First, the virtual identity of criminal and police councils, and their similar means of conducting a manhunt. Lang makes that point satirically—but a Hitler might have been stirred by the resemblance and thought how naturally a street gang could become the force of authority. The second point concerns the character of the murderer. His torrential confession is the cinema's first recognition of uncontrollable impulse in the criminal, an acting out of social schizophrenia. Of course, this murderer's plea can be attacked as the neat defense of mitigating irresponsibility, too eloquent for someone really distraught. But it is a speech in a work of the imagination, it describes the separation of thought and action, and it may remind us of two Kanes, or of ourselves imagining ourselves as someone else:

> MURDERER: Always . . . always, there's this evil force inside me. . . . It's there all the time, driving me out to wander through the streets . . . following me . . . silently, but I can feel it there. . . . It's me, pursuing myself, because . . .
> SCHRANKER: You mean to say you *have* to murder?
> MURDERER: I want to escape . . . to escape from myself! . . . but it's impossible. I can't. I can't escape. I have to obey it. I have to run . . . run . . . streets . . . endless streets. I want to escape. I want to get away. And I am pursued by ghosts. Ghosts of mothers. And of those chil-

dren. . . . They never leave me. They are there, there, always, always. Always . . . except . . . except when I do it . . . when I . . . Then I can't remember anything. . . . And afterwards I see those posters and I read what I've done . . . I read . . . and . . . and read. . . . Did I do that? But I can't remember anything about it. . . . But who will believe me? Who knows what it feels like to be me?

That last unanswered question is the cry of the psychopath, but it sometimes occurs to the wholesome in today's city, and it might be the quandary of the moviegoer. What would Nazism find relevant in that heartfelt but histrionic defense? At the time, probably no more than sharper antipathy toward the "pervert" and a more urgent call for authority. But how easily the murderer's divided soul anticipates the separation of action and conscience that Nazis invoked as their defense. Too easy to say that plea was specious and cowardly, if it is heartrending when uttered by Lorre. Perhaps Nazi atrocities could only have occurred within a psychic climate of riven souls. The ghoulish vision of society in the best crime film is not just social irony but a sense of man's alienation leading to an everyday mania. Lang's piercingly analytic style turns the city into a nightmare grid on which the chase is a macabre game between sensitive paranoid and the brutal mass.

When Lang came to America, he was allowed to resume that theme in *Fury*. The director's fresh memory of Germany and his wish to warn oblivious America are stronger motives than any special awareness of American problems. But Lang in America never lost the limpid coldness of plot progression, or the preference for sets that one attributes to Germany. *Fury* does have a Germanic tone, but in hindsight it seems an uncanny hunch about America.

Fury begins with an everyman and his girl: Spencer Tracy and Sylvia Sidney. They are too poor to be married, and in

1936 that was an obstacle to people in fact and fiction. Tracy is picked up in a small town for a crime he did not commit, and the people there work themselves up into a lynch mob. They storm the jail and set fire to it. It seems that Tracy has been killed in the fire. But he reappears, unforgettably changed—"I could smell my arm burning"—his decency now scorched by anger and the need for revenge. Amiability has become malice, and that recurring plot movement hints at the suppressed discontent of the common man. Tracy plans a court case against the mob leaders and organizes it from his place of hiding. Shut away, he becomes as malignant as the people he is attacking and who, in court, are horrified by the newsreel evidence of themselves at the head of the mob. The MGM story has Tracy relent at the end: He leaves the moral to the world and gathers Sylvia Sidney in a redeemed embrace. But the tidy restoration of kindness is less convincing than the onset of malice in a wronged man. *Fury* shows how easily everyman can become a brute, how quickly he can be detached from his fellows and how that inert community can accomplish mindless destruction. *Fury* is a melodrama, but it rests on an acidulous portrait of a spiteful, unprincipled crowd—the huddled mass ready to break out.

In Lang's next film, *You Only Live Once,* Henry Fonda is the first romanticized criminal whose outlawry is not Cagney's need to expend energy, but the despondent retreat of an honest, benighted man. The Warners criminals— Cagney, Robinson, Raft, and Bogart—were ready for their fate: They sneered and laughed at it face-to-face, and their glittering confidence left them hardly in need of our sentimental support. Fonda has a different screen character, seldom used as a villain. In the late thirties, he was an idealist, tender to women and with safe political attitudes. Because he is so much more good-looking than Cagney, and so much more slow-moving and introspective, his criminal life seems considered, rational, and the response of a hurt sensibility. In addition, the Fonda character in *You Only Live Once* is dogged by the bad luck of mistaken identity, and forced to flee with his pregnant wife—Sylvia Sidney again. In their car, pursued toward death, they are an American ideal rejected by their own society—the back seat is piled with foodstuffs and consumer products. Fonda dies, and the ending is tragic, for the sentiment of the audience has been drawn toward the abyss by his dismay at the closed paths of society. The film's title underlines the single chance man must take—by one means or another.

The war years reduced the quantity of urban crime pictures. Positiveness filled the screen; energy was harnessed to the war; and every effort was made to look away from trouble at home—that suggests how far this sort of film is a tacit measure of social tensions. Nevertheless, the direction initiated in *You Only Live Once* does persist, most intriguingly in the character of Humphrey Bogart. In the late thirties, Bogart was a rather coarse, uneasy screen frightener, without the assurance of Cagney and apparently not comfortable as an unambiguous villain. One reason for that could be an actor's reluctance to be "bad," or to detract from his own estimate of himself. A new ease settles on Bogart as soon as his material treats him with more respect and discovers a world-weary outsider, hardened against fate and society and trusting only himself and Hemingway's code of grace under pressure.

The film that admitted Bogart to his own kingdom was *High Sierra,* directed by Raoul Walsh. It begins with him coming out of prison—lean, gray-haired, and pale—taking deliberate pleasure in grass and open spaces. He is met by former associates and a continued life of crime seems automatic. A friend from the old days recalls Dillinger's remark about a generation of gangsters "just rushing toward death," but Bogart longs to "crash out" of this criminal pattern and live ordinarily. He meets and befriends a man with a crippled daughter and pays for the operation that helps her to walk again. But once on her feet she abandons him and sets out to catch up with fun. This disappointment drives Bogart deeper into fatal crime, into a grudging affair with an embittered moll—Ida Lupino—and, finally, pursued by the police, to the desolate sierra where he is shot down. Bogart regards his fate with sardonic regret, but no surprise.

In *Casablanca*, the same attitude motivates Rick, the adroit handler of delicate situations, the loner more fond of Ingrid Bergman than of the Allied cause, but eventually coaxed out of his neutralism by the pressure of militant team spirit—"Buy War Bonds as you leave this theater" is the punch line to many movies of the period. *Casablanca* is not an urban crime picture, but it shows a character from that genre taking on definition, ready for the splendid isolation of *The Big Sleep*.

The source for that is Raymond Chandler's novel, as well as director Howard Hawks's legend of self-sufficient professionals granted the company of a cool doll and keeping up a line of amusing chatter through thick and thin. *The Big Sleep* is a private-eye film, but the privacy is more telling than the detection. The mystery of the film is tortuous and impossible: The audience does not follow it, but accepts that menace and treachery beset this world in the way shadow crowds in on every frame. The darkness and the idea of sleep invoke an impenetrable chaos that only the witty and skilled detachment of a Bogart can combat. The police have nearly vanished and everyone lies, betrays, or double-crosses. The solving of the mystery holds no more value than persevering with a puzzle. Real confusion can never be unraveled: The honorable man can only try to stay sane. That now seems the point of *The Big Sleep,* and the companionship of Bogart and Bacall is its assertion of human values. It goes without saying that the private eye adopts nearly every ploy of the criminals: The need to remain private and intact permits any tactic.

The Big Sleep is a foundation for the film *noir,* a genre in which the mystery that requires a detective turns into an impossible riddle that the individual risks his stability in trying to answer. Within the scope of the entertainment movie, the hope of reason in the world has been fatalistically abandoned. Thus, we now regard Bogart's solitariness as existential, courageous, and admirable.

Solitariness of an insane pitch characterizes one of the last old-fashioned gangster films: *White Heat,* made by Walsh for Warners in 1949 and starring a bulkier Cagney as Cody Jarrett. Jarrett still has a gang, and they hold up a train in the film's first sequence. But once back in their hideout it is clear that Jarrett is unbalanced, violent and unpredictable, and a mystery to his own gang. He has overwhelming headaches, during which only his mother can comfort him. Their relationship threatens the acceptable limits of the entertainment film; it is touching but grotesque. They have a private toast—"Top of the world"—which is a deranged version of the success motif and the senseless destination for Jarrett's energy. However, Cagney now shows us how far motion is an attempt to escape reality and the headaches.

Still, Jarrett is the hero, and he has to suffer a slut wife—Virginia Mayo—and a disaffected gang. The bond with his mother is admitted to be psychopathic: As a child, Jarrett faked headaches to get her attention; now they are real. Without her he would go berserk, but with her he is a deadly infant withdrawn from reality and development. Though older, Cagney has become more childlike and in one scene he weeps and huddles on his mother's lap. Every woman in the film is unsound, and the attack on motherhood is direct enough to need no other meaning. But it also stands for the fallacy of conventional family order and the deluding shelter that protection has given to Jarrett. He goes to prison and, while there, he hears that his mother has died—we learn later that Mayo and her lover were responsible for her death. Jarrett has a spectacular fit, staggering along the top of the prison dining-room table, demolishing guard after guard, and finally being carried away, screaming and writhing, by four guards. Cagney's unabated physical passion turns this into a frightening vision of a machine running amok, and the hushed silence in the dining room afterward stands for the audience's awe.

Thereafter, Jarrett's cunning never obscures self-destructive mania. He breaks out of prison, kills Mayo's lover, and plans another robbery. But the police are on to him—the job is a trap and Jarrett dies, gibbering, astride an oil tank that bursts into huge flame with his exultant cry, "Top of the world, Ma!" He is the last independent gangster, as crazy as private enterprise in the corporate state. His mania is personal and clinical, but it separates him from the new ways, and the last great gasp of flame has been likened to the new prospect of nuclear explosion. The pessimism is considerable: There is not a reliable or healthy human relationship in the film; instead, people are restlessly vicious and untrustworthy; fate impels the hero toward disaster, as the only release from psychopathy and grotesque hopes of success. "Top of the world" may respond to a very competitive materialism and the facelessness that settles on all losers. It is every bit as disastrous as Kane's seclusion in Xanadu, and it says a great deal for Cagney's inner warmth that Jarrett is never a monster but only a maddened protagonist.

One subtlety in *White Heat*, and a sign of new ways, is the character played by Edmond O'Brien. He is a policeman who volunteers to be planted in Jarrett's prison cell to learn the whereabouts of earlier loot. He befriends Jarrett, breaks out with him, and is a reluctant confidant when the killer meditates on the preciousness of his mother. Thus O'Brien is another betrayer, and it is he who arranges the trap in the last job. The film does not challenge O'Brien, but the audience flinches from his duplicity and never warms to the cold-blooded and efficient performance of the police throughout the film.

Yet O'Brien is the new policeman. After the war there was a run of films that carried the crime movie into real city streets and dealt laboriously with the methods of crime-fighting. Cinematically, the example of Italian neorealism beckoned American pictures onto the streets and *The Naked City, Panic in the Streets, Call Northside 777,* and *The House on 92nd Street* have a semidocumentary tone. At a time of cold war and internal fear of radicalism and red peril, the crime picture moved firmly behind authoritarianism and gave it as much substance as possible. These policemen are not prominent characters, but dutiful organization men who culminate in *The FBI Story,* made in 1957, and the origin of a long-running television series. While the cinema grew distracted and nervy, and Eisenhower's America became more determined to retain its frail security, so the urban thriller became a fixture of TV. In that icebox, the system has been seen—monotonously and inaccurately—working. That only shows how much less candid and adventurous a form TV has been.

In the cinema, several important crime films appeared in the fifties. Shortly before he was forced to quit America by the hostility of McCarthyism, Joseph Losey remade Lang's *M* in Los Angeles. It owes much to Lang's picture, but it is the more naturalistic because of its real city and the extra psychological detail in David Wayne's moving performance as the murderer. Above all, it reveals the criminal organization's repressive control of the city. Never before had films suggested the structure of syndicated crime, though this too is a theme that develops in the fifties as the lone or star criminal recedes along with the commanding policeman. In hindsight, we can see that growth referring not just to crime systems, but to the stealthy influence of legal corporations, be they the FBI or large commercial enterprises. Other good films that observe this tendency are *Force of Evil, Murder Inc., The Big Combo,* and *The Phenix City Story,* all of which emphasize the resemblance of crime and business.

A climax in this line is Samuel Fuller's *Underworld USA* in which a rogue hoodlum pursuing private vendetta eliminates the syndicate leadership. Along the way, the film charts an underworld of big business and executives who pay their taxes, contribute to charity, and market goods the people want. What more does America need, they seem to ask, with genuine hurt that their trade and persons should be disturbed. Respectability and prosperity have now obscured the moral distinction between one setup and another.

Fritz Lang touched on this in *The Big Heat,* his last study of the individual and the system. The central character is a police detective, played by Glenn Ford, set on removing the crime syndicate in the city—there is no locality, only the urban generality that Lang always predicted for the future. In one scene, Ford visits the boss, and their night meeting is set against a backdrop of skyscrapers and illuminated windows, all of which, the boss indicates, are his—and are orderly, prosperous, and purposeful. Indeed, the policeman is resented by the boss as a threat to equilibrium, and there is a hint that the other policemen are accomplices to the boss. In other words, the affinity revealed in *M* has turned into a tacit alliance—as has occurred in some American cities.

The boss warns the detective, and when he pays no heed his car is made into a booby-trap that kills his wife instead. Vengeance now carries Ford beyond the circumscribed methods of the police, and he eventually routs the boss and his corrupt organization, with the aid of a moll, Gloria Grahame, whose sadistic lover, Lee Marvin, has disfigured her face with scalding coffee. It is rare in the urban thriller for pain to be made so disturbing; more often it is disguised. The "heat" in this instance is the appalling cruelty; but the "big heat" is criminal slang for a large-scale investigation and an allusion to the hellish state of the city.

At the end of *The Big Heat,* Ford rejoins the shamefaced police, and the film closes with the suggestion that the city is safe as long as there is integrity in the police. But Lang is not an optimist, and his analyses always outlast commercial overlays. There is no good cheer in *The Big Heat.* The logic of the city requires a boss to make the unwieldy place function, and the detective's nobility fits a morality play rather than a real man tried to the point of despair.

The sympathetic treatment of how policemen behave finds unexpected confirmation in Orson Welles's *Touch of Evil,* in which Welles plays the bloated and spiritually devastated police chief of an American town near the Mexican border. As another character admits, he is a good detective but a bad cop. He has a sour intuition of human nature, and if he thinks a guilty man is likely to be saved by lack of evidence or niceties of the law, he will frame the man. How many policemen, frustrated by the complexity of their work, the idealism of what they protest, and the larger indifference of society that goes with their fantasy support for fictional cops, have rigged a case to fit their hunch? Welles's cop is found out—by a clever, younger, bureaucratic policeman— and dies with the blood of his only friend on his hands, toppling into the trashy edge of a stagnant river—nature beginning to be fouled by the city.

Some fifteen years later, Clint Eastwood's *Dirty Harry* went to a sump pit on the edge of the uncontrollable city and hurled away his police badge, despairing of the contradictions in the job.* The cinema offers no policemen to be

---

* Box-office success made Harry think again, and he was restored to the badge in *Magnum Force* and *The Enforcer,* though unconvinced by bureaucratic chiefs and liberal laws. Eastwood's distress as Harry Callahan should not disguise the way his own company, Malpaso, made these very profitable sequels.

proud of now, and they are not likely in an age taught to mistrust CIA, FBI, as well as local police, or in a society that sees less wrong in the regular breaking of laws involving automobiles, drugs, income tax, or sexual behavior. It is not an obedient or lawful society. In New York the individual sometimes carries a gun to be his own policeman and may not report a crime to the harassed police, so remote is the chance of conviction. In *Death Wish,* Charles Bronson had audiences cheering as he turned himself into a decoy for muggers; and that film no longer noticed the irony of his own violence and criminality. The city is so fearful that we question the wisdom of going to the neighborhood cinema at night—film *noir* has crept out of the theater and into the street.

American cinema of the last decade has cultivated the criminal: He is profitable; he permits some of the sharpest commentaries on the politics of America; and to the most creative directors he is an especially intriguing American. Still, the need to release energy and to find oneself, in cinema, generates violence and the perpetual difficulty of understanding antisocial behavior. Crime in the movies is like a car crash: The spectacle and sensation, on screen, make for melodrama and plastic excitement, whereas the reality is hideous, painful, and shattering. The safety-conscious bourgeois so often attending to cinematic enactments of crime are mesmerized by the object of a real anxiety that has surpassed the Bomb, broken families, or unemployment. Crime is no longer a symptom of our aggression or of social malfunction; it stems from what we fear may be an inherent disorder in crowded democracies, a dissociation of action and consequence that has its *locus classicus* in the concentration camps.

Arthur Penn is a director who has strived to ask the significance of violence in America. In *The Chase*—already referred to in this book—he triggered our memories of the killing of Lee Harvey Oswald and employed a rural setting, with a sheriff in a hat, to demonstrate the untenable position of the law officer and the rabid sensationalism of the populace. In *The Chase,* the criminals are decent, hunted animals, and society—in whose name the sheriff serves—is amoral and decadent. Thus the sheriff leaves the town to its own cruel amusements.

A year later, Penn reinvested the legend of the thirties gangster with a feeling for youth affected by the protest movement of the sixties: Faye Dunaway's Bonnie was much nearer the fraught beauty of Joan Baez than sister of the sullen Bonnie Parker. *Bonnie and Clyde* are romantically idealized, beautiful, vital and, in their own terms, as honest as the world they pillage is deceitful, gross, and stupid. The young gangsters help a displaced farmer to shoot up the sign of the bank that has confiscated his home; and when they are on the run and wounded they are helped by an encampment of derelicts—Joads, perhaps, who never reached California. But the most striking quality of *Bonnie and Clyde* is their yearning to be known. To emerge from the huddled mass, and find themselves in the newspapers, is a pressing ambition; Bonnie is tempted by the movies and the Gold Diggers. It is when she has a doggerel verse account of their lives published that Clyde overcomes his impotence and shouts with joy, "You've told my story." Moments later, the young couple go through a death roll that is sensual, terrible, but exultant, and stresses their need to be recognized before dying.

That same compulsion activates *Point Blank,* remarkably the work of an English director, John Boorman, who found in Los Angeles the city of his imagination. *Point Blank* has an elliptical, cerebral form and brutal internal momentum. Lee Marvin, the vicious thug in *The Big Heat,* is the seasoned hero in *Point Blank,* evidence of our growing taste for hardened men. As the film begins, in the strange context of the abandoned Alcatraz prison, an elaborate criminal job is being wound up. But, at the climax, Marvin is betrayed by his wife and friend, and left for dead as they go off with the money.

What follows is an odyssey of the remaining energy in stranded individualism, or the speculative reconstruction of a defeated man. The film shows Marvin, badly wounded, swimming to the mainland, and then setting out on a re-morseless pursuit of his money that destroys most of the leaders of the syndicate. One clerical syndicate executive actually uses Marvin's vendetta to clear away the boardroom for his own greater power. Finally, when Marvin has the opportunity of recovering his money, it comes to him at night, back on Alcatraz. The new tycoon stands in a court-yard with a searchlight on him as a helicopter drops out of the darkness with the packet of money. He calls to Marvin to come and get it, but the Marvin who lurked in the shadows a moment before never materializes. There are several viable interpretations: He fears another trap—the syndicate marks-man is also present and might have shot Marvin as he stepped into the light; he is so disgusted with the system that at the last step he withdraws in a negation of earlier single-minded-ness; or, he dies, his fantasy submerged in darkness.

All of *Point Blank* could be Marvin's thoughts to stave off dying—the impulse of *Citizen Kane*. Much of the film has a hallucinatory or sleepwalking quality; the return to Alca-traz is more ritualistic than credible; and, all through, we have the feeling of watching a pregnant allegory, a dream marooned in wakeful consciousness. *Point Blank* is the sad ballad of Los Angeles, and the quest Marvin follows touches the parts of the city to explain how it works: used car lot, nightclub, tower building and penthouse, the sewer system, suburban model house. The city is a citadel of the American dream, so that Marvin's cold dismantling of it also shows contempt for American life-style. The film is so charged with social disgust that Marvin's considerable violence seems cleansing and his solitariness a virtue. The girl in the film, Angie Dickinson, is used as sexual bait for a trap, and when she and Marvin make love the coupling is nearly mute, but obligatory, as if the ideological dictates of romance confronted the incompatibility of people.

Since then, the urban crime picture has come into its own as a paradigm of alienation and breakdown, as a political and social condition, and as a particular human predicament. In a later chapter, I shall discuss the unwitting extent of their separation in *All the President's Men,* perhaps the most striking confusion of real America with the melodrama of the crime movie. For the moment, a few other pictures must be mentioned as illustrations of the dismembered society.

Francis Ford Coppola's *The Conversation* begins with a brilliant plan of moral dislocation. It picks out a rare sort of technical connection to show the deep lack of contact or understanding within the crowd. From a high angle, we close in on a busy sunlit public square in San Francisco. It transpires that one couple in the square are being bugged—in a virtuoso feat of electronic expertise their conversation is recorded and separated from the hubbub of noise in the square. The bugger-in-chief—the best on the West Coast—is Harry Caul, played by Gene Hackman, a private and suspicious man who lives with as little traceable human reference as possible, as if fearful of the threat of surveillance. He has dehumanized himself in the thought that humanity is what makes men suffer. Sounds are his only pleasure, and secure in his hermetic apartment he relaxes by playing (or miming) the saxophone to taped music. The characterization is highly original in American terms, yet the writing and the acting are exact enough to show us Americans we know (but have seldom met on the screen) and at the same time to refer to the universal isolation of Kafka's work. Like all spies, Caul's duty to himself is to be unobtrusive and repressed.

Caul makes a tape of the conversation to deliver to his client, but the edgy tone in the talk and his seeing the couple in the client's office building tug at his clenched conscience. He wonders if he is abetting a crime, and ineptly tries to protect the couple—easily made to seem appealing by the camera. In fact, the couple murder the client—an austere tycoon, tended by Doberman pinscher and smooth young aides—and Caul is warned to forget what he knows. That call comes on the phone he thought no one knew existed: His own sanctuary has been bugged, his impregnability is gone. The film ends with a silent Caul ripping the apartment to pieces in a vain attempt to find the bug, and going deeper into mania.

The double meaning in "bugger" is never forgotten in *The Conversation* and part of the final humiliation is of a suppressed homosexual being magically raped. This is not the only reference to sexual perversion in the contemporary crime picture. In *Chinatown,* for instance, incest—between John Huston and his daughter Faye Dunaway—is the climax of a moral and political incestuousness that infects Los Angeles. Thus, the sexual glamour of the detective figure is deflated. Whereas Bogart in *The Big Sleep* seems always on the point of bedding Bacall, in *Chinatown* the famous attractiveness of Jack Nicholson is depleted—by his director slitting his nose, by Dunaway appearing behind him (the bugger's position) as he tells his story of screwing like a Chinaman, and because of the prior interference with Faye by the man he is tracking down. *Chinatown* is an outstanding film *noir* and when Nicholson loses Faye and the chance of exposing the conspiracy a friend murmurs to him, "It's only Chinatown," as if they stood on the brink of the narcotic drowsiness of unreason.

The American diagnosis of mania in its own blood is most clearly acknowledged in the crime movie. Martin Scorsese's *Taxi Driver* presents a character who has especially disconcerted America in recent years: the man from the street who finds fame by shooting down a celebrity. The way in which Bonnie and Clyde strove to escape obscurity is echoed in *Taxi Driver,* where we are reminded of the brief notoriety achieved by Lee Harvey Oswald or Arthur Bremer.

The central character is Travis Bickle, played by Robert De Niro. At the start of the film he looks exhausted, unstable, and at the end of his tether. He was a marine in Vietnam, and he cannot sleep. So he takes night work as a taxi driver who will go to any part of the city, New York. As he drives, he talks to himself, incoherently angry with the sordid city. Travis is not sophisticated; he does not understand his own experience; but he is not callous, and the sadness of the city raises a desperate pity in him. Paul Schrader, who wrote the script, has called it a film "about a car as the symbol of urban loneliness, a metal coffin." Travis talks of a rain one day that will wash the city clean.

The subtlety of this portrait is in allying decent but helpless instincts with the violence of free-enterprise fascism. Travis tries to reach out of his own torment toward an anodyne blonde campaigning for a hollow presidential candidate. Their relationship fails, and Travis goes further into himself until he sees a child prostitute whose fate grips him. He reverts to marine training, equips himself with guns and knives, fails to assassinate the candidate, and instead "frees" the child in a frenzy of blood that kills three men and leaves himself badly wounded, with an empty gun that cannot put a last bullet in his own head. He survives as a press hero; the girl's father sends him a thank-you letter; even the blonde respects his fame; and he is still driving a taxi, as haunted by his own face in the rearview mirror as Jekyll was by Hyde.

Taxi Driver is a fearful movie, and who can reprove those people nervous of seeing it? Reality is bad enough now, they argue, for us not to need such savagery as entertainment. It in an earnest plea—more pained than ever it was in *Sullivan's Travels*—and those who make it can always see *The Godfather* instead.

The two parts of *The Godfather* comprise an overwhelming period piece. This is not just the care with which clothes and cars trace the twentieth century. Not simply the recollections of New York new to Sicilians or of a Babylonian Hollywood before it was sold off in lots; not only the Las Vegas billboards for Patti Page and Martin and Lewis or the poster for Dewey that smiles on a street brawl. Nor is it confined to the re-creation of color photography that is shadowy indoors and a little overexposed in the open, characteristic of the late forties. What really makes *The Godfather* a regression is the confidence with which it is made, and the uncomplicated support for capitalism, conservative attitudes, family solidarity, and such unlikely subjects in 1972–73 as loyalty, love, success, and the status quo. Not since Andy Hardy had an American film shown such unshadowed love between father and sons. All the treachery and bloodletting is devoted to one object—reputedly close to the hearts of our silent majority—the defense of the old order, business stability, domestic virtues, and the hope for decency.

A policeman appears in Part I, a corrupt man in whose formal execution we willingly aid and abet. Otherwise, the world of *The Godfather* is one that the Corleones are epically struggling to hold together. Of course, they profit from that themselves, although it is stressed that they live modestly, crowding around a lower-middle-class table to eat pasta and meat sauce. In return for power and the respect of their people, the Corleones protect the surrogate members of their family. In a country short of welfare services and skeptical of understanding in doctors, priests, teachers, lawyers, or social workers, the Corleones can smooth the paths through life of their family. This may entail professional advice and service, or the unofficial pressure that eases a fading actor into the one role that can save his career.

Why do we enjoy *The Godfather*? Why is it one of the most profitable films ever made? Because we identify with the Corleones, father and sons, and because their steady faith in social order allays our fears that the world is on the edge of decay and chaos. American cinema for the last twenty years has offered heroes overcome by their tasks, ultimately daunted by the problems of bedlam.

But Marlon Brando, reestablished as a master impersonator in his portrait of Don Corleone, is a wonderfully reassuring father figure. Old age has not been observed with such tenderness in an American film for many years. When he is shot down in the street what is he doing but buying fruit for Christmas? And when he eventually dies it is from the exertion of playing with his enchanting grandson among his own tomato plants. Don Corleone cherishes his offspring and conditions our response to them; he lives without extravagance and goes to church with the gratitude proper in a lucky immigrant. More than that, he is the source of respect, honor, and trust in a ramshackle community fearful of disorder.

It is natural that the success of *The Godfather* launched a sequel; just as inevitably, corporations perpetuate themselves at the heart of America. Those servicemen returning from Vietnam, and those millions of Americans aching for calm, needed a setting fit for heroes, that holds to the dignified life, to family meals, to church services and the near papal benevolence of a healing godfather. The election claims of Richard Nixon were barely distinguishable from the policies of Don Corleone: peace on the streets, the freedom of business to expand and be prosperous, honor in profit and hard work, distaste for narcotics, support of a Christian moral and social ethic, belief in neighborliness, and the schizoid inability to relate wholesome ends and a crook's methods. In *The Godfather,* the assembled mobsters congratulate themselves on their patriotic sentiments—"After all, we're not Communists."

I have stated this point more baldly than either the book or the film of *The Godfather* allows, but the message is implicit in both, and it is only public acclaim that has exposed it. But the message is alarming and cynical because the makers of the film do not admit it and thus evade the choice of denying or abiding by it. *The Godfather* is a subject for Luis Buñuel, short only of the humor with which the Spaniard's films dissect bourgeois hypocrisy. The one serious entertainment omission of the film is that of humor, almost as if it were afraid to smile in case it could not stop crying.

What would Buñuel have made of this Catholic, bourgeois ruling class that issues orders for murder during a marriage party? The last sequence of Part I, in which the new young godfather, Michael Corleone, professes his Catholic faith at a baptism, is intercut with shots of the murder of his rivals, a process he has himself ordered. Michael and the film are numbed by the contrast, and it ought to be sufficient to reduce the audience to helpless laughter or to send them out into the street to tear down every vestige of our decrepit order. Buñuel would have cheered both reactions. But *The Godfather* holds itself tense and still at the end so as not to provoke its audience beyond the immediate gratification of the wish to belong to the Corleone family.

In *L'Age d'Or,* forty years earlier, Buñuel showed a bourgeois gathering that tolerated a gamekeeper who shot his own son out of pique, ignored the fire burning in the kitchen quarters yet repudiated one couple intent on lovemaking. How pleased he would have been to have invented that last equation of religious ritual and the social preservative of slaughter. How near *The Godfather* comes to the burning criticism of Buñuel. To take but one strand, it is a work preoccupied with eating, an image that runs through Buñuel's work. In *The Discreet Charm of the Bourgeoisie,* it is the inability of the chic socialites to sit down and complete a social meal that crystallizes their anxiety. The Corleones are forever enjoying their pasta; the meal table is their place of communion; eating together, with women cooking for the men, is the affirmation of family solidarity and female subordination.

The crucial scene in which Michael kills a rival gangster and the corrupt policeman takes place in an Italian restaurant. As the three men eat and discuss a reconciliation, Michael goes to the lavatory. He knows that a gun has been left on the cistern so that he can kill the other two. The association of food with unity and the lavatory with purging violence is one that Buñuel would have delighted in. Socially and psychologically, *The Godfather* holds the seeds of an outrageous satire on our society. But it does not feed the seed to, say, the ripeness of the tomatoes amid which Don Corleone expires. Instead, the movie is content to be a comfortable entertainment, rather than agitate or divide audiences. The world of the Corleones, its use of melodrama to disguise crime, and its sly subversion of morality, has consumed the system that produced the film. The magisterial triumph of the movie is deadly evidence of our insecurity. What trade Italian restaurants must have done next door to cinemas, for the connection between blood and tomato paste has never been more piquant.

VII

WOMAN'S REALM
AND MAN'S CASTLE

> *The convention of romance is anyway*
> *still a power although a weakened one;*
> *and especially so in the United States,*
> *as is made entirely clear from the facil-*
> *ity and frequency of American divorce*
> *which of course is a profoundly* moral
> custom.
> —JOHN COWPER POWYS, *Dostoievsky,*
>   1946

NOW THAT FILM IS NOT THE REGULAR STAPLE OF FICTION, WE have begun to fret over the "effects" it has. For fifty years few reflected on its deeper influence. But in the last twenty we have endured reproachful surveys of the example for our children—and even for ourselves, since children risk becoming us—of acts of violence presented on the screen. We are seldom clear how such surveys are compiled, and we take it for granted that violence means killings and beatings, not cuts in continuity, or the indifference and contempt in a form that has withdrawn reality from us. We only complain at the way film-makers "exploit" violence and at the melodrama that cushions it. But it may be that we luxuriate in melodrama. Violent impulses and impossible attitudes may be the "forbidden" fruits allowed in this Eden.

If we were shrewder, we might recognize that the concern with violence demonstrates how far we watch a medium, rather than messages or human activity rendered through it. Indeed, it is hardly possible to watch dramatized violence without the triggered and protective wondering about what it is doing to *us*. In *Taxi Driver* we do not admit responsibility for Travis Bickle—that fictional persona is sealed off, and we know he is not real—or for Robert De Niro—since he has only made his outward signs available to fiction. But we stare at the imprint those two ghosts leave in our sky— for we may yet be real, even if Bickles and De Niros do not know us. The voyeur has been made less ashamed of himself. An entire era and culture arranged around his self-centeredness implies that he is excusable and natural.

In that frame of mind, it is likely that we do not respond directly to the hurts or joys felt by film characters; how can we, when they are inaccessible and immaterial? Instead, we flinch at the violence of the film itself, the aggressiveness in the showing and the impression made on minds exposed to this visible illusion. Consider the loss of dignity in the petulant loathing every night when a new commercial goads the bitter helplessness of "What do they take us for?" There speaks the addict, whose easeful sinking back into fantasy has institutionalized the abandonment of truths. Personal fulfillment once promised a great liberty, but we are trapped in it and by the knowledge that we have been taken for isolated fools, narrow explorers of private feeling unable to establish connections outside ourselves. The human being has become more intellectual, more fantasizing, free only in the cell of his own mind. That projection of Romantic idealism has separated him from his world as much as Kane is cut off from meaning.

If we have to imagine the pain, then our capacity for imagining acquires a priority that supersedes reality. Imagining becomes the elementary mode of human cognition, not feeling, experiencing, or knowing. Knowledge, experience, and emotion are then all reaches of the imagination. Of course, all appeals to the imagination lay the ground for this recession in identity—I imagine, therefore I am—but moving imagery carries the process to a special intensity because of its totality of audience and the bewildering imitation of life it provides. In this chapter, I want to consider the resulting confusion of a feeling we call love with images and inducements in what is known as the weepie, the melodrama, or the women's picture, genres aimed at the female audience and associated with the emotional travails of women.

Those are not clear-cut terms, whatever students of genre may say in defense of folkloric forms or against the rigidities of Hollywood. Crying in the cinema is less proof of a distinct genre than evidence of real emotions being inspired by unreal situations and characters. For instance, I have wept at the harsh treatment of Lassie, the final blizzard in *Scott of the Antarctic,* the revelation at the end of *Kane,* the dull man made luminous by cancer in Kurosawa's *Living,* as well as at some films that play the heartstrings: *Three Comrades, To Each His Own, Stella Dallas, Mr. Skeffington, Letter from an Unknown Woman,* or, less obviously, *East of Eden.*

The range of that assortment requires investigation. First of all, people certainly weep in cinemas: Perhaps women do so more openly, but men also cry, and may feel special release from the overbearing social pressure that men ought not to cry. Cinema managers once had the tact to restore light be-latedly after a very poignant conclusion, so that deep feelings in the voyeurs might be protected. The commonest cause of tears in the cinema, I think, is the calculated organizing of tragic events to achieve pathos. That is a hallowed sense in the viewer of a personal sorrow casting an influential shadow. It is contrived in most instances by some obstacle to the happy destiny of characters with whom we have been made to identify. We lodge our affections and sympathetic support with a character who is then thwarted by the action of the film. This often centers on death and the retrospective but useless wish to have behaved differently, in a way that might have averted the loss or failure. In mythic terms, the weepie is not just a lamentation for unrequited loves but intolerance of death, aging, the passing of time, and every mistake we make. "Oh! how ashamed you will be of this afterwards!" cries Myshkin in *The Idiot,* sensing the frenzied mood of impulse and remorse.

By that scheme, *Citizen Kane* is a weepie, involving a man's ingenious mourning for the ways his life went wrong, and the redemption by pathos that finds a fragile coherence. "What might have been" absolves and sharpens the tragedy of Kane's life, just as it does the estrangement of mother and child in *Stella Dallas,* and the wife's guilt toward her blinded and betrayed husband in *Mr. Skeffington.* Time and again, tears are prompted by imagination carrying us over the bar-riers of death, time, separation, and estrangement. In real life, it is crying for the death of someone who was often difficult and tedious when alive. Like all cinema, the weepie is subjunctive; feelings there are more searing than real, indicative emotions. The characters in a film have to endure the delicious agony of separation from one another that we try to surpass in involving ourselves on their behalf. The most urgent spring of tears is that we cannot touch or be beside Joan Crawford or Margaret Sullavan; in the same way, love poetry is seldom written when the lovers live happily together.

Consider *East of Eden* as an illustration—a film not ordinarily classified as a weepie. In Elia Kazan's version of Steinbeck's novel, it has been turned into a study of denied affection, of feelings blocked, and of the anguish that arises in consequence. Indeed, cinema excels at and can become hysterical over the way suppressed or refused emotions constitute a lost reality.

To avoid the biblical allusions that beset *East of Eden,* I will describe it in terms of the actors involved. A father, Raymond Massey, has two sons: the clean-cut, upright Dick Davalos; and the shabby, furtive but passionate James Dean. The brothers have been told their mother is dead, but in fact she is Jo Van Fleet, the madam of a brothel in a nearby town, a reclusive arthritic businesswoman (and further proof of how much more absorbing characters can be in American movies if they are damned). Dean knows of her existence when the film begins; his turbulent energy is close to intuition. He feels bound to protect his brother from knowledge of their mother, because Davalos is privileged—his father smiles on him, he makes an easier way in the world, he has none of the adolescent's awkwardness, he is like a young saint in a maidenly religious painting, and he has the endearing Julie Harris as a girl friend.

Kazan's compelling, if emphatic, realization of this psychological situation uses physical and spatial connections or barriers, and that very engrossing cinematic activity—watching. Whereas Massey and Davalos are content with their lives in rural Salinas, Dean makes the journey to the town, Monterey. They are neither sensitive nor acute, but he is as watchful as a cat. The distance between Salinas and Monterey is not just geographical; it is a measure of the willingness to be concerned with difficult things outside oneself.

Dean makes the journey on the perilous and exposed roof

of a train, hunched up against the chill. In Monterey, he watches and follows his mother as she goes to her bank. This is on a misty morning, and the indistinct distances and secrecy express the voyeur in pursuit of the mystery that may explain himself. Dean's nervy wariness makes a trembling picture of adolescence, but it is also consistent with a larger inquiry about the world. The spatial links in Dean trailing Van Fleet, sitting on a curb as she walks past in a black veil, are gripping because of the repetition of our own concentration on the passing spectacle. Just as we are imagining ourselves Dean—and his stardom rests in persuading us to do that—so he is speculating on this mother whose dark respectability seems depraved to the sheltered life he has led.

She knows she is being followed (he gets his sharp instinct from her) and has him roughly warned off. But Dean goes back to the brothel-saloon in the evening and adventures down the dark corridor to his mother's office. The resemblance of that corridor to a womb betrays Kazan's over-obvious manner, and the scene could be crude without the visual tension of narrow corridor and CinemaScope width. He comes to the door of the office, and looks in for a moment at his weary, pained mother before she notices him. I have elaborated this treatment in order to demonstrate the brimming emotionalism possible in cinema: The form of the sequence draws us into a deprived boy's yearning for parental recognition, and for what the film and our psychologically attuned culture would call love.

Dean's emotional need and courage have bridged the separation of his parents, and an uneasy relationship develops between mother and son. He goes back to Salinas and the attempt to span emotional distance is maintained in the sequence in which he follows Davalos and Harris, half playing with the idea of telling his brother about their mother, while darting in and out of the trees where they are walking. They go into Massey's new icehouse, and Dean spies on the other two, envious, excluded and sexually inquisitive. The rudiments of plot are dwarfed by the emotional and psychic implications of the image. Dean's attempt to gain his father's attention by hurling the iceblocks out of the house and down the chute is an onset of infantilism, an act of destructiveness that conveys the torment of unrequited feelings.

Massey's scheme to refrigerate lettuce allows Dean to feel useful: He steals a coal chute to assist the lettuce-sorting. But the first trainload of vegetables is held up, the lettuces are sodden as with tears, and Massey's pioneering investment is lost along with his dreams of invention. Dean then asks his mother for a loan and goes into the bean-growing business, foreseeing that America must soon be in the Great War, at which time the demand for beans will increase. I emphasize this commerce in lettuce and beans because part of the accuracy of *East of Eden* is in intermingling money and feelings.

War comes, beans flourish—encouraged by their young grower's fond attention—and Dean makes a lot of money, which he presents to his father, wrapped in pretty paper, for his birthday. But by then Massey is on the town draft board, sending young men to their death. Though briefly touched by the gift, he rejects it as war-profiteering. Dean's pain is so terrible as to reduce him to tears in front of Harris, Davalos, and Massey. He clings to his father, pleading for recognition and respect, but the frigid Massey is alarmed by the emotionalism. We, in the audience, share Dean's distress and understand the spasm anger that immediately drags off the innocent but complacent Davalos to meet his mother.

It is a test of maturity in the brothers that Dean was not shocked to find his mother and has struck up a relationship with her, whereas Davalos's shallow personality is devastated by the discovery. He goes on a drunk, abandons his stuffy pacifism, and enlists in the army. On the train before leaving, Massey tries to stop him. But in a stupor of liquor and resentment, Davalos crashes his head through the carriage window

—breaking the invisible barrier. Fragments hit Massey and he has a stroke. This crisis is clearly emotional, less psychosomatic than the dramatic collapse of a man whose life is in ruins.

Dean and Harris attend Massey in what may be a fatal condition. At the bedside, Dean tries to win a word or gesture from his stricken father, but Massey remains inert and staring. Then Harris speaks to him and explains how much Dean needs a sign of affection. Dean returns to the bedside and the father does whisper to him—to get rid of the officious nurse. The emotional tension is released and we feel that Dean will now be his father's chief comfort and at-long-last recipient of parental love. Harris is there in the background, to empty the bedpans, cook the meals, and be the evident and nourishing lover of Dean. Music, by Leonard Rosenman, makes its gentle claim of epic fulfillment, and a sort of tranquillity brings separation and thwarting to a state of tearful union and discovery.

Now, *East of Eden,* made in 1955, has many elements of "adult" cinema. Its normal classification is as "drama." The place and period are convincing and integral: The still-provincial California and the moods of 1915–17 steadily contribute to the movie reality. The feelings of the characters seem the more natural because of so thoroughly believable a world. The acting is very striking. Kazan's skill at harnessing the emotions of his players is evident in all but the wooden Davalos. Above all, the imagery is like vibrato in music: Composition, movement, and color constitute feeling, and usually without the sort of symbolism already mentioned. Kazan has always stressed the importance of conviction—his need to believe in and feel for his material—and whenever he attains that moviegoer's absorption he is capable of a superficial but very effective power in which the forms of a movie represent his own identity with emotional characters unable to express or find satisfaction in feelings. He is in the mainstream of cinema, for his method suits the medium's creation of a plausible context worthy of our bursting wish to belong.

In other words, the impetus to watch is a passionate regret over alienation or misunderstanding. The resolution leads always to the terminus literary people deride in all films, and which is supposedly a mark of rawness in movies—the happy ending—when the weeping violin gives way to the orchestration of satisfied sentiment. The adultness of *East of Eden* can easily be dismantled. Dean was always a dark, disturbing presence, who reminds us of the biblical references to Cain in his character. The moment when he "seduces" Davalos to see the mother is sinister and shows Dean as a hurt child verging on a devil. Further, how easily can we dismiss Davalos and Van Fleet from our thoughts, both of whom have been used—by Dean and by the film—ostensibly in the name of feelings, but actually with callous detachment. Will Dean continue to visit his mother? What happens when Davalos—decent, if not distinguished—comes back from the war, or can we count on his inconvenience being permanently removed? Is it credible that the benign-natured Julie Harris will tame and hold Dean? And will Dean and Massey enjoy a prolonged sick-room communion? Will Massey even rise up and walk again, cured by the unhampered love of father and son?

East of Eden has the prestige of Steinbeck's name, strength of feeling in its subject, background authenticity, and Kazan's imaginative engagement. Yet it is a weepie, immersed in the melodramatic deeps of cinema. All its virtues gather behind a sentimental punch at a point of emotional crisis. It sees intense feelings coming to turning points; it believes in the rise and fall of pressured emotion; and that, ironically, amounts to stability in melodrama, just as waves are characteristic of the sea. What might be required in a novel as a plausible working out of artistic purpose and human nature is subordinated to the restrained hysteria of withheld feeling. The voyeur is allowed to see emotion, and then that prospect recedes, becoming the more agonizing, unrequited, and difficult. And cinema here conforms to the principle that the more unobtainable a thing is, the more desirable it becomes. We grieve because our sensibility has been concentrated on the need for feeling, and in the way that feeling is aroused, then denied. The affinity with the induced envy and frustration of advertising is horribly clear, and Dean's impact must be seen in terms of the drama of prevented feelings. An adult, he played adolescents and extracted the adolescent frustration in audiences of all ages.

These are essential conditions of the "weepie," and proof that we often get a "good cry" from films other than labeled weepies. Not only the form's preying upon immature response—the channeling of all energy into sentiment—need be remarked upon. It is useful to explain how far marketed narrative fictions as a whole have explored this stimulation of unreal feelings, for cinema often reproduces the historic development of the novel. Sentimentality is a concept that comes to us from the first novels of the eighteenth century. What we take for the glory of that form was then widely disapproved of for teaching readers the indulgence of emotional fantasy—escaping themselves by identifying with the concocted existence of nonexistent characters. But to be moved by a book has been interpreted as imaginative fineness; it is the human sensibility that E. M. Forster saw making a necessary "connection" with the world. If, philosophically, we are enclosed and selfish, then imagination redeems us by permitting us to "feel for" others. But perhaps that "feeling for" depends upon the manipulation of fiction, the cold-bloodedness of voyeurism, and an increasing inability to believe in the reality of others.

The industry of tearful tales that began in the eighteenth century was originally directed at a female readership. It persists today in what is called the "romantic novel," a product seldom reviewed but limp from use in libraries. Very early, sentimental fiction found one of its most devious exponents in Laurence Sterne, an entranced victim of his own ability to slip from sham tears to real distress. In Sterne's life and work—uneasy and spasmodic as they were— there is a dilemma fully realized in cinema: that we are moved more by the thought of things than by things themselves. And since the market in popular fiction is not much more than 250 years old, it must be underlined that the form proposes a threat to cultural integrity—that we feel more strongly through the imagination. Thus, we feel what we lack, we love what we do not have, and emotions cling to impossibility. As a culture, we have wearied of reality and fastened on fiction.

Sterne wanted to feel. He was emotionally promiscuous, but could never find relationships to withstand his own imaginings; and in his writings he is alert to the way feeling flares up when it is hindered. His most fevered and significant work in a vain search for stability is the *Journal to Eliza,* a diary written for (or at) a woman he had known in London but who returned to a dull husband in India. As she sailed away, so his love grew with the friction of writing about it. I think that the generative power of impossibility for Sterne is central to the weepie movie and to the entire condition of hopeless participation that cinema inspires. In addition, Sterne was dying, of consumption and of absurd but consuming passion. Let me quote one passage in which the sickly rapture evokes something of our response to movies:

> I have been within the verge of the gates of death.— I was ill the last time I wrote to you; and apprehensive of what would be the consequence.—My fears were but too well founded; for in ten minutes after I despatched

my letter, this poor, fine-spun frame of Yorick's gave way, and I broke a vessel in my breast, and could not stop the loss of blood till four this morning. I have filled all thy India handkerchiefs with it.—It came, I think, from my heart! I fell asleep through weakness. At six I awoke, with the bosom of my shirt steeped in tears. I dreamt I was sitting under the canopy of Indolence, and that thou camest into the room, with a shaul in thy hand, and told me, my spirit had flown to thee in the Downs, with tidings of my fate; and that you were come to administer what consolation filial affection could bestow, and to receive my parting breath and blessing.—With that you folded the shaul about my waist, and, kneeling, supplicated my attention. I awoke; but in what a frame! Oh! my God "But thou wilt number my tears, and put them all into thy bottle."—Dear girl! I see thee,—thou art for ever present to my fancy.

The women's picture is still a pejorative term, with suggestions of unworthy films shown in disreputable places to gullible audiences. In some academic circles, it is talked of in the same tone that despairs of television commercials. But such disparagement often overlooks its own familiarity with the object of scorn. How many professors retreat exhausted from their departments to be soothed by the evening lullaby for the new Chevette or a better burger? As many, I suspect, as there are stranded housewives who attend with desperate contempt to soap operas. If we are weary, unhappy, unpeaceful, or alone, we are susceptible to the plaintive appeal to unsatisfied emotions and self-pity that exists in pop music, advertising, and the women's picture.

Hollywood and Madison Avenue have channeled sentiment into manageable, shallow pools where once, perhaps, as the Romantic Age asserted, there were sublime oceans. In the novels of Dostoevski, one sees the melodrama of psychic insight and neurosis intruding on Romanticism. The women's picture, it is often alleged, debases sentiment. It may only be that, better than any other form, it recognizes our loss of constant, unequivocal sentiments. To be in love with Gene Tierney or Ray Milland, without any hope of meeting them, is enough to make us wistful and love unsound. In the movies, and especially in the women's picture, we live on a trick—that the lifelike equals life—which makes us skeptical of all feeling.

When cinema is studied seriously today, no sort of film raises as many problems as the women's picture. Film departments are often recruited from disenchanted or heretical literature teachers and while they admit the compulsive thrill of moving images in the dark, they flinch from the women's picture. Can that overflavored stew be respectable? Once one has known *Emma* and *Middlemarch,* is one obliged to mock the immoderate *Love Is a Many Splendored Thing,* and assume that the coiners of such titles are vulgarians? The titles seem to spring from abject commercialism. They smack of mawkishness and the calculated play upon feelings as unsteady as jelly.

Film studies therefore fight shy of *All That Heaven Allows, History Is Made at Night,* or *Dark Victory,* because of the swooning titles, and the allegedly febrile emotions they boast. But if we have lost faith in feelings, may artificial sentiments not reflect our experience? Important critics prefer the subtitled complexity of *Persona* or *Belle de Jour.* But Bergman and Buñuel employ themes and ideas from the women's picture. Both those celebrated films explore the emotional fantasies of unhappy women. One is grim, the other sardonic, but both admit the impossibility of natural, spontaneous feelings. If we can respond to this in *Belle de Jour,* then may we not discern the loveless hollows in loving protestation in American pictures? *Persona* and *Belle de Jour* juxtapose moments of actuality and passages of fantasy, whereas the Hollywood women's picture rejected such contrasts and found a form in which the real and the fantastic were combined in every image. Both types of film rely on the darkness in cinema, in order that the plangent imagery will pierce our defenses. This furtiveness is described in a rapturous remark from Bette Davis in *Hush, Hush . . . Sweet Charlotte* that might also apply to our most intimate and precious experiences: "It only works in the dark."

Yet I cannot shrug off complaints about the women's picture, or ignore the perils in treating it seriously. It is an offensive label employed by a male-dominated film industry, whether the box-office scorekeepers on *Variety* or the production bosses at the big studios. It was orthodox policy that an audience waited for films dwelling on the emotional long-suffering of women. They might be virgins misled and betrayed, wives double-crossed, or mothers devoted to wastrel sons; they might even be decent girls, pushed by circumstances into thinking and working for themselves. It was accepted that such films pleased women. But men have always watched women's pictures, just as, invariably, they have made them. Even if the audience was as much as sixty percent female, the films would have flopped without the forty percent of men. Cinema's tortured attitude to women may only stand for the confused lust and guilt in men, and some women's pictures are maddened extensions of the western cult of the madonna. The form, it seems to me, is manly: It projects and protects men's dreams of emotional life and is colored by men's private shame—that they do not feel as intensely as women do; that women's stamina gives continuity and warmth to the world.

Feminists despise the caricature of women and the restrictive treatment of love, marriage, and emotional happiness that sees women as beautiful but stoical faces down which shining tears will always slide—it is an idiom as persistent and mistaken as men's readiness to fight. Most provocative of all, the women's picture came from an industry that has confined women to jobs or roles that sustain a man's notion of what life ought to be. The woman in the film industry is the bespectacled continuity girl or production secretary who mothers the genius director; the embittered, veteran script-writer, such as Scott Fitzgerald offers in *The Last Tycoon*, and Eve Arden might have played; the doting and credulous member of the audience; or the goddess who submits to the grinding inspection of a male audience watching movies to catch lovely women unawares. Garbo, according to gossip-column folklore, retreated from this scrutiny with the wish to be alone; yet, in truth, it was the solitude of stardom that most weighed on the gods and goddesses. They were alone— like the audience—eventually distressed by the cinema's blaring legend of community.

The women's picture is an American phenomenon, a line adopted by the industry and the star system and supported by a mass audience. It uses American cinema's appeal to the mind's eye in a visual code that outflanks censorship and the industry's own wish not to unsettle its market. Therein lies much of D. W. Griffith's work, particularly the smaller melo-dramas—*True Heart Susie, Broken Blossoms,* and *Way Down East*—and *Intolerance*'s hinging the fate of civilization on Mae Marsh's determination to prove her husband innocent. It is the bulk of Garbo's films in which she is a figurehead of impossible eroticism—a Queen Christina sailing into abdi-cation, from the affairs of men and affairs with men, Camille dying of consumption after she has given up the healthy Robert Taylor. It covers the careers of Joan Crawford and Bette Davis, the one a gypsy madonna, the other an angry Pekingese, both as harrowed by elusive satisfaction as Mick Jagger. But the women's picture also includes the consistent vision of director Frank Borzage and such re-markable pictures as *A Man's Castle; Stella Dallas,* directed by King Vidor; Mitchell Leisen's *To Each His Own;* John Stahl's *Leave Her to Heaven;* Michael Curtiz's *Mildred Pierce.* It is a genre enlivened by the lyrically frail courage of Margaret Sullavan, the battered pride of Joan Crawford, so often invaded by somber shadow, the shining plight of Lillian Gish, and the willful but ridiculous depravity of Dorothy Malone in *Written on the Wind.*

Not every film about a woman was a women's picture; many pictures ostensibly dealing with men are sticky with the sentimentality attributed to the women's picture. In the 1930s, especially, there were women in films who were intelligent, feeling beings, different from but as capable, witty, impulsive, or misguided as men. The most assured is still the fatalistic Marlene Dietrich, her surreal pencil eyebrows arching over a rueful smile at the inescapable absurdity of sex. The films she made with Josef von Sternberg at Paramount are satires on emotional dishonesty in which only woman stays lucid. Dietrich sometimes approaches the camp exaggeration of a tyrant mistress, but the quality of *Morocco, Shanghai Express, The Scarlet Empress,* and *The Devil Is a Woman* lies in her visible authority and the disharmony of relationships: Beauty does not flow tranquilly into romance, as cinema usually contended. When men talk to Dietrich in these films there is only misunderstanding and the pained silences of lovers who cannot communicate. Von Sternberg's movies have a chilly meaning: that we may look at one another, but not reach another person, never rid ourselves of solitude.

Dietrich's films are European in tone. At a more American level, the thirties ripple with the headstrong glory of Katharine Hepburn, Carole Lombard, and Barbara Stanwyck, as daft as men in screwball comedies, spared the surliness that now clouds Jane Fonda's strenuous independence. We can go to the films of Howard Hawks and George Cukor to find men and women putting up with one another as equals: In *Twentieth Century* there is no gap in cunning or deceit between Lombard and John Barrymore; in *Philadelphia Story*, Cary Grant and Hepburn are equally capable of making fools of themselves, torn between feelings and saving face.

Elsewhere, we must concede maudlinism in the "men's picture": the Warner Brothers gangster film, the Paul Muni biopics, the war movie, and the John Ford smokeroom film in which women are dreadfully relegated, treated as stooges, roughed up, given over to Greer Garson, or told to be plucky little skivvies who must have the slippers ready when the heroes lurch home. What is Bogart in *Casablanca*, hunched over a bottle, cosseted by self-pity and Sam's obedience at the piano, but the replica of the woman torturing herself over a lost love, like Bette Davis in *The Letter* discovering that "even my agony was a kind of joy"?

There again, cinema catches a modern neurosis, the capacity to replay unhappiness until abjectness becomes a reason to live. In *The Idiot*, Myshkin detects an attitude to suffering in Nastasia that we sometimes feel in screen heroines: "You are proud, Nastasia Philipovna, and perhaps you have really suffered so much that you imagine yourself to be a desperately guilty woman." At times the screen seems to regularize regret and grief for the huddled masses. Indeed, the cinema suggests that we identify most quickly with the forlorn, and cling to unhappiness in ourselves as a structure for identity. The darkness of the cinema may remind the disappointed of a church, while the movies can be an apologia for failure.

In the suburban stage of film education, D. W. Griffith has succumbed to the well-intentioned rehabilitation that takes him ever further from his context. The wish to make someone responsible for the crystallization of quicker narrative techniques has fixed on Griffith—whereas, as I have suggested, his real novelty was commercial. And since Griffith played a prominent part in coaxing the medium beyond early sensation and bluster, it is assumed that the content of his films is valuable, personal, and better than bluster. But he straddles popular theater at the turn of the century and film's capacity for melodrama. In his "large" pictures Griffith was a grandiloquent defender of man's fate and history, but what fascinates him is the suspenseful ordeal of waiting women and particularly the spiral of eager emotions, puritanism, and a fate worse than death. Movies have always shuddered at the threat of rape—hence their powerful association of death and orgasm.

Griffith cherished women and had an intuition of how to film them so as to persuade a spectator that he had rescued a character's inner mood from neglect and solitude. His company of players revolved around the actresses, and his films are a series of trials and tribulations for womankind. But he was restricted by his own condescending and censorious attitudes toward women. His young female fits into one of three categories: the rapturous virgin in danger of deflowering and disgrace; the scarlet or fallen woman—who is the first category after one unlucky encounter, without a chance of recrossing that frontier; and the comic, ugly sister who serves as light relief to everyone else. In literary terms, there is not a three-dimensional woman in Griffith's work, not one who asks more than the fond sigh or stern hiss of melodramatic performance. They are all driven on by the frantic activity of the films, with no time to reflect or respond, only the need to react.

But there is more going on in these films than old-fashioned and moralizing plots. The images have subtler effects. And Griffith might not have persisted with sanctimonious trials of virtue endangered if he was not, within himself, unconvinced about such virtues. Early cinema claims reverence for protected virginity and social stability built on love and marriage, but it regularly shows us how interesting the alternative is. Like the yellow press, it illustrates depravity, debauchery, and the white slave trade by insisting on their wickedness. There is a seething sexual imprecision in Griffith's work, which I suspect he never noticed. It comes out of the preying upon women with a camera that makes them lovely, tethered victims. The camera always bestows a sort of bondage, essential to so many erotic fantasies and underlining—or introducing—the power plays involved in sexuality.

For instance, early in *Way Down East,* the simple country girl, Lillian Gish, goes to the city. The film was made in 1920, yet Griffith still endorsed the cliché about the gulf between rural prudence and urban abandon. She meets an older man, instantly recognizable to everyone except Gish as a seducer. He is as touched by her innocence as he is aroused by her beauty. As the titles tell us, he lusts after her but is awed by her purity—until he catches a glimpse of her leg. That dissolves restraint in him; and what does it do to us? For Griffith daintily serves up that leg in one of his innovative close-ups. The visual treatment is more equivocal than the story line. The plot sees no reason not to condemn Gish for being seduced, even if the tone is paternal. But the form of the film simultaneously puts us in her position and in that of the seducer. Thus the movies actually destroy moral steadfastness by allowing us everyone's point of view.

Exactly the same thing occurred in the early novel. Samuel Richardson's *Pamela,* published in 1740, is an extended description of how a servant girl manages to marry her master only by keeping her body intact against him. There is the same uneasy flux of puritanism and prurience, and the form permits Richardson all manner of attempted outrages that are still disturbing today. Real sexual experience is evaded; the book concentrates on fearful speculation and barely avoided rape. We learn nothing of Pamela's sex life after she marries—perhaps her own undoubted but covert libido goes into the reading of books. And in Griffith's films, the blanket solution "happily ever after" quickly descends on the interesting subject of how people live together when they are happy, or stay happy when they cohabit. We never feel the growth of character or intelligence in a prolonged relationship. Instead, the film turns on the question-begging of integrity being locked up in virginity.

But melodrama requires not faces so much as fixed masks. In Victorian theater, the virgin was armored with austere white makeup, the villain curled moustaches and leered, while the young man was carved from soap and marble. Early movies continue those traditions. Griffith's villains are unmistakable but unfathomed. His heroes have the unflawed nobility of Robert Harron and Richard Barthelmess. Yet once he looks at women, he sees so much more. In *Intolerance,* there is a fallen woman, played by Miriam Cooper. She is only a supporting character in the story dominated by Mae Marsh as the blonde wife desperate to save her husband. Miriam Cooper is dark and sad; she looks ill, as if suffering physically from living with a man outside marriage. The plot allows her to know that the husband has been framed, and that her own man is the real culprit. She becomes the most adult person in *Intolerance* because she struggles with recognizable doubts, torn between a sense of justice and her love for a rotten man. The dilemma is simplified, but the close-ups of her dismay are absorbing. Griffith's virgins so seldom know doubt, yet doubt is the abiding condition of real people.

Again, in *Way Down East,* the long shots relay the melodrama, full with the posturing and grimaces that served as acting. But then comes a close-up of Gish with a corona around her disheveled hair so that the features are in half-light. Instantly, it is Sousa replaced by Mozart. The strident stereotype of melodrama collapses with the evident spectacle of real human thought processes. Seeing Griffith today one must be patient with antiquated attitudes and laborious plots, and wait for sights of the future. Those moments are invariably privileged glimpses into the spirit of a troubled woman.

Frank Borzage is not as well known a director as Griffith, and the preservation of old films has not always appreciated the need to collect his. He was born in 1893, and he worked steadily as a director between 1916 and 1948, after which he made only three more pictures before his death in 1962. In his heyday—mid-twenties to about 1940—Hollywood admired him for craft and box-office returns. But neither Borzage nor anyone else regarded him as an artist, and in the late thirties Scott Fitzgerald thought he was typical of the established and once freer director now handed assignments by the studio and reduced to the status of obedient professional. Indeed, Broaca * is as likely to be derived from Borzage as from anyone else, for Borzage directed *Three Comrades,* the one film that Fitzgerald took pride in as an author.

Part of Borzage's merit lies in the diversity of his appeal. He did a job that Hollywood respected; yet he made romance a lyrical tribute to *l'amour fou* identified by the French surrealists. Borzage's imagery uncovers poetic and psychic forces in what can be a trite convention. But he uses stories in which emotion defies a set of obstacles, including the Depression and poverty, political tyranny, illness and death. The popularity of cinema in the thirties should not obscure its appeal to some sections of the avant-garde. They delighted in the manifestations of absurd realism (the life-like that has no existence) and such command of the public

* See p. 71.

imagination that millions were participating in the sort of waking dream the surrealists aspired to. Of course, Hollywood leaned heavily on naturalism and plots that fitted together tidily. But André Breton, a leading surrealist, liked to go into cinemas while films were showing and leave as soon as the dull plot insisted on being understood. For a few moments he could revel in the liberty of an automatic but inexplicable phantom of life. Being so strict, he would not stay once a plot obtruded, and he did not see that Hollywood films retained that sensational embodiment of fantasy even when plots emerged like railway lines out of the mist.

In Borzage's best work, passion, visual eroticism, and fidelity to the ideal of love produce imagery so psychically material as to make story lines only pretexts. He trusts the audience's willingness to lift ardent characters out of crushing circumstances: The events of life that separate his lovers stimulate the chivalry of our imaginations. In *Three Comrades,* the setting is Germany beset by a foreboding fascism in which three friends are devoted satellites of Margaret Sullavan. The men are ciphers, only as forthrightly good-looking as Roberts Taylor and Young and Franchot Tone. But Sullavan as seen by Borzage is an extraordinary actress. No other Hollywood beauty seems to attend so intelligently and feelingly to what is being said or happening. She had a vulnerability that naturally played invalids, but easily extended to the fear that all precious things—life, love, and liberty—were at risk. Risk, a living element in life, easily looks false in films, perhaps because everything is written and rehearsed before filming, and because many stars had enough complacency and self-love to subdue it. Sullavan's tremulousness reminds us of risk in the least movement or the largest decision. A catch in her voice conveys fearful hesitation. In *Three Comrades,* her family has been stricken financially by the First World War. Against the coming tide of the second war she faces love, tuberculosis, and the stress between personal fulfillment and social breakdown. Without any announced intention, Borzage allies the personal and political levels of existence. She dies at the end, willingly, and the cause of love and liberty is made all the more glowing because of her generosity.

It is the avoidance of happy endings that shows Borzage's commitment to sentiment. In *The Mortal Storm,* Sullavan is the daughter of a university professor who is sent to a concentration camp. Her love for James Stewart unites the couple in antagonism to brutal authoritarianism, and there is one scene of them standing together, still and unmartial, amid a forest of aggressive fascist salutes. It is an emblem of Borzage's faith in love as an ideological stance.

Perhaps he was fortunate to live between wars and under the shadow of the Depression. It is remarkable how far the women's picture can contain—without their deliberate insertion—attitudes that address the reality of an age more cogently than other genres managed. Two other Borzage films, from widely differing sources, describe war blighting but enhancing love: *Seventh Heaven* and *A Farewell to Arms.* In the first, a pair of lovers are separated when the man goes off to war. He is reported missing and presumed dead. But she—Janet Gaynor—insists on his enduring emotional presence, and her faith is rewarded. He does come back, blinded. But such love needs no visible reassurance. Implicitly, this is akin to cinema's imaginary conjuring of love persisting in our mind after the screen has gone blank.

The Hemingway material is unexpected. But as one reflects, it is easier to see that the proclaimed toughness in Hemingway trembles with sentiment. That novel is a hymn to private feelings being more worthwhile than affairs of state, and what is the fateful rain at the end of the book but the tears of prevented love? Borzage largely dispenses with military combat and concentrates on the lovers' doomed idyll. For instance, when Gary Cooper is wounded, the camera tracks into the hospital as if from his stretcher, all the way past faces until Helen Hayes appears, ecstatically dipping down to kiss the camera. Their love scenes consist of close-ups and two-shots that must be seen to feel the achieved warmth between the couple.

Above all, Borzage has confidence in love transcending separation and death. When Hayes dies, Cooper lifts her body from the bed. Her dress makes an elegiac curve as he turns away to present her to the window and to birds seen flying in the last shot while he murmurs "Peace." These could be the elements of hokum, but Borzage's eye and the purity of feeling give the ending a spiritual force utterly different from the repressed sentimentality of Hemingway's conclusion. In passing, it is worth mentioning that the music used at this point is the love duet from *Tristan and Isolde,* the music Buñuel added to the sound track of *Un Chien Andalou,* along with a domineering tango. And though the means, tone, and purpose of those two directors are far apart, their works believe in the same chance of human ecstasy.

Borzage was no less resourceful in handling the opposition of love and the Depression. *Little Man, What Now?* is set in Germany, with Margaret Sullavan and Douglass Montgomery as a couple resisting the demoralization of poverty and unemployment. She is a stronger figure than he is, and visually she motivates the action. Their scenes together involve her in radiant, reflective close-up with him looking into the frame like someone sniffing a rose. Such shots signal love, admiration and mutual nourishment, but they are also sexually suggestive. Without alarming chaste censors, Borzage films lovers in ways that treasure the prospect of sexual communion, just as closing the eyes in prayer summons a god. Very few film-makers share Borzage's belief in vital experiences that cannot be seen or shown. Not everything in the world is visible, and remorseless naked couplings on screen only remind us that copulation is ungainly, incredible, and no guarantee of love. Borzage knows that sexuality is a state of being, and his images steadily look forward to it.

A Man's Castle is set in New York, a city made insecure by the Depression. The central characters, who become lovers, are Loretta Young and Spencer Tracy, both impoverished to the point of vagrancy. Borzage treats their love not just as human idealism surviving social breakdown, but as evidence of the necessary surrender of independence. Tracy has been made brusque and nomadic by the Depression; he does not want to settle down. Whereas Loretta Young yearns for stability. This struggle between home and ostensible freedom runs through the film and eliminates the danger of sweetness in the treatment of the couple. It is resolved ambiguously, with the two riding the railroad to some new town, in one another's arms in the straw in a boxcar. The image is very beautiful, taken from a high angle, and it has a variety of suggestions—that a man's castle is freedom; or that freedom is his toy, while his strength comes from woman.

A Man's Castle is a short film, with a clear situation, yet its characters and sense are subtle. Best of all, it is a women's picture with a self-sufficient man. There is a hardness in Tracy that tells of concealed pains, an assumed toughness to avoid tenderness that actually makes feeling more vibrant. There are other things to see: the way in which the plot moves in sections, taking us deeper into its study of love; the bleak view of the Depression, and of people pushed to the end of their tether; the matter-of-fact assessment of crime and prostitution as consequences of slump; the uncoy admission of sexuality between the couple; the wild humor in the exposure of hypocrisy; the call of train sirens on the sound track; the symbolism of the window in their Hooverville home, opening on far more than one square of sky; the way in which love goes unadmitted, a thing beyond words yet always alive in the affectionate tone of the images.

Mildred Pierce is set in a California town, a locale fully defined in TV commercials of the next two decades, but scarcely seen in cinema before 1945. Mildred lives in a street where all the houses look alike, and the residents are proud of that: large bungalows with cars in the garage and orderly gardens—it is suburbia, and it is new in the movies. The 1930s had known only the big city and the countryside. The film is narrated by Mildred, and as we see this new world we hear her account of herself: "I was always in the kitchen. I felt as though I'd been born in a kitchen and lived there all of my life, except for the few hours it took to get married. I married Bert when I was seventeen, and never knew any other kind of life. Just cooking, washing, having children." This is not a bitter complaint, such as feminists would write for a Mildred twenty years later. But it is a story to win women's understanding, and the basis in everyday experience is new. For the first time, despite Crawford's brooding glamour, the woman on the screen is the woman in the movie house.

Mildred has two daughters, one an adolescent, Vida, played by Ann Blyth. Her husband is evidently weaker than she is: In *Mildred Pierce* the men are spineless, coarse, or treacherous, while Mildred is a model of energetic decency. The husband is cheated by his partner, out of a job and into a consoling affair. He and Mildred quarrel and the husband leaves her to cope on her own. She wants a good life for her children and now has to earn and establish it. That draws the film back to melodrama, albeit a smoother version of it than Griffith achieved. *Mildred Pierce* is significant because of the straight-faced but patronizing view of this woman's definition of a good life. In hindsight, it becomes a piece of social criticism—more subtle than Warners or director Michael Curtiz recognized, I suspect. But the blandness of Mildred's ambitions now looks sterile, and her misfortune seems the result of limited attitudes.

She takes a job as a waitress in a downtown restaurant and is quickly promoted by the manager, Eve Arden. She likes working and every evening bakes pies at home to sell over the counter. Vida finds out and is humiliated that her mother should be working for her living, and working in so demeaning a place. But Mildred prospers and opens her own restaurant. The property she leases is owned by Zachary Scott, a playboy with just the moustache melodrama expects. There is then a scene reminiscent of *Way Down East*. Mildred is getting the place ready to open as a restaurant. She is sitting on a stepladder fixing a light and the frame is so composed that we see only her legs in the top part of the frame and the door behind her. Scott comes in, looks at what we can see, and says he has come to "check on his investment." The sexual innuendo is the same, but now sex hinges on ownership and the commercial instinct. All through *Mildred Pierce,* love is masked by issues of class and money. Mildred and Monty (the Zachary Scott character) become lovers: They are seen in the rain together and sitting in front of a fire to dry. In 1945, no one would have misread that code, and anyone could have speculated on the bodily encounter for himself.

But Mildred dominates. Her business expands and Monty squanders the proceeds. "Everything I touched turned to money," Mildred tells us. "I needed it for Vida. She was growing up." Monty is taking Vida out, as well as being Mildred's lover. He buys Vida a car with Mildred's money and Mildred then warns him to keep away from her daughter. This dialogue follows:

MILDRED: Vida's drifting away from me. She hardly speaks

to me anymore except to ask for money. You look down on me because I work for a living, don't you?

MONTY: Yes, I take money from you. But not enough to make me like kitchens or cooking. They both smell of grease.

Mildred breaks with Monty, and Vida runs away from home. She is discovered singing in a nightclub—code for having turned to prostitution. The monetary impulse in happiness and contentment is underlined when Mildred asks Monty to marry her to make Vida come home. This triangle is grotesque but true to any life measured by its barriers. Mildred has become the man figure. Love has been made a means of currency. The good life is corrupted by compromise. In the end, the fickle Monty tells Vida to get lost and she shoots him dead: All through, she has been mercilessly spiteful and grasping, coldly exploiting Mildred's sacrifices. The family and mother love are both undermined. Suburbia inextricably confuses happiness and the dollar.

In retrospect, one knows Mildred and her world—Mary Hartman lives there now. She is fighting to keep her looks; she likes a tasteful, tidy home; and—here is the sidelong question that pins her down—"How good are Mildred Pierce's pies?" See the film today and one knows that she makes the sort of pies that sooner or later would have been bought out by a chain bakery, the name retained and the pies gradually made more synthetic, more sweet, more uniform—Mildred's Original Home-Baked Pies, made in Jersey City factories, three million a day, wrapped in plastic, the fitting dessert for a better burger. Mildred comes on with the smart, brisk optimism of women in TV commercials, and her home has that insipid airiness we associate with quick-and-easy furniture polish, tasty trouble-free foods, this bank and that insurance scheme.

For 1945, *Mildred Pierce* predicts a world to come. It is still a melodrama: Mildred is only telling the story, in flashback, to a policeman who suspects her of killing Monty. The film works in the classic way of the women's picture, asking us to admire and be moved by Mildred's attempt to be independent, only to suffer a vicious daughter, unworthy men, and the cold comfort of money. But beneath this form there lurks the suspicion that her ideal is misguided. The film is sharply divided into day and night sequences. By day, we see her in a sunny home, on the beach, or in the restaurant. These scenes try to convey hopes of affluence and contentment: They look like commercials. But more memorable are the night sequences: the killing and Mildred at the police station. This is Warners night, day for night, a lustrous, velvety darkness. There is a sequence in which Mildred paces the waterfront before going to the police to confess to the killing her daughter did. She wears a fur coat and a fashionable hat; moisture is hanging in the studio moonlight. She looks like a duchess sleepwalking, or like a high-class hooker. The fur at her throat glistens with damp, and the hat drops a slanting shadow across her face. The pensiveness in Joan Crawford's eyes and the mordant feel of the image are the core of *Mildred Pierce* and they are signs of a dread reckoning that suburbia has been misled. And woman—the object of feeling and the source of loving kindness—is the fall guy.

Within a decade of *Mildred Pierce,* her home would have contained several television sets—consolation, perhaps, with both daughters dead and only enervated men for company. Television soon took over the material of the women's picture and now shows it when women are reckoned to be in the home, on their own, bored and free. TV then cements the melodramas with miniature, inspirational movies that urge us to consume and take comfort against any sadness. What will become of this surburban afternoon? The extramural enterprise of *Belle de Jour,* or the slack hold of game shows and soap opera?

The cinema has hardly touched the genre for a dozen years. But in the 1950s there was a last flourish in the convention with the films made by Douglas Sirk at Universal: *Magnificent Obsession, All That Heaven Allows, Written on the Wind,* and *Imitation of Life.* Sirk was evidently more intelligent than his material: He had been a prominent director in the German theater in the twenties and thirties, and his films and his comments on them show a cultivated and serious man. He was also among the most fluent of stylists: The gliding facility of his camera, the liquid coherence of design, color, and music all add to the problematic efficacy of melodrama. Compared with Borzage, I do not think Sirk has the same compassion for lovers. I am not sure that his films even believe in love. But he could redeem trash with elegance of description, and he recognized the blend of hysterical behavior, contrived predicaments, precision in style, and melting music that exists in all cinema, but especially in the melody of heightened dramas.

Sirk's films have been interpreted as social criticism of an America losing heart and soul in a time of neurotic materialism. But that history is glib, and even if the comfortable analysis of disapproval can be made I doubt that it exists in the films. Admittedly, *All That Heaven Allows* contrasts rigid middle-class frigidity with natural, Thoreau-like vitality. So, too, *Written on the Wind* shows a retreat into alcohol, violence, and depression on the part of the dispiritedly successful. But the criticism is decorative, and never amounts to an attitude. Sirk's critique is the wintriness of high style distancing people. His own glossy presentation is frighteningly like the middle-class salon settings of the films: a picture-book full of cavities. The films are possessed by a pessimism denied Borzage's faith in people and their imaginations; they are hypnotized by the onset of decadence in the

1950s. And it is something like decadence—or mannerism—for these tales to be told with such erroneous grace. Sirk is fascinating because his films illustrate the rift between style and substance endemic in America. He is a serving victim of Hollywood's warping attitude to love, but unable to believe in the degraded ideal.

Hollywood searched out romance in films, making it a test of human or social virtue. But it suppressed sex as if it were subversive, and it only tolerated lovers as beings apart. The standard final kiss was all we saw of companionship, argument, and caring. In the long term nothing may be more influential than its inducement to love, and its separation of love from life and judgment. It set love within a framework of melodrama so that it was made to be neurotic, emotional, and instinctive (which it may be), and not rational, intellectual, and personal (which it is also). Love became a spasm reaction rather than the response of an intelligent, moral sensibility. The women's picture stressed happiness as a securable asset, yet left audiences aware of their tenuous hold on it. Men and women in such films had little other preoccupation than romance and the carefully codified allusions to sex. The role of women was glorified but localized by the movies, while men could only be husband, betrayer, or constrained sexual companion. Endless wooing was the state of love, and closed-mouth kisses constituted rapture. Sexual splendor was a never-reached nirvana beyond the happy ending, while marriage was a restful, comic condition of the middle-aged. Thus in Hollywood pictures, lovers seldom talk together, overcome problems, or change one another—they are long-lost twins, wonderfully reunited and blissful no longer to be without one another.

I wonder whether the effect of movie love is not more debilitating than the possible encouragement to violence. To entangle anyone in the illusion of violence might lead to perplexity rather than damaging action. But to make a similar mesh from love may have left us in love with screen-play love, rather than attached to other people. If we are more helplessly angry than we were, it could be because of that second trap. Murder, after all, is most common in the home and between people once in love. Lost love may be so great a risk that we hesitate before embarking on it. The natural and fruitful adoration that men and women in-herited from Romanticism as an expectation is so much more lasting in cinema if lovers never meet. And the movies do touch us without making real connections.

VIII

BLANDNESS AND DIFFICULTY

Life's not like anything I've seen before.
—Remark in *The Missouri Breaks*

IN HIS EARLY THIRTIES, THE CHILD REACHED AMERICA. HE HAD looked forward to it as fervently as some immigrants. But he came over the Canadian border painlessly, driving from Montreal the same day he landed there and into a Vermont that might have been founded on an attempt to render English rural beauty more purely and just a little more emphatically—as a location for a movie about England.

I lived and worked in New Hampshire for a year, offering film studies to American students. It was pleasant for me; I was never disarmed or perplexed by strangeness—difficulties

I have met in France or Spain, countries much nearer England. My expectations of America were confirmed. I felt at ease in the country, partly because easiness is one of its treasured idioms, but also because the cinema proved a very useful training for America—I could see in the dark.

Americans do not admire or readily tolerate a kind of reserve or difficulty of personality that is honored in Europe. Despite the legend of violence and disruption bristling from America, it is an orderly country. It makes great efforts to be understandable and believes in clarity. Perhaps its history necessitated a public iconography accessible to people of all tongues; it may also show the longing to subdue the imaginative threat of so much space—but it is not easy to be lost in America. Whatever the intensity of New York, it is a numbered grid in which you can get anywhere from anywhere simply by counting. Equally, if the comment does not betray brief experience in this glib European, it sometimes seems that Americans do not explore their own nature but proffer a visible, communicable personality—one that is easygoing and tidy, and surely charms the Englishman depressed by his nation's and his own introspection. "Have a good day," Americans will say, but Englishmen flinch at the kindness and worry that deeper feelings are neglected by surface pleasantry.

Of course, as soon as I began to notice this cheerful tic, I was reminded of a film: *Invasion of the Body Snatchers,* a science fiction allegory made by Don Siegel in 1956, about sinister pods that germinate while people are sleeping and take over their bodies. These new creatures reproduce the snatched humans exactly—they are indistinguishably lifelike and are played by the same pre-pod actors—but they have no feelings. Siegel's film was originally exciting and entertaining. Some years later, its makers and enthusiasts saw it as a commentary on McCarthyist America. I now wonder how far it alludes to insubstantial amiability; and while I have been writing, it occurs to me that it is also a plan of cinema: humanoids without souls gradually promoting soullessness.

No one remembering as many American films as I did should have been allowed into America. It only encourages a superficial conclusion that one understands the country and impudent "warnings" that it might try to be a little more complicated. How swiftly my own hypothesis dissolves as I reduce friendly Americans to dismay and hurt. I should have listened to those who made moving pictures, and who were adamant that they were not to be taken seriously—even if making profitable pictures was a serious business. Such moguls vehemently proclaimed lightness, warmth, an appeal to the heart, and a good show, and fought off any greater gravity in the product. In *Picture,* Lillian Ross's account of the making of *The Red Badge of Courage,* there is a scene between Louis B. Mayer and one of his producers, Arthur Freed, in which Mayer summed up the necessary bluntness of the movies:

> "Entertainment!" he cried, transfixed by what he seemed to see on that screen, and he made the face of a man who was emotionally stirred by what he was watching. "It's good enough for you and I and the box office," he said, turning back to Freed. "Not for the smart alecks. It's not good enough anymore," he went on, whining coyly, in imitation of someone saying that winning the heart of the audience was not good enough. He pounded a commanding fist on his desk and looked at me. "Let me tell you something!" he said. "Prizes! Awards! Ribbons! We had two pictures here. An Andy Hardy picture with little Mickey Rooney, and *Ninotchka,* with Greta Garbo. *Ninotchka* got the prizes. *Blue* ribbons! *Purple* ribbons! Nine bells and seven stars! Which picture made

the money? Andy Hardy made the money. Why? Because it won praise from the heart. No ribbons!"

And only a little later, Freed uttered this limpid defense of the Hollywood system—"Thoreau said most of us lead lives of quiet desperation. Pictures should make you feel better, not worse"—an attitude embedded in American popular entertainment and which it is difficult to question without sounding perverse and un-American. A version of it faced me in teaching a course on Hollywood when I asked the class how far they thought Hollywood had affected their attitudes. Little or not at all, some said, for the simple reason that they knew the movies were not to be taken seriously. This was not a dismissal of all films, but the ingrained conviction that Hollywood movies were as crass as the Mayers had made them.

There has been a widespread belief in America that you can't trust American movies. They are superficial entertainment, a warm bath, a diversion from Thoreau's grim melancholy, the sort of rosy alternative to hard times that *Sullivan's Travels* opts for. Some of my students told me that it was customary to relax in the movies, but fruitless to look for significance there. You go to the movies to have a good time and forget your troubles. But if that is so, then the influence on Americans is all the greater for going unnoticed. The student today in America is likely to have spent twenty thousand hours by the age of twenty-one relaxing in the flow of moving images. In which case, film may have instilled one profound attitude: to take it easy, to take nothing seriously. What else explains the everyday prominence of so trivial a medium?

Now, that is a smart-aleck conclusion—but film has passed into the arena of academic wisdom. I was teaching kids whose parents were probably startled by film in a college curriculum. Both Mayer and Freed are dead; the MGM lion is now in the zoo of posterity, withdrawn from the competitive jungle. Not for years has an American film breathed or shone with its studio of origin. The studio insignia on films now only refer to premises used, a source of finance, or the distributive process. The majority of films are set up by individuals, and they undoubtedly have a creative freedom not known in the great days of unrivaled cinema. But films are still intruded upon—by financiers and distributors, and by their directors' wish to be successful. Film keeps faith with narrative methods that once worked at the box office—*The Godfather* and *Jaws,* two of the most profitable films ever made, insist on popular spectacle and encourage film-makers that the people are eager to be spellbound.

Nevertheless, since 1945 the advance of education has made it easier for an American to take film seriously. It has been suggested that until Orson Welles spent that year at RKO watching whatever he could of the archive of cinema, no one saw anything except new films of the moment. Movie houses were plied with the current product, and old films were kept in storage or dumped to make room for the new. Only a few societies showed old films and then, invariably, foreign films that the American intelligentsia were inclined to respect on the shaky premises that they were "truer" to life and made under less commercial pressure—a Mayer would have said they were boring, sordid, and out of focus. Welles, therefore, was the first film student in America; and it is fitting that his debut is still the most regularly examined of American films in college.

By now, the American film student is legion. In 1975, the American Film Institute published a *Guide to College Courses in Film and Television,* 286 pages long and listing nearly 800 institutions where such courses were taught. Over 30,000 students were working for degrees in film or television, while well over 100,000 were taking a film course as part of studies majoring in some other subject. With more or less success, film education teaches the history of the cinema, the chance of art and artistic satisfaction, and breaks down the technological mystique that had kept film-making at a distance for anyone outside the film industry. There is a bias toward practical work, so that the role of production factories once filled by Warners, MGM, Paramount, Universal, and Fox may have been taken over by New York University, the University of California, and the campuses of Ohio, Illinois, and Wisconsin. At NYU, for instance, there are 350 undergraduates and 120 graduates studying film, with courses in all technical matters and in history, aesthetics, theory, and production, as well as seminars on every director from Renoir to Michael Snow.

No one is too comfortable about where these students will find jobs, let alone a release for awakened creative urges; and few places of higher education can ignore the cost of tuition and residence being measured against the prospect of a paying job. Nor is there much evidence that America is becoming more "visually literate," or that the history of moving images is being taken to heart. But America is proud of its new respect for movies, and the students must form the heart of a more alert and demanding audience, just as a few star or heretical pupils are actually making films for the millions. Still, there is a disparity between the movies and the university. I recollect the shock I caused in forsaking Oxford, and I can imagine Louis Mayer's scorn at show business being led astray by art. And the ogre would be right. It will be a sad day if academics ever drain away the sensational from cinema.

Film education is already an empire, just as much as Hollywood was. It has evolved its own cliques and doctrines in imitation of the city-state studios. There are three main approaches to film in education and all arouse the mirth of anyone working in the film industry. A teacher of or writer about film must try to absorb all three approaches—it is certain disaster to espouse only one of them—and I know that they have affected this book, even if I have reservations about all of them. The most arcane theory simplifies as soon as it excludes the value of other approaches. The cinema cannot appeal to so many different sorts of people without being beyond the restraining tidiness of any one theory.

The first is the *auteur* theory. It derives from France and the reevaluation of American cinema by a group of young French critics, many of whom went on to become directors themselves—François Truffaut, Jean-Luc Godard, Claude Chabrol, Eric Rohmer, Jacques Rivette. During the 1950s, they spelled out what no one now denies: that out of the diligently mercenary scheme of Hollywood there emerged impressive and imaginative works "belonging to" their authors, the directors. This helped establish a pantheon of authors who were celebrated in ways kept for the traditionally accepted and safely dead artists of the world. We therefore see character, consistency, and quality in Hitchcock, Hawks, Ford, Von Sternberg, Nicholas Ray, Minnelli, Anthony Mann, and many others. The identification of authors rescued films that earlier critical attitudes had patronized or ignored; it stressed the dependence of film on visual realization—as opposed to literary or thematic intention; and it helped those young Frenchmen to validate a job and opportunity they were themselves longing to take. For them, and soon after for a young generation in America, the *auteur* theory was an encouragement even in the shabbiest compromises with distributors. Nothing prompts creative earnestness and application more than the thought that one might be an artist. Today, directors know they have a following and wonder about posterity.

But the elevation of the film director presented problems. It was hero-worship that could embarrass heroes with interpretations they had never imagined and with "jewels" in a work that were due to others, or which the heroes might still regard as blemishes. It is not possible to produce a commercial film single-handed, and few can make their vision prevail upon all the essential collaborators. The crucial lead of an individual is not ruled out by the participation of honest but unbrilliant, or even cunning and pretentious craftsmen. But it does require cohesion in the creative process, and assertion or command from the director. There are still too few thorough accounts of the making of particular films that measure this balance of authorship. The task would require constant surveillance and such knowledge of all the crafts involved that the author might himself direct. Even then, the book would be long and laborious. But such a salutary work is needed, to offset the optimistic glorification of directors and to give substance to the growing willingness to allow enough credit to writers, actors, or technicians in what is a mixed medium or a compromised art.

If film is at best cooperative, and at worst a struggle, can it ever equal the profundity or purity of other forms of art in which one man is both initiator and craftsman, possibly pursuing his obsession to the point of poverty? (And the film director is an affluent fellow.) Some criticism in the *auteur* vein has compared Hollywood directors with novelists, poets, composers, and painters. While it may be helpful to suggest an affinity in tone or theme between one art and another, it seems to me idle and fanciful to make such claims. I know because I have made them. But the child from the garden of Hollywood has become a writer, more and more troubled by our culture's readiness to forsake literature for moving imagery. I wish that I could believe the cinema has the vitality, the responsiveness to wide experience, the susceptibility to doubt and compassion, the searching intelligence, the easy association of the personal and the universal, or the same commitment to human nature and its fictional imprint of, say, Dickens, Tolstoi, Dostoevski, Melville, Cowper Powys, Faulkner, or Nabokov.

Authorship is a cultural ideal of the Renaissance and the humanist tradition. We do not know "who" made the Gothic cathedrals, Angkor Wat, *Beowulf,* Romanesque paintings, African masks, or the stone circles. But their effects upon our imaginations are so great that we "know" these things without actually encountering them. We regard them as coming out of a darkness in which uniformity and anonymity characterized culture. Such art has a collective origin and reveals a "huddling" in which imaginative experience was overawed but shared. For the last four hundred years, our faith in individualism and private property has wanted to attribute art to authors and insight to ourselves. Suppose that history is moving into another period of indistinct massiveness, then Hollywood movies might be a pioneering of that darkness. Hollywood cinema and television often seem the outpouring of a system, an age, and a way of marketing fictions that outweighs individual authors. The commercial structure and the style and meaning inherent in the medium may be more influential than the "signature" of individuals. Even the most ambitious of directors makes a film that manifests the system —I have tried to indicate that in the "wayward" *Citizen Kane.*

Herein lies the second doctrine of film studies: that popular cinema mirrors the collective unconscious. Thus industrial fictions are scrutinized as confessions of hopes, fears, ideals, and doubts pervading society. Not only film critics, but also sociologists, anthropologists, psychologists, and historians study genres to find fresh and rewarding access to popular ideology. Something of that method is incorporated in the chapters on the urban crime film and the women's picture, though both are written in the spirit of speculative interpretation rather than rigorous science. That is still the surest approach when it is so difficult to find a practical and exact way of studying what happens to people in cinemas.

Studios sometimes give sneak previews for their new films and ask the audience to fill in simple questionnaires afterward. Those reactions may result in a film being promoted with energy, trimmed, cut apart and remade, or even shelved. They may still be the most thorough survey of audience feelings ever made. Yet some audiences dash through the questions, reply frivolously, or deliberately lie. There is no way of knowing whether a spectator has spoken candidly or intelligently about his responses to a movie—especially if he has been taught to believe movies are for "fun." Nor is there any chance of wiring him for changes in pulse, temperature, or brain waves. Movies may not merely be for fun, but they cannot bear such ponderous examination. The darkness in the movie theater permits privacy, and both scientists and censors remain uncertain about what is happening in the mind of the viewer.

The interpretation of genres also begs one important question. Does popular cinema reflect or generate a mood? Hollywood self-righteously proclaimed its wish to give the people what they wanted. But any study of its history shows a more complicated reality. The system was anxious to know what the public wanted, and it would repeat any proved successes. But, like all of us, it was more fearful of not being wanted than confident of divining a general but unexpressed taste. It made what it could, and what it reckoned would ensure steady business. I have tried to indicate how that took forms embodying experiences and states of mind beyond the mass of the public. It may have identified values held in common in America, but the cinema also introduced a pattern of fantasy and frustration that confirms the situation of the huddled mass and the alienated victim. There are few states as disenchanting as that of the buttered-up and disappointed customer. In the cinema that plight is more acute than it is in the supermarket. There, the pocket, appetite and constitution are being affected. But in the cinema the soul, conscience, and imagination are played upon. Again, it is possible that all genres are natural extensions of the medium's detachment from inhabitable reality.

The third approach to cinema concentrates on the properties of the medium and on the various "sign" systems contained in moving imagery. "Semiotics," as it is called, examines the meanings we derive from film—rather than from films. It tries to amass a dictionary of film forms and signs. Unfortunately, it has quickly grown a dense jargon, and much writing of this kind is impenetrable. It also tends to forget the overall quality or effect of a film in specifying and isolating the contributory signs. Semiotics can make films sound much more elusive than they are by overlooking the initial coherence we feel before sitting down to an array of signs—that we are going to see a movie.

Still, there is one valuable task shared by semiotics and old-fashioned, impressionistic commentary on films: the close description of the work itself, or textual analysis. Film reviewing in the popular press is still often an excuse for smart chatter. Even in its more responsible moments, it treats films as if they were books or plays, with the inane addition of "beautifully photographed." It is impossible to divine the effects of film without basing one's account on the text of a film itself, and without rudimentary knowledge of film as a language.

But is film a language, or only an alternative form, verbal descriptions of which are irrelevant? Do films have "texts," or does that terminology only reveal our limits? Anyone teaching or writing about film knows the fundamental compromise in the decision to speak about films. Film does pertain to a sensation, to the impact on several senses simultaneously, and to a confusion of reality and unreality that surpasses verbal delicacy. It is a commonplace among film teachers to talk of "visual literacy," implying a need to train people in the elements of language in moving imagery so that they may have more sense of what is happening to them. But "visual literacy" is a verbal construct and a literary idea. Perhaps moving images are not literate or understandable. In trying to describe a brief passage from *Un Chien Andalou*, I hoped to illustrate how film scatters order and works through threatened disruption.

After all, we would hardly talk about "literate visibility," thinking to extract a visual equivalent for written works. We have labored long enough with "film and the novel" to know that there is no reliable connection between the two. You cannot film novels, good or bad, except by filming the pages. You can only take novels as pretexts for films. Similarly, can one really write down the effectiveness of a film, or is the only chance the sort of evocation of a film that we already mistrust as a cinematic treatment of literature?

Perhaps "visual literacy" is a nonsensical conception. Perhaps moving imagery has no grammar, no syntax, no law—perhaps it is without even the lack of those things. Then it might have no meaning, in the sense of something we can narrow down and depend upon. Perhaps film is a sensation that instructs us to submit ourselves to experience, impact, and the sensational without any hope of "understanding" it. Nothing would confirm the huddle or the massiveness of society so much as the thought that experience was beyond comprehension but could only be endured, just as the camera helplessly conveys what happens in front of it. That ends the humanist tradition, and explains the frenzy with which Kane hunts for significance. But if we refute the chance of visual literacy we not only make film criticism futile; we also begin to relinquish the hope of shared meanings in life. Yet the confrontation of shining light and darkened masses does contain many suggestions of monolithic participation in sensation without reliable conclusion.

I have to stop and start again, having come so close to demolishing my own basis. My years in the garden of Hollywood have left me with a passion for films, only lately tempered by a compassion for the society that has been made by them. The cinema still beckons me and gives me pleasure. But perhaps cinema has made us more lonely, more anxious, more insecure, and more imaginatively alienated than we might have been. That is why it seems irresponsible to "dismiss" film as an art and not face the confusions of a form that has excited political dictators and tycoons of commerce as well as sometimes simulating the heady effects of art.

It is a forlorn resort to write about film. But an upbringing in the darkness instilled imagination and persuaded me to invent and write. I found that I loved words, sentences, and the tempting hope of explaining things. In time, it occurred to me that film and literature were examples of the delight man can find in fiction. But it would be easier to be delighted if we lived in Elysian times. No other age has had to be aware of so much suffering "elsewhere," beside which fiction can seem a craven or narcotic distraction. If there is no way of "belonging" in the various forms of fiction, then its practitioners are idlers and frauds, all the unhappier if they cannot believe in any of the political creeds that offer conviction. The only purpose I can accept is that of language and imagery connecting individuals and owning up to the remaining hope of a shared fund of feeling thought out of which the human race might proceed without cruelty, restriction, or indifference to one another.

But it is not easy to believe in that. Whatever the chance

or desirability of our becoming visually literate, there must be fears of receding verbal literacy. In America, an alarming proportion of college students do not possess their own language. They rarely read for imaginative nourishment. They write chaotically. Their spoken language willfully abandons the subtlety and precision of words. Instead, it regresses toward signals of moods and feelings—words, sounds, and gestures—sometimes called "body language" and actually typical of a culture moving *toward* verbal articulacy. Furthermore, the institutional sources of language—politics, the media, business, law, science—are spreading deeper mistrust of devastating cliché, slipshod vagueness, and tortuous difficulty. We do not share a fluent, natural, and supple English. One can easily succumb to pessimism that language is more obscure. Do we really talk to one another, in the wider cultural sense? Surely, the feeling that we do not helps account for music and film dominating the creative energies of young people who once might have thought of writing.

Despite threats to independence, seriousness, and useful treatment of human difficulty, cinema and television offer the most potent of lures—an audience so large that it is, effectively, the people. Detach the first part of that brutal assertion from *Citizen Kane* and "The people will think" remains a hope to be fulfilled in the media reaching and stimulating the masses. Consider the pressures on a talented young filmmaker: To make a hit will furnish the accessories of success that his precarious society respects; it also provides the chance of addressing the people with a dramatic truth. Perhaps the two cannot be managed together; that may be the cinema's burden. But the challenge is absorbing, and it has been taken up in a way hardly matched anywhere else in the world by a generation of film-makers in America. American movies draw large audiences still. They are more serious, more testing, and more dangerous than they have ever been.

They are beautiful—allowing that that judgment has any utility—and more concerned with the felt nature of America than previous film. They are even reversing the decline in audiences that has gone on for twenty-five years in competition with television.

There is no need to paint a golden age of geniuses or propose that America has its "new wave." We can surely go further than the rigid precept that *auteurs* are heroes who make only great films. Instead, let us recognize talented, stubborn, and prickly individuals trying to deal with the dilemma outlined in the previous paragraph: to be a movie director and to be good in the light of eternity, or a few years. There are no unflawed films coming out of America, but it may be a step toward maturity not to need flawlessness so much as lively and controversial untidiness. Still, all of the following directors are more or less functioning in America (more or less because no director is sure where his next film is coming from), and most of them deal with recognizably American material.

Arthur Penn made a series of distressed studies of violence in American history, as a reality shaping society and a suggestive legend affecting the mind. While all but *Mickey One* can be fitted into the box office's scheme of genres, his films are as personal and as much a visual realization of an attitude as, say, Mailer's writing. Indeed, there is the same emphatic and poetic reason in that author and in *The Left-Handed Gun, The Miracle Worker, Mickey One, The Chase, Bonnie and Clyde, Alice's Restaurant, Little Big Man, Night Moves,* and *The Missouri Breaks.*

Sam Peckinpah's capacity for violence, and his sympathy for violent men, has often made him brutal, but *Major Dundee* is the ruins of an intriguing allegory about Vietnam, and *The Ballad of Cable Hogue, Pat Garrett and Billy the Kid,* and *Bring Me the Head of Alfredo Garcia* are westerns with a somber philosophical dimension, studies of the man of action betrayed by activity and confused purpose and ending in humor, tragedy, or nihilism.

Robert Altman is possibly the most pretentious of current American directors, either a formal innovator or a helplessly inept narrator, depending upon point of view and particular film. Whether by design or failure, he has made us more conscious of the frailty of coherence than any other director, especially in *McCabe and Mrs. Miller, The Long Goodbye, California Split,* and *Nashville.*

Those are three men of about the same middle age, all of whom began their careers in movies in the middle fifties. There is a later generation, all still close to forty and drawing upon the new film graduates in America. Several of them either hold degrees in film studies or have taught the subject or written about it. Peter Bogdanovich was one of the first American critics to reflect the influence of the French new wave, and he has gone on to be a versatile director—*Targets, The Last Picture Show, What's Up, Doc?, Paper Moon, Daisy Miller, Nickelodeon.* Monte Hellman and Francis Ford Coppola studied film in California, and while Hellman has become nearly an underground film-maker—so hermetic are *The Shooting, Two-Lane Blacktop,* and *Cockfighter*—Coppola has taken on the tests of lavish success with both parts of *The Godfather* and put the profits and prestige from them toward less comfortable films—for example, *The Conversation.* Martin Scorsese studied and taught at New York University before directing *Mean Streets, Alice Doesn't Live Here Anymore,* and *Taxi Driver.*

There are others of the same generation and quality, if not with the same academic background. Steven Spielberg's colossal box-office success with *Jaws* confirms the great narrative flair in *Duel* and *Sugarland Express.* Indeed, *Jaws* reminds us that accelerating and cathartic narrative is itself an American myth and seldom likely to be forsaken by American movies. Terrence Malick's one film, *Badlands,* is

a combination of news-story offhandedness and surreal fantasy, a ballad of a casual killer who wants to be known, to
have his brief glory out of the huddled crowd.

Perhaps the best of them all is Bob Rafelson, who has
shown an awareness of uncontrived eccentricity in character,
setting, and action in *Five Easy Pieces, The King of Marvin
Gardens,* and *Stay Hungry.* Rafelson is the director most
likely to surprise without being shocking, coy, or pretentious.
In *Marvin Gardens,* within the context of a silly but credible
family tragedy, he discerns a paradox in American character
appropriate to the condition of the movies. The film is about
two brothers, Jack Nicholson and Bruce Dern. Nicholson is
subdued, depressive, and introverted; he has a late-night radio
show during which he sits in the dark spinning monologues.
Dern is extravert, flashy, and lunging at the future with giddy
plans for big deals. Both men are fantasists, in opposite
modes. At one point Nicholson is disturbed in the john by
one of his brother's girls. She retires from him and his tape
recorder with the murmured understanding that, of course,
he is an artist. But the flamboyant Dern, an operator and a
cheerful crazy, may be the more characteristic American
artist and a passable portrait of the drive, charm, and nerve
that are required for making it in the movies.

America still provides a sanctuary for aliens and refugees.
John Boorman has made his best films there, and since the
late 1960s the Czech director, Milos Forman, has slowly acquired a sense of America so that *One Flew Over the
Cuckoo's Nest* was unmistakably American in its ribaldry,
its outrageous hero, and its scorn for stupid institutions. But
it was made graver by Forman's recollection of a more practical tyranny in eastern Europe.

I saw *Cuckoo's Nest* the week it opened and on a first visit
to New York City so that the film and the city inevitably reflected on one another. It was playing at the Paramount, a
cinema beneath the ground at the foot of the Gulf & West-

ern building, to a swell of laughter, applause, and roars of encouragement and woe that one might hear at a football game or a political meeting. The week I saw it, New Yorkers were getting ready for Thanksgiving and President Ford's cautious admission that he would refinance them. As in any other week, they were living on the brink of violence and breakdown. New Yorkers are like people who live near the Sphinx; they all have their own stories of the riddle and carry them like pass-cards. A publisher told me there was only one sound rule: to know the kind crazies from the unkind.

Ken Kesey's novel in the hands of Milos Forman did not seem promising. Forman's Czech films are sensitive and observant chamber studies. *Taking Off,* his other American film, is hazy with charm, and it suffers from laziness, prettification, and a superficial identity with youth. Kesey's novel is fantastical, declaratory, awkward, redolent of the sixties, and only a pretext for a film—albeit a pretext that had apparently grown slowly in the minds of Kirk Douglas and his son, Michael, one of the eventual producers of *Cuckoo's Nest.*

The film takes place inside an institution for the mentally disturbed—blurred, inefficient, and ill-funded—not unlike a New Yorker's idea of New York. The routine is listless and deadly: recreation hours of unadventurous pursuits; all things subordinate to the smooth functioning of the institution; grotesque therapy sessions conducted by the blandly oppressive Nurse Ratched; kindly but distant doctors who view the patients as if they were fish in a tank; sadistic male nurses, rogue cops with straitjackets. And most of the inmates are there voluntarily, able to leave if they can only muster the will, courage, and independence to ask to be let out.

Such a system might go on forever, numbing everness even. No doubt there are institutions all over the world where people of problematic stability and instability are kept in safe, dead neutrality, where alleged illness of the mind excuses lack of vitality in the spirit. But this institution draws into itself the sanely disruptive figure of R. P. Mc-Murphy, played by Jack Nicholson—the presence of the moment allows the hope that we are something more than the daily evidence suggests.

In New York, the audience chattered with delight as soon as Nicholson appeared on the threshold of the institution, handcuffed and wearing a blue woolen hat, clowning his way into the "nuthouse" and into our hearts. He plays a shabby reprobate and casual philosopher, a man who likes to fight and screw, and who has been carried in and out of jail by that primitive energy. The real coarseness of such a man is cleaned away by the screened movie and made acceptable by Nicholson's very negotiable personality. Having "raped" a fifteen-year-old—his confession is persuasive enough for any father of teen-agers in the audience—he is committed to the institution for observation, one of the very few who cannot leave of his own volition.

At first, the film is content to be hilarious as Nicholson plays deadpan tease to the doctors who examine him. At these moments one is conscious of a supreme comedian whose wit lies in that special American vein—the dry answer to a stupid question. Nicholson's timing is exaggerated, naturalistic, and loving, and a film full of stutterers and shambling loonies naturally gathers around his easiness. We would not laugh as freely as we do at mental derangement if Nicholson was not so evidently a source of intelligence and feeling. The film was made at the Oregon State Hospital, but any experience of visiting hospitals brings home the film's thorough alteration of the nature of a hospital—narrative is always an orderly form when set against life.

Gradually Nicholson tries to civilize the institution and

extend the shriveled inmates. The antagonism he forms with Nurse Ratched turns into a wager that Nicholson will invert the system and ram it up her arse. The merry approval of this endeavor in the Paramount cannot simply mean that so many New Yorkers have suffered in such institutions; unless one grants that the institutions are now too few for the disturbed, so that any city has to handle its disconcerted masses with Nurse Ratched's bleak care. The feeling in the Paramount was of wild glee that here was a film that knew how lousy the system makes us feel.

The benign outlaw repudiates the ghastly order of the institution. This is nothing less than the anarchy of Groucho and Harpo, the volatility of Cagney and the muttering search for the self in Brando. In other words, the Nicholson character embraces several American heroes, the shrewd, instinctive, laconic antisocial, appealing despite his scorn of appeal. He agitates to have the World Series on TV, rather than endless Mantovani on record. Ratched calls for a vote and cheats when she loses. Whereupon, Nicholson sits in front of the blank set and reacts to the invisible baseball with such zest that the inmates join in and wonder what they can or cannot see—since they're not sane. Nicholson works on a giant deaf-mute Red Indian to teach him basketball. This not only defeats the male nurses at that game, but also encourages the Chief to speak—he had only withdrawn from pointless human communication. It is the Chief who helps Nicholson over the fence, so that he can hijack the bus provided for genteel rides. Instead, Nicholson takes the group to the coast, hires a boat, recruits a girl, and has the gang go fishing for a day. When the boat owner seems suspicious, Nicholson explains that they are all doctors from the hospital and the camera pans across these newly appraised faces with a lovely wonder.

Nicholson gets ECT for his violence to the system, and no film has conveyed what violence ECT does to our system so graphically. He lurches back to the ward, like Karloff as the monster in *Frankenstein,* then collapses in mirth—still play-acting, still beating the repressive order.

The final battle between threatened human vitality and Ratched's administration comes in a one-night orgy when Nicholson gets girls and booze into the ward. The kid who stuttered rigid from sexual hang-ups has a night with a broad and emerges—magically—pleased and fluent. The rest get drunk, tear the ward to pieces, and have themselves the time of their sad lives.

Next day, Ratched comes in with the male nurse and re-duces the kid to stuttering again with the dulcet unkindness that she will have to tell his mother. The kid cuts his throat and the ward subsides. Nicholson is removed for more treat-ment and brought back late one night. The Chief thinks he's still kidding, but this time Nicholson has been lobotomized: There is a dotted line across his brow, and he is in for as long as he lives. The impact of this moment combines distress and anger. New Yorkers were roaring at the placid screen with the dismay of people who would revolt if only they could see a safe way of doing so. But in New York you cannot revolt since you are the future.

The film ends with a weird harking back to the western. In the ward washroom there is a marble stand that Nicholson had once attempted to shift—"At least I tried." Now the Chief lifts it, staggers with it to the window, and hurls it out so that it carries the window frame with it. He leaps after it and runs into a misty blue landscape of forest and moun-tains, as if he were the last of the Mohicans. This is a land-scape not previously seen outside the institution, the lost wilderness that no one in New York now credits.

Cuckoo's Nest measures the transformation that has oc-curred in American cinema since the virtual abdication of Mayer's imperial condescension toward his audience. Ken Kesey may have profited very little from it. He may have disowned the film. But still it deals with, or through, the notion of insanity. That was once anathema to Hollywood, save for an occasional exercise in tasteful melodrama, such as *The Snake Pit. Cuckoo's Nest* treats mental disturbance as a natural condition, and as a means of entertainment and example. This combination is more disturbing than the protest about harsh institutions. The film shows men disfigured by neurosis and brain damage—in that respect, it goes beyond the Hollywood norm of handsomeness. As a portrait of an institution it frightens the potential inmate in us. By showing us shock treatment, it achieves that tightening of the gut we have all felt in hospitals. It is also a tragedy in which a life-loving man is crushed by the bureaucratic custodians of order. Yet those unsettling qualities did not mar an eventual triumph at the box office, or its scooping up of an armful of Oscars in March 1976 when the Academy of Motion Picture Arts and Sciences continued its undignified attempt to keep show biz abreast of the times.

That congratulatory evening disclosed uncomfortable traces of the compromises in making big movies. The glossy, overjoyed, and enriched men who produced the film were more evidently aware of being on a well-oiled wagon than of the tragic subject of their film. Achievement is an understandable idol in America, and there is no shame or reticence in remarking upon it in oneself. At one level, *One Flew Over the Cuckoo's Nest* is a success story. Even before its set of Oscars the movie had the desirability of a coup: It was an "event" in the entertainment world and a film that one had to see. Yet, remorselessly, American cinema saps its own best intentions and most searching effects with the pressing need for success.

McMurphy cannot be defeated because he is Jack Nicholson, and there was Nicholson on that Academy evening, wearing dark glasses in the audience, but removing them as he stepped up to receive the Oscar for best actor. It was a deserved win. His was the most striking performance of the five nominees. All through the evening the television coverage was backing him. In recent years he had come so near so often that there was an inevitability in winning. But would McMurphy have taken a prize for his actions at the hospital? And is not Nicholson's image very close to the untamed, down-to-earth pith of that part? In recent years, both Brando and George C. Scott have stood Oscar up. Some people must have wondered if Nicholson would see Ratcheds everywhere and not knuckle under. Perhaps Nicholson himself was in two minds about what he would say until the last moment.

There was an awkward disharmony in Nicholson as Mc-Murphy, lobotomized, inert, and smothered by the merciful Chief, and Nicholson as Nicholson, unsure whether he despised or wanted the Oscar he handled so casually. This struggle emerged in a grinning, mercenary reference to Mary Pickford as someone who had always stood up for actors getting a larger cut of the cake. If various available sentiments confused Nicholson, he settled for money—guessing that it was the most widely shared ideology before him. Earlier in the evening, the Academy had given the retired actress an Oscar for overall achievement, and a camera had gone with the statuette to Pickfair, that stately home where she and Doug once lived. Mary was there still, in one of the lounges, perched in the corner of an antique sofa, hunched and shaking with palsy, uttering sounds of thanks that were interpreted by her husband, Buddy Rogers. A Mary less successful might have spent her last years in a ward like that in *Cuckoo's Nest*, even the actual Oregon hospital, weird provider of authenticity and show-biz sensation. Nicholson's sense of money reminded one that his undeniable role as part-author on some of today's best films means that he can now ask one million dollars for a film in which he will play the spirit of wry, cheerful failure: Homespun is still a manufactured cloth.

I do not mean to call Nicholson a hypocrite until I have shared his predicament. But at least one can point to the rocks of self-deception and contradiction. They will emerge again when *Cuckoo's Nest* comes up for showing on television. No matter that millions will have seen it in cinemas, its transmission into nearly every home in America will wait upon the skillful deletion of certain images and words. During 1976, another Nicholson film—*The Last Detail*—underwent a similar indignity as its naval idiom was reduced to a more acceptable version of "strong language."

And, with the neatness of one of Mr. Carson's transitions, that brings us to television. That medium is not just the logical development of moving images, so that more people can see them more easily. It institutionalizes the cultural modes inherent in cinema: the detachment of the viewer from reality; the fictionalization of experience; the safe anonymity of the viewer; the duplication of life with imitations of it; a code that makes narrative an imprisoning form; and the outward signs of polish, grace, and orderliness that muffle every threat of breakdown in the material on television.

I have time and space to deal with only a few aspects of television. First, the extent to which it has become a domestic comforter, no longer watched or closely attended to, but furniture as necessary as sedatives. Television does not dominate or insist, as movies do. It is not sensational, but taken for granted. Insistence would destroy it, for its message is so dire that it relies on being the background drone that counters silence. For most of us, it is something turned on and off as we would the light. It is a service, not a luxury or a thing of choice. Sets turned on are likely to stay on long after the program that prompted the first decision. We sometimes wake up in the cold small hours with the persistent lines still doing what they can to warm us. Television has taught us not to be discriminating, no matter that a majority of people having sets feel victims of the medium, and think and talk of it with

a hostility that extends to their own part as writhing re-
cipients. Television is like growing older—unnoticed but
insidious.

Second, its quantity easily surpasses that of the cinema.
As a persistent filmgoer—albeit with some other things to
do—I sometimes see three hundred films a year: Let us say
six hundred hours in front of moving images. Yet that is less
than two hours a day of television, and ask yourself how many
hours a day the set is on in your presence. There are people
who watch over ten hours a day, and children are among
them since the TV set is often used to divert or pacify bored
infants.

Within those very rich hours there is a fragmentation of
genres not dared in cinema. Formally, television is restlessly
experimental and the unwitting embodiment of interrup-
tion, a device used much more circumspectly in other media.
In any evening we are jostled by going in and out of the
room where the television is, by household talk overlapping
with screen talk, and by the swapping of channels—everyman's editing machine. We have to adjust to the meticulous
perfection of the commercial; the similar but less urgent style
in old movies, cut to fit time-slots and accommodate advertising; TV's own situation comedy or romance series; live
outside broadcasts; newscasts and their mélange of scripted
reports and film credited to immediate and precarious van-
tages but impossible to verify—the calm of Howard K. Smith's
summary and the visual incoherence of some far-flung part
of the earth on film, as rough and jerky as the newsreel
obituary of Charles Foster Kane. The discreet place of TV
in the home does not limit its exhausting turmoil of forms,
a test of our resources if we try to watch closely and enough
to make us feel that the material on television is untrustworthy and unmanageable.

Third, to take only one genre among many, the urban
crime picture. While I was in America, all of these series

were running: *The FBI, Harry O, Baretta, SWAT, Bert D'Angelo, Starsky and Hutch, Police Woman, The Streets of San Francisco, Hawaii Five-O, Ironside, The Rookies, Bionic Woman, Six-Million Dollar Man, Cannon, The Blue Knight, Kojak, Colombo, Macmillan and Wife, McCloud,* and at least another half a dozen that I have forgotten. Their collective impact can only be wondered at. Nearly all of them feature leading figures belonging to recognizable police forces. The series are mostly shown in the evening—a time when crime occurs most heavily—and are therefore likely to fill the weary audience with alarm about the danger to property and security. They endorse the work of the police, no matter that their screen violence is calculated to keep people awake for the commercials—which also urge us to take care of ourselves and gather more property. The brutality is artificial, but constant, shocking, and not as worrisome to censors as language and sexual candor. But the largest lie perpetrated by these series is that, in this unending struggle to preserve law, order, decency, and property, the forces of law invariably triumph. All over America the police concede rising quantities of unsolved crimes and the consequent increase in unreported crimes. Yet the heroes in the crime series dismiss difficulty and danger—only poor ratings would carry them off.

The form of this exaggeration is crucial, for the crime series resolve all the complexity of crime and the cities in the trite confrontation of cops and rogues. Confrontation is the rhythm of television, whether the miracle washing powder or brand X in a commercial; the Boston Red Sox or the Cincinnati Reds in a World Series stretching into the night and forcing the abandonment of waiting programs; host and guest in a talk show; rival protagonists in a debate; quiz master and contestants in game shows; network against network in the scheduling; or even Jimmy Carter and Gerald Ford in the medium's version of democratic decision-making.

The flux and difficulty of a country of diversity striving to sustain equality and harmony is evaded by the simpleminded reiteration of entertaining polarity in all things—a fake issue that makes decisiveness a mania while it takes away the power of real discrimination and undermines the necessary variety of America. Melodrama has suppressed all texture, and in the next section I want to make an extended analysis of a recent film that sacrifices life for just such a lifelike polarity.

All the President's Men begins with a massive contrast of dark and light, the one violent image in this account of the most significant constitutional violence in modern America. On a paper-white screen, a typewriter hammers the date so that the paper shudders and ink oozes like blood. Then we cut to original TV news coverage as Nixon lands in a helicopter on the White House lawn and enters an applauding Congress. I saw the film once with a friend who wondered whether this scene was out of focus, not recognizing the dilute colors and rough grain of television images. Then we go from Nixon in exultant TV close-up to the lustrous darkness of cinema, of film *noir* and Alan J. Pakula's smooth handling of men by night breaking into offices in a sleeping steel and glass tower, the Watergate, now as evocative of a culture as the Acropolis or the Eiffel Tower—but, unlike them, an unfamiliar and indistinct building.

The film that follows—and it takes 138 minutes—is riveting yet incoherent. It is so confusing that I would rather it had not been made; Watergate is no topic for half-baked thrill. But nothing I could say would have prevented an enormous bicentennial box-office success sending decent people out of the cinemas heartened that the "idea" of America still works. That "idea" can be made so glossy as to persuade us to overlook all the president's men in the face of two tousled investigative reporters pretending to be Robert Redford and Dustin Hoffman.

One must not blame Bob Woodward and Carl Bernstein for not being Gore Vidal and John Kenneth Galbraith; but we need not forget the gap. Nor am I trying to discredit their persistence or shrewdness in beginning to uncover the scandals that escaped efficient concealment that night at the Watergate. It is possible that the iceberg of iniquity would have slipped by but for them; it is likely, even now, that, as with all icebergs, we have appreciated only a fraction of it. The method of *All the President's Men* is naïve to the point of neglect in its attitude toward icebergs. The uneasy mixture of newsreel and melodrama should not conceal how old-fashioned a film it is, or how blithe a policy it advocates for sailing in cold seas.

Take away the length of the film, the apparent bravery in tackling notoriety so soon after it occurred, take away Pakula's dark-colored deftness with intrigue and the absence of any substantial villains (or any damaged victims), and this becomes a 1930s movie about crusading reporters. It is more plausible: We accept that reporters did work in that way, just as we take it on faith that the studio re-creation of the *Washington Post* newsroom was exact enough to deceive the paper's editor, Ben Bradlee.

But was Bradlee equally perplexed by Jason Robards's effortless shot at the Oscar for best supporting actor, playing none other than Ben Bradlee? Robards is a gray eminence to the young reporters and the shirt-sleeved managing editors, Jack Warden and Martin Balsam (twenty years ago, two of the *Twelve Angry Men*). He dresses better than anyone else on the paper. No one doubts his instinct for substance, verification, or prose when he puts his feet on a desk and wearily takes a red pencil to Woodstein's draft. He makes scathing jokes and, when the crunch comes, he backs the kids, tells them to print it like it is, and wanders out of the newsroom making dreamy motions with his arms, like a gray eminence recollecting his own young escapades.

Robards's performance is from the depths of Hollywood: It glamorizes a wry distaste for the world; it is wisdom according to show biz, and why should we not come away thinking that Robards-Bradlee would make an honorable President in these hard times? Better Robards than a faded star, the ingratiating whine of cleanliness or an evident extra given the star part. The sour knowingness of Robards, plus the dogged beauty of the young leads, serve to protect the Constitution in this movie. But in the world itself, they are not enough.

The film starts with much on its side: most fatal of all, the assumption that we all know the story. That is a fallacy, but it permits a ruinous freedom: The film does not bother to tell the story. I have seen it with a ten-year-old who was cheerfully carried along by the "excitement," but who admitted afterward that she had not the first idea of what actually happened, other than that the President had done a bad thing, which *The Washington Post* resourcefully pulled into the light of day. The unintelligibility of a film is not necessarily a failing. I am reminded of the way Bogart, Howard Hawks, William Faulkner, and Raymond Chandler could not explain one dark turn in the plot of *The Big Sleep* and finally gave up trying. They were right not to worry, for the essence of that film is disillusioned lucidity holding back a chaotic mystery—like a flashlight in a labyrinth.

Yet that only hints at how far *All the President's Men* is rooted in the 1940s thriller. When the subject is so momentous, and the political source so clear, the resort to melodrama is evasive. After the self-righteous battering that Woodstein have given the Nixon apparatus, one must notice the ethical confusion of reporters who turn themselves and their story into an entertainment. One has as much right to expect professional duty—as well as personal ambition—in a newspaper reporter as in a White House aide. The most troubling thing about the film, and about the admiration poured on the two reporters, is that it so closely repeats the overlapping of self-interest and larger concern in which the Nixon White House foundered.

There are two ways in which the film shirks its own story. First, apart from the outline sketch of large-scale corruption, with the puppy hounds from the *Post* agitating the ground for scraps of evidence to lay at Bradlee's feet, the film assists our unfounded feeling of knowing what "Watergate" means. Again, this is the method of *The Big Sleep,* which rests on the droll contrast of vicious and stupid people being dealt with by Bogart's disenchanted grace. *All the President's Men* omits chunks of its own material, knowing we will hardly notice because we are not keeping up with the density of the action. For all of us, there came a time when the surfeit of Watergate and faith in the iceberg factor turned it from a reality into a horror of mythic proportion. This enabled us to give up the chase and enjoy the drama. All fresh details could be thrown into the pattern, without close attention or the wearisome legal tracking down that real crime requires. The final laziness was the President being pardoned before trial, as if a man's wounded pride were more sacrosanct than trampled constitutions. The lack of stamina aided and abetted our wish to fictionalize the whole affair. In that sense, the film is the story of events the public has cheerfully inflated out of narrative or reality.

The second failure is more important. If it had been remedied, then the first omission would not have been as damaging. It is that, dramatically, we have not *all* the President's men, but hardly any of them. Nixon, Agnew, Kleindienst, and Ford are shown briefly on TV screens. But that sets them in a remote world that never blends with the studio *Washington Post.* John Mitchell is heard groaning on the phone— the abode of so many of the characters. Otherwise, the film provides only Hugh Sloan, treasurer of CREEP, Donald Segretti, a dirty-tricks specialist, and a few anguished secretaries. These scenes are the most humanly upsetting and a pointer to the proper subject: the personality of the ordinary or extraordinary people who, knowingly, unknowingly, or having to smother their own qualms, perverted a constitution in which they all thought they believed.

This is like saying that the thought processes of a Hitler are no more significant than those of a little man in extermination. The greatest risk that *All the President's Men* could have taken was to show us ourselves in the list of names in CREEP. But the film only flirts with that chance. The Sloan household has a few vivid moments. Sloan is upright and childishly good-looking, and his wife a tense bun of a girl who opens the door and tells Woodstein fiercely, "This is an honest house." So it proves, despite an earlier view of smart Washington homes sitting smugly in the sun as Woodward comments, "Isn't it strange to think of such people living in these houses." The film makes Sloan an unhappy man, hurt by what he had to do and prepared to allow the half-hints or pregnant silences that Woodstein can interpret. He is also in decline: When we first see him he has just resigned, but on the second visit the house has shrunk and Sloan is in the kitchen while his wife is delivered of their child. The reporters, having won a little more material from Sloan, congratulate the new father. The bonhomie of this platitude is macabre, but the film is unaware of the hypocrisy: To admit it would make Woodstein something other than wholesome gatherers of truth.

Another muffled scene is the long "interrogation" of Sloan's secretary, so well played by Jane Alexander. Of course, it is a part of the film's self-protection that she is as thoroughbred as Miss Alexander, long in the neck, haughtily perched between loyalty and candor. Mysteriously, her sister admits Hoffman-Bernstein when everyone else in CREEP is stonewalling. One feels within touching distance here of a family that is agonizing over the matter, but the sister only makes coffee while Alexander talks for hours about her allegiance and bit by bit divulges what the boys want.

Best of all is the Segretti scene. He opens the door to Bernstein like a convalescent snake recognizing the mongoose. The playing here is brilliant: Robert Walden's expression, tone, and gesture, and the cold-blooded taste of the bachelor pad, all contribute toward the essential creep. Segretti is like someone from Dostoevski: half boasting and half tearful about his ploys to smear Democrats—the alleged bastard child of Hubert Humphrey, and the cunning disclaimer (at which we all laugh) that it would only have improved HHH's image. With alarming speed Segretti breaks down, claiming that he was a fine lawyer who knows he's going to jail. Adroit writing, a good set, and a gloating performance convey the nasty mixture of malice, invention, and self-justification in Nixonville. Sleaziness breathes out of the film and we begin to understand the mood of that wobbling White House. Significantly, Bernstein becomes invisible, or no more prominent than the shadowy Thompson who interviews the people stranded by the death of Charles Foster Kane.

That seems the proper way to present Woodward and Bernstein in this film. It detracts from what they discovered if they are elevated as coltish heroes. The film only uses them as hollow characters, but insistent, noble presences—sadly like the people in advertisements. We know nothing of the two reporters, save that they live like Kafka protagonists in untidy rooms, spending their days in search of justice. I do not want to know them better, but I do not want the effete starriness of Redford and Hoffman hovering over these shells. Woodstein, I daresay, deserved the Pulitzer prize they won for investigative reporting. They do not deserve anything out of the way for their writing, and they have no right to allow themselves to be presented as corduroy-jacketed vigilantes for the Constitution. The film begs one substantial question by keeping the two reporters so much on camera. It implies that they did love justice, and loses sight of two lowly reporters who must soon have realized that they were on to a very juicy story. I do not mean to disparage the boys in wondering whether, in the spirit of American success, they ever foresaw the plush lining to so much hard work: two books and a movie, and such fame that they can hardly ever investigate again now that they are "public" eyes. For, as the film hints, it was their insignificance that got them as far into the story without being trodden on. Still, once investigation is done, the story does require political understanding and not the amalgam of adventure, dramatized documentary, and melodrama.

The melodrama is there from the beginning in the thunder of the typewriter and the slick crosscutting of Nixon bellowing probity while his suave operators make a hash at the Watergate. This tone carries through the accelerating detective-story structure, abruptly cut off before the participation of Sam Ervin, Archibald Cox, or Leon Jaworski, long before the discovery that this President had kept souvenir recordings of all his utterances. The inquiry is glorified: It becomes central to the polarity of good and evil, and the camera gives it grandeur, as when Pakula dissolves to higher and higher views of the two boys sorting through cards at the Library of Congress, revealing the circular form of that reading room as the imprint of conspiracy.

That sequence in the library is symptomatic of the film's director, Alan Pakula, maker of *Klute* and *The Parallax View*, films that whisper with the threat of sinister conspiracy in the world. It is instructive to remember the most frightening moments in *Klute:* in the apartment, when Donald Sutherland murmurs to Jane Fonda that there is someone on the roof listening to them; and in the garment factory when Fonda realizes that she is alone with the killer. Pakula is an able stylist with an undeniable skill at producing something more menacing in a spatial relationship than meets the eye. He films tense with the knowledge of living in a voyeurist society, and that is what makes *All the President's Men* so compelling. The rising views in the library not only comment on the search, but also suggest that Woodstein are themselves being watched. Again, it is unnerving when one CREEP secretary is in tears at the repeated visits of Woodstein because "they" may be watching. A tourist taking snaps in Washington is easily made to seem a security agent recording meetings for "their" files.

But the greatest melodrama, and the most blatant trickery, concerns the appearances of "Deep Throat," so suspect a device that he makes Linda Lovelace look like a Daughter of the American Revolution.

Deep Throat is Bob Woodward's inside source of information. Allegedly he had helped Woodward on other stories, and in the early stages of Watergate Woodward contacts him again. Without explanation, Deep Throat at first wants nothing to do with this story, but then agrees to see Woodward and talk—though it is less talking than listening and nodding to confirm or deny. In the movie, Deep Throat is Hal Holbrook, a gaunt figure who clings to the shadow of an underground parking lot at night. This is a classic setting of melodrama, and it is so theatrical that the reality of such places being home ground for muggers has been omitted.

Except that Holbrook and Deep Throat are mugging like crazy. The low key of the scenes is fondly composed and worthy of a Fritz Lang film. But Deep Throat's taste for dread enigma suits a college production of *Oedipus*. As the film advances, and Woodstein get nearer to the nerve of what is described as a sheer, omniscient system, so Deep Throat develops cold feet. He might have thought of that before, and he might have avoided underground parking lots. But at last he realizes their lives are in danger. Whereupon, an unseen car in a corner of the lot revs up and drives away.

The startled Woodward watches it go; when he turns around a second later Deep Throat has vanished—swallowed himself, no doubt.

Woodward then leaves the parking lot and hurries away through deserted night-town. The camera tracks behind him —it is a trick as old as Hitchcock, but one that always works —and the audience feels the terrible clutch of danger. Like an assassin, the camera zooms in, and Woodward turns fearfully to see only an empty street. At this he rushes back to Bernstein, turns on the stereo, and types out the warning that they may be under surveillance. The irony of nagging reporters themselves turning paranoid is not owned up to, and the film soon escapes into the headlines that tell the rest of the story.

A real Deep Throat need not have behaved as portentously as Hal Holbrook does. But a "real" Deep Throat is not easy to credit. No one doubts that senior members of the administration could have known enough to be Deep Throat and felt disturbed enough to want to bring the rotten castle down. But it keeps such a figure in the hothouse of melodrama to believe that he chose to feed confirmations to a minor reporter in so dangerous a setting. And if we must continue to see Deep Throat in the light of melodrama—and Woodstein say they will not identify him until he dies—then why did someone not "eliminate" him, the fate of stool pigeons in melodrama, especially when they make as much fuss about talking as Holbrook does?

A skeptic, and someone in the newspaper business, might wonder if Deep Throat ever existed. It is farfetched that the hardboiled Bradlee would not have insisted on meeting him. It is possible that *The Washington Post,* or Woodstein, knowing they had a story they could not quite prove, invoked the god in the parking lot who tells no lie as the necessary verification to push their story home.

There may have been a Deep Throat: I don't know. But

I'm sure that he never resembled the movie's cloak-and-dagger version of him. It could also be that he was a fraud. He might even be like the expensive lawyer who appears at the first hearing of the Watergate burglars and says—and is both mocked and criticized for saying—"I'm not here."

And here we come to the most serious deficiency of the film: its double standard, which deplores duplicity and furtiveness in some, but employs the same methods and makes them out as amusing, clever, and necessary. I must add, lest anyone jump to the conclusion, that I am not shifting blame from Haldeman to Woodstein. Yet politicians and reporters can be judged by similar standards. While the movie neglects the temperament and philosophy of the President's men, it unwittingly shows us a good deal about the press.

I have already touched on the way Woodstein's expediency sometimes seems more dangerous than the film realizes. Still, anyone could reasonably argue that men in public life should expect to be harried by *The Washington Post*. Nor is it immediately suspect that Woodstein frame questions in such a way that people can more easily keep a clear conscience about yielding secrets: "I'll count to ten, and if it's all right [true], don't say anything, but don't hang up." There are nastier moments when even this easy-riding film begins to make moral remark. The list of CREEP personnel is obtained by putting pressure on a *Post* secretary to set up a meeting with her ex-fiancé, who works for CREEP. She resents the proposal, and the film does not show that meeting, only the slap of the envelope as the girl drops it without a word on Woodward's typewriter. Then we are off again, without time to reflect how much this tactic would have appealed to the sly Segretti.

In other words, Woodward and Bernstein use people, and are not fully conscious of the shaded means they sometimes employ. How trenchant a film it might have been if the feeling had been conveyed of the same blurring of scruple at the *Post* and the White House. It would require a dash of *Front Page* bitters in Woodstein's root beer. It would have needed more than a Pakula, and more than producer Robert Redford's simpleminded buying of Woodstein's integrity. The real subject of the film is the warping of integrity throughout our system. It is hard to imagine any director grasping this barbed subject within the mock-documentary framework. One thinks of Billy Wilder or the Otto Preminger of fifteen years ago: They might have made a truly sardonic film that gave warning of the climate of administration.

That film would have needed to escape the heavy intrusion of personality that has obscured Watergate, and that has turned two serving journalists into media stars. There is some irony in their stories being often based on "deep background"—the anonymous source, a sea of deep throats, the alleged confessing lips that might so easily turn into the gullibly digestive mouths of the public. Names should be named, then the camouflage of personality could be abandoned. That would allow us to see Watergate as an illustration of ends and means tangled in democratic administrations. Bernstein and Woodward are not worthy of our attention; they have not begun to acquire a personal significance. And the humiliating personal gossip of their second book, *The Final Days,* is again the material of melodrama—soap opera this time—obscuring the point that the Presidency is more important than the individuals who occupy it.

The pardoning of Nixon and the celebrity of Woodstein are signs of America interpreting Watergate as a drama of individuals and not as a revelation of society and government. How often can we rely upon the sprightly enterprise of young reporters before we recognize the pressure on moral authority in a free but careless society?

All the President's Men was advertised as "the greatest detective story of the century." That is hyperbole ushering in early apocalypse to protect its own rashness. Watergate was not a detective story. Yet within a few years its obscure events have been clarified as a popular myth. As a bicentennial phenomenon it has all the relevance of the digestible answer foisted on infinite difficulty. As a film made in the superficial spirit of crusade, it is a trivial reassurance. Cinema's capacity for depleting our sense of reality is made terribly clear. Yet, ironically, it was the abused medium of television that spread doubts in Americans about their administration. The prolonged live coverage of the Ervin Committee sometimes resembled courtroom drama, but it showed responsibility and persistence to the point of tedium. Eventually, it impressed on Americans the mentality of Nixonism, just as twenty-five years earlier Senator McCarthy had been unraveled by television coverage of his conflict with the United States Army.

There is a lesson here, I think. Moving imagery is most free, expressive, and useful when recording and transmitting live events. The deathly shadow in finely wrought and preserved records of the past eventually undermines our sense of life and our involvement in it: That is a fearful legacy of cinema, and it hampers my own love of the medium. Television, too, has succumbed to it, and is less lively when it employs safeguards to restrain spontaneity. The world at large, and our own far smaller spheres of experience, are uncertain and open to doubt. Television has no more demanding duty than to reproduce that.

What do I propose to that end? Measures that are "absurd" or "unthinkable." Television should show no fiction, other than "records" of other fictions—films or plays—on channels known as archives. It should show as much live material as possible. It should abandon the regular injection of encouragements to us to buy marketed products—the commercials. That would require a new means of financing itself, which would make the ownership of the medium a public concern. It should have channels kept available for uninterrupted live coverage of the various governmental processes. It should have no set schedule—this is the most important of all, for not knowing what was on when would require of us a new and more attentive way of using the medium. There would be conversations that went on much longer than expected and news programs that ceased after only a few minutes—if only to destroy the habit that talk and news are of fixed duration and significance. There should be pauses, gaps, and unexplained interruptions. The ruinous tidiness of television must be dispelled if we are to be fit to face our own difficulties.

The cinema seems to have been eased toward seriousness and art by television's catering to the total audience. To go to the cinema now is to exercise choice, and it can be rewarded by the quality of much recent American film. But the cinema still gathers huge audiences and has now added to its range of sensations extreme degrees of pornography and violence. For all its new sophistication, the cinema is still about sex and violence—the enactment of attractiveness and antagonism—about melodrama and visible things. At best, a film allows us to relate to a state of mind. At worst, it encourages the wasteful fantasy involvement that appeases immaturity. It seldom deals adequately with ideas, or with the mesh of thought, feeling, impulse, and doubt that really besets us. To accept that life can be made visible is to tolerate hopeless privacy within the crowd. To persist with patterns of melodramatic confrontation and with the coherence of people in films is to suppress the full range of experience and reflection. The people in films are not like us. They have an integrity we can never equal. The cinema still resembles itself more than it does life, and it has turned the lifelike into a cultural model.

Cinema may be so melodramatic a situation that it cannot abandon that vein. Perhaps the dark cannot free itself from heightened speculation. In which case it must eventually yield to the political or sociological authoritarianism implicit. in the shining light and the huddled mass. But film may yet rid itself of the oppressive company of stars, big budgets, and perfect realization. It is now a facility within the reach of millions: It has become amateur, and that might shatter professionalism. Films need not look as polished as Hollywood has led us to expect; and the medium's nature could alter if stylishness became less of a requirement. Films might then be exchanged between people like letters. They are not obliged to keep the length of feature films: They can be seconds long or run like wakefulness.

There are films like that already. "Underground" cinema explores a much greater range of lengths and ignores the conventions of technical acceptability. It makes more enclosed, private films, flawed, untidy, obscure works. Very often, it is as dedicated and pretentious as poetry or music. That avoids many dangers in commercial cinema. But I cannot resist the allure of the garden, no matter that I know a serpent lives there. Nor will Rafelson, Scorsese, and others abandon the chance of making movies that reach the people and express themselves.

But in those directors there must be some recognition of the duplicity of cinema as a form. We must not trust it. It does not tell stories about the world. It is concerned with the difficulty of looking at things and understanding—or of seeing and agreeing that one cannot know. Cinema must gently attend to itself as its own proper subject. To that extent, the urge to entertain must also be educative. The films made in that spirit need not be dull or dry. Let me end with a tribute to one more American film, symptomatic of what might be done—Andy Warhol's *Blue Movie*.

Although I attribute it to Warhol, the film is not the work of a deliberate or possessive author; only the attitude toward the medium shows us Warhol, not specific uses of it. It is a film of two people, Viva and Louis, talking and making love. They are recorded by a camera put down in the corner of a room, as uninterfered with as possible, certainly not composed or lit. If we are moved visually it is by the sight of sunlight on sheets and bodies. The couple talk, endlessly, formlessly, spontaneously, sometimes tediously and unintelligibly, with no more wit or insight than one might hear in a real conversation. Because no dramatic situation has been imposed upon them, we feel the openness of real people. We do not have to judge them; we are free to observe.

But the topic of lovemaking—true to one of the movies' recurring subjects, and a version of the other *—leads to a philosophical game. In films, we have long since become confused as to whether people are doing things or pretending to do them. Indeed, film has taught us that in our lives to "do" a thing we have to perform it if the doing is to be communicated. In *Blue Movie,* just as the bodies curl in and out of one another, so the ideas of reality and simulation are entwined together. It is a model of cinema, and at one point Louis manifests the riddle that we must ask the serpent before it teases our natural curiosity with nonexistent fruit. As Louis undresses to make love again, Viva says: "I thought I was supposed to be your wife in this movie," and Louis replies with a paradox that assures us life is more than the lifelike:

> What movie? There ain't no movie. You think I'd do this in front of—in a *movie?*

Of course, he is trapped in the paradox, but he knows and admits it. *Blue Movie* is not about sex or humans, but one of the things that relates us with sex, the blue movie. The cinema notes the passing of definition in things, of ideological stillness, and reproduces our continued but bewildering relationship with them. Movement, change, and passing time are all we know.

---

* On film, sexual relations are always and only physical; thus they tend to be a "clash" of bodies. More and more, movies treat sex as a violent form of expression. The more gentle it was, the less visible it would be.

FILMOGRAPHY

THIS LISTS THOSE FILMS DISCUSSED AT LENGTH IN THE TEXT
and provides their principal credits:

All the President's Men (1976, Wildwood/Warners). Directed
  by Alan J. Pakula, produced by Walter Coblenz, written
  by William Goldman from the book by Carl Bernstein
  and Bob Woodward, photographed by Gordon Willis,
  music by David Shire, with Dustin Hoffman, Robert Redford, Jason Robards, Hal Holbrook, Jane Alexander.

Angels with Dirty Faces (1938, Warners). Directed by
  Michael Curtiz, written by John Wexley and Warren
  Duff, photographed by Sol Polito, music by Max Steiner,
  with James Cagney, Pat O'Brien, Humphrey Bogart, Ann
  Sheridan, George Bancroft.

The Bad and the Beautiful (1952, MGM). Directed by Vincente Minnelli, produced by John Houseman, written by
  Charles Schnee, photographed by Robert Surtees, music
  by David Raksin, with Kirk Douglas, Lana Turner, Dick
  Powell, Walter Pidgeon, Gloria Grahame.

The Big Heat (1953, Columbia). Directed by Fritz Lang,
  produced by Robert Arthur, written by Sidney Boehm,

photographed by Charles Lang, music by Daniele Amfi-theatrof, with Glenn Ford, Gloria Grahame, Jocelyn Brando, Alexander Scourby, Lee Marvin.

The Big Sleep (1946, Warners). Directed and produced by Howard Hawks, written by Jules Furthman, Leigh Brackett, and William Faulkner from the novel by Raymond Chandler, photographed by Sid Hickox, music by Max Steiner, with Humphrey Bogart, Lauren Bacall, John Ridgely, Martha Vickers, Dorothy Malone.

The Birth of a Nation (1915). Directed by D. W. Griffith, written by Griffith and Frank Woods from *The Clansman* by Thomas Dixon, photographed by Billy Bitzer, with Lillian Gish, Mae Marsh, Henry Walthall, Miriam Cooper, Robert Harron, and Raoul Walsh (as John Wilkes Booth).

Blue Movie (1969). Directed, produced, and photographed by Andy Warhol, with Viva, Louis Waldron.

Un Chien Andalou (1928). Directed by Luis Buñuel, produced by Buñuel, written by Buñuel and Salvador Dali, photographed by Albert Dubergen, with Simone Mareuil, Pierre Batcheff.

Chinatown (1974, Paramount/Penthouse). Directed by Roman Polanski, produced by Robert Evans, written by Robert Towne, photographed by John Alonso, music by Jerry Goldsmith, with Jack Nicholson, Faye Dunaway, John Huston.

Citizen Kane (1941, Mercury/RKO). Directed and produced by Orson Welles, written by Herman J. Mankiewicz and Welles, photographed by Gregg Toland, music by Bernard Herrmann, with Welles, Joseph Cotten, Everett Sloane, Dorothy Comingore, Ruth Warrick, Ray Collins, Agnes Moorehead.

The Conversation (1974, Coppola/Paramount). Directed, produced, and written by Francis Ford Coppola, photographed by Bill Butler, music by David Shire, with Gene Hackman, John Cazale, Cindy Williams, Robert Duvall.

East of Eden (1955, Warners). Directed and produced by Elia Kazan, written by Paul Osborn from the novel by John Steinbeck, photographed by Ted McCord, music by Leonard Rosenman, with James Dean, Raymond Massey, Julie Harris, Dick Davalos, Burl Ives, Jo Van Fleet.

A Farewell to Arms (1932, Paramount). Directed by Frank Borzage, written by Benjamin Glazer, Oliver Garrett, and Laurence Stallings from the novel by Ernest Hemingway, photographed by Charles Lang, with Gary Cooper, Helen Hayes, Adolphe Menjou.

The Flame and the Arrow (1950, Warners). Directed by Jacques Tourneur, written by Waldo Salt, photographed by Ernest Haller, music by Max Steiner, with Burt Lancaster, Virginia Mayo.

Fury (1936, MGM). Directed by Fritz Lang, produced by Joseph L. Mankiewicz, written by Bartlett Cormack from a story by Norman Krasna, photographed by Joseph Ruttenberg, music by Franz Waxman, with Spencer Tracy, Sylvia Sidney, Bruce Cabot, Walter Brennan.

The Godfather, Part I (1971, Alfran), Part II (1974, Coppola/Paramount). Both directed by Francis Ford Coppola, Part I produced by Albert Ruddy, Part II produced by Coppola, both written by Coppola and Mario Puzo from the novel by Puzo, both photographed by Gordon Willis, music for both by Nino Rota, with Marlon Brando, Al Pacino, James Caan, Robert Duvall, Sterling Hayden, Diane Keaton, Robert De Niro, John Cazale, Talia Shire, Lee Strasberg.

Gone With the Wind (1939, Selznick International). Directed by Victor Fleming, Sam Wood, and George Cukor, produced by David O. Selznick, written by Sidney Howard and Selznick from the novel by Margaret Mitchell, photographed by Ernest Haller, music by Max Steiner, with Clark Gable, Vivien Leigh, Leslie Howard, Olivia de Havilland.

Greed (1923, MGM). Directed and written by Erich von Stroheim from the novel by Frank Norris, photographed by Ben Reynolds and William Daniels, with Zasu Pitts, Gibson Gowland, Jean Hersholt.

Hard to Handle (1933, Warners). Directed by Mervyn LeRoy, written by Wilson Mizner and Robert Lord, with James Cagney, Ruth Donnelly, Allen Jenkins.

High Sierra (1941, Warners). Directed by Raoul Walsh, produced by Mark Hellinger, written by W. R. Burnett and John Huston, photographed by Tony Gaudio, with Humphrey Bogart, Ida Lupino.

I Am a Fugitive from a Chain Gang (1932, Warners). Directed by Mervyn LeRoy, produced by Hal Wallis, photographed by Sol Polito, with Paul Muni.

Intolerance (1916). Directed by D. W. Griffith, photographed by Billy Bitzer, with Mae Marsh, Robert Harron, Miriam Cooper.

Invasion of the Body Snatchers (1956, Allied Artists). Directed by Donald Siegel, produced by Walter Wanger, written by Daniel Mainwaring, photographed by Ellsworth Fredericks, music by Carmen Dragon, with Kevin McCarthy, Dana Wynter.

Lust for Life (1956, MGM). Directed by Vincente Minnelli, produced by John Houseman, written by Norman Corwin from the novel by Irving Stone, photographed by Frederick Young and Russell Harlan, music by Miklos Rozsa, with Kirk Douglas, Anthony Quinn, James Donald.

M (1931, Nero-Film). Directed by Fritz Lang, produced by Seymour Nebenzal, written by Lang and Thea von Harbou, photographed by Fritz Arno Wagner and Gustav Rathje, with Peter Lorre.

A Man's Castle (1933, Columbia). Directed by Frank Borzage, written by Jo Swerling, photographed by Joseph August, with Spencer Tracy, Loretta Young.

Metropolis (1927, UFA). Directed by Fritz Lang, written by Lang and Thea von Harbou, photographed by Karl Freund and Gunther Rittau, with Brigitte Helm, Alfred Abel, Gustave Fröhlich, Rudolph Klein-Rogge.

Mildred Pierce (1945, Warners). Directed by Michael Curtiz, produced by Jerry Wald, written by Ranald MacDougall from the novel by James M. Cain, photographed by Ernest Haller, music by Max Steiner, with Joan Crawford, Zachary Scott, Ann Blyth, Jack Carson, Eve Arden.

The Mortal Storm (1940, MGM). Directed by Frank Borzage, produced by Victor Saville, photographed by William Daniels, with Margaret Sullavan, James Stewart, Frank Morgan, Robert Young.

One Flew Over the Cuckoo's Nest (1975, Fantasy). Directed by Milos Forman, produced by Saul Zaentz and Michael Douglas, written by Lawrence Hauben and Bo Goldman from the novel by Ken Kesey, photographed by Haskell Wexler, Bill Butler, and William Fraker, music by Jack Nitzsche, with Jack Nicholson, Louise Fletcher.

Point Blank (1967). Directed by John Boorman, produced by Robert Chartoff and Judd Bernhard, written by Alex

Jacobs from the novel by Richard Stark, photographed by Philip Lathrop, music by Johnny Mandel, with Lee Marvin, Angie Dickinson, John Vernon, Keenan Wynn, Carroll O'Connor.

Public Enemy (1931, Warners). Directed by William Wellman, written by Kubec Glasmon, John Bright, and Harvey Thew, with James Cagney, Jean Harlow, Edward Woods, Joan Blondell.

Rear Window (1954, Paramount). Directed and produced by Alfred Hitchcock, written by John Michael Hayes, photographed by Robert Burks, music by Franz Waxman, with James Stewart, Grace Kelly, Wendell Corey, Thelma Ritter, Raymond Burr.

Rebel Without a Cause (1955, Warners). Directed by Nicholas Ray, produced by David Weisbart, written by Stewart Stern, photographed by Ernest Haller, music by Leonard Rosenman, with James Dean, Natalie Wood, Sal Mineo, Jim Backus.

Red River (1948, Monterey). Directed and produced by Howard Hawks, written by Borden Chase and Charles Schnee, photographed by Russell Harlan, music by Dimitri Tiomkin, with John Wayne, Montgomery Clift, Joanne Dru, Walter Brennan, John Ireland.

Rio Bravo (1959, Armada). Directed and produced by Howard Hawks, written by Jules Furthman and Leigh Brackett, photographed by Russell Harlan, music by Dimitri Tiomkin, with John Wayne, Dean Martin, Angie Dickinson, Ricky Nelson, Walter Brennan.

Samson and Delilah (1949, Paramount). Directed and produced by Cecil B. De Mille, photographed by George Barnes, music by Victor Young, with Victor Mature, Hedy Lamarr, George Sanders.

Seventh Heaven (1927, Fox). Directed by Frank Borzage, written by Benjamin Glazer, photographed by Ernest Palmer, with Janet Gaynor, Charles Farrell.

Sullivan's Travels (1941, Paramount). Directed and written by Preston Sturges, photographed by John Seitz, with Joel McCrea, Veronica Lake.

Taxi Driver (1976, Italo-Judeo). Directed by Martin Scorsese, produced by Michael and Julia Phillips, written by Paul Schrader, photographed by Michael Chapman, music by Bernard Herrmann, with Robert De Niro, Cybill Shepherd, Jodie Foster, Peter Boyle, Harvey Keitel.

Three Comrades (1938, MGM). Directed by Frank Borzage, produced by Joseph L. Mankiewicz, written by F. Scott Fitzgerald from the novel by Erich Maria Remarque, photographed by Joseph Ruttenberg, music by Franz Waxman, with Margaret Sullavan, Robert Taylor, Robert Young, Franchot Tone.

Touch of Evil (1958, Universal). Directed and written by Orson Welles, produced by Albert Zugsmith, photographed by Russell Metty, music by Henry Mancini, with Welles, Charlton Heston, Janet Leigh, Joseph Calleia, Akim Tamiroff, Marlene Dietrich.

Way Down East (1920). Directed by D. W. Griffith, written by Anthony Paul Kelley, photographed by Billy Bitzer and Hendrick Sartov, with Lillian Gish, Lowell Sherman, Richard Barthelmess.

White Heat (1949, Warners). Directed by Raoul Walsh, written by Ben Roberts and Ivan Goff, photographed by Sid Hickox, music by Max Steiner, with James Cagney, Margaret Wycherly, Virginia Mayo, Edmond O'Brien, Steve Cochran.

Written on the Wind (1956, Universal International). Directed by Douglas Sirk, produced by Albert Zugsmith, written by George Zuckerman from the novel by Robert Wilder, photographed by Russell Metty, music by Frank Skinner, with Rock Hudson, Robert Stack, Lauren Bacall, Dorothy Malone.

You Only Live Once (1937, Wanger). Directed by Fritz Lang, produced by Walter Wanger, written by Gene Towne and Graham Baker, photographed by Leon Shamroy, music by Alfred Newman, with Henry Fonda, Sylvia Sidney.

BIBLIOGRAPHY

THERE ARE FAR TOO MANY BOOKS ON HOLLYWOOD—FROM the academic to the scurrilous. After seventy years, very few are penetrating, accurate, and readable—perhaps the subject is beyond words. This is a list of those works that have been most useful in writing this book.

HISTORY

ANGER, KENNETH. *Hollywood Babylon*. Phoenix, Ariz., 1965. A history of Hollywood scandals shamelessly imitating the manner of lurid fan magazines, written by one of the leading experimental film-makers in America.

BAXTER, JOHN. *The Hollywood Exiles*. New York, 1976. The story of European exiles at work in the American film industry.

BROWNLOW, KEVIN. *The Parade's Gone By*. London, 1968. A well-researched patchwork account of Hollywood before the coming of sound.

CROWTHER, BOSLEY. *The Lion's Share: The Story of an Entertainment Empire*. New York, 1957. The history of Metro-Goldwyn-Mayer.

FRENCH, PHILIP. *The Movie Moguls*. London, 1969. Short but informative account of the major studios and their founders.

GOODMAN, EZRA. *The Fifty Year Decline and Fall of Holly-wood.* New York, 1961.

JACOBS, LEWIS. *The Rise of the American Film.* New York, 1939.

POWDERMAKER, HORTENSE. *Hollywood the Dream Factory.* Boston, 1950. An anthropological view.

RAMSAYE, TERRY. *A Million and One Nights.* New York, 1926.

ROSTEN, LEO C. *Hollywood: The Movie Colony, The Movie Makers.* New York, 1941.

THORP, MARGARET. *America at the Movies.* New Haven, Conn., 1937.

INDIVIDUALS

BOGDANOVICH, PETER. *Allan Dwan.* London, 1971.

———. *Fritz Lang in America.* London, 1967.

———. Interview with Howard Hawks, *Movie,* no. 5 (December 1962).

BEHLMER, RUDY, ed. *Memo From: David O. Selznick.* New York, 1972.

CHAPLIN, CHARLES. *My Autobiography.* London, 1964.

CHIERICHETTI, DAVID. *Hollywood Director: The Career of Mitchell Leisen.* Teaneck, N.J., 1973.

CLARENS, CARLOS. *Cukor.* New York, 1977.

GARNHAM, NICHOLAS. *Samuel Fuller.* London, 1971.

HALLIDAY, JON. *Sirk on Sirk.* London, 1971. Also, Halliday, Jon, and Mulvey, Laura, eds. *Douglas Sirk.* Edinburgh, 1972.

HENDERSON, ROBERT M. *D. W. Griffith: His Life and Work.* New York, 1972.

HOUSEMAN, JOHN. *Run-Through.* New York, 1972.

LAMBERT, GAVIN. *On Cukor.* New York, 1972.

MAILER, NORMAN. *Marilyn.* New York, 1973.

McBRIDE, JOSEPH. *Orson Welles.* London, 1972.

McGILLIGAN, PATRICK. *Cagney: The Actor as Auteur.* Cranbury, N.J., 1975.

MILNE, TOM, ed. *Losey on Losey.* London, 1967.

SCHICKEL, RICHARD. *Douglas Fairbanks, The First Celebrity.* New York, 1973.

SIEGEL, JOEL E. *Val Lewton: The Reality of Terror.* London, 1972.

STERNBERG, JOSEF VON. *Fun in a Chinese Laundry.* New York, 1965.

Take One. Issue on Nicholas Ray, vol. 5, no. 6 (January 1977). Also on Ray, *Movie,* no. 9 (May 1963).

THOMAS, BOB. *Selznick.* New York, 1970.

TRUFFAUT, FRANÇOIS. *Hitchcock.* New York, 1967.

WOOD, ROBIN. *Arthur Penn.* London, 1967.

———. *Howard Hawks.* London, 1968.

FILMS

Blue Movie, screenplay. New York, 1970.

Un Chien Andalou, screenplay. London, 1968.

KAEL, PAULINE. *The Citizen Kane Book.* New York, 1971.

KNOX, DONALD. *The Magic Factory.* New York, 1974. On the making of *An American in Paris.*

LAMBERT, GAVIN. *The Making of Gone with the Wind.* Boston, 1973.

M, screenplay. London, 1968.

MAILER, NORMAN. *Maidstone,* screenplay with essay, "A Course in Film-Making." New York, 1971.

Metropolis, screenplay. London, 1973.

ROSS, LILLIAN. *Picture.* New York, 1952. On the making of *The Red Badge of Courage.*

GENRES AND SOCIETY

American Film Institute. *Guide to College Courses in Film and Television.* Washington, D.C., 1975.

BANHAM, REYNER. *Los Angeles: The Architecture of Four Ecologies.* London, 1971.

BARNOUW, ERIK. *Tube of Plenty: The Evolution of American Television.* New York, 1976.

BERGER, JOHN. *Ways of Seeing.* London, 1972.

HASKELL, MOLLY. *From Reverence to Rape: The Treatment of Women in the Movies.* New York, 1974.

KITSES, JIM. *Horizons West.* Bloomington, Ind., 1970.

McARTHUR, COLIN. *Underworld USA.* London, 1972.

McCANN, RICHARD DYER, ed. *Film and Society.* New York, 1964.

SITNEY, P. ADAMS. *Visionary Film: The American Avant-Garde.* New York, 1974.

SKLAR, ROBERT. *Movie-Made America.* New York, 1975.

TYLER, PARKER. *Magic and Myth of the Movies.* New York, 1947.

———. *Sex Psyche Etcetera in the Film.* New York, 1969.

WOOD, MICHAEL. *America in the Movies.* New York, 1975.

WRIGHT, WILL. *Sixguns and Society.* Berkeley, Calif., 1975.

CRITICAL APPROACHES TO FILM

ANDREW, J. DUDLEY. *The Major Film Theories.* New York, 1976.

BAZIN, ANDRÉ. *What Is Cinema?* 2 vols. Berkeley, Calif., 1967, 1971.

BLUESTONE, GEORGE. *Novels into Film.* Berkeley, Calif., 1957.

BURCH, NOEL. *Theory of Film Practice.* New York, 1973.

CORLISS, RICHARD. *Talking Pictures.* New York, 1974.

McCONNELL, FRANK D. *The Spoken Seen: Film and the Romantic Imagination.* Baltimore, Md., 1975.

METZ, CHRISTIAN. *Film Language: A Semiotics of the Cinema.* New York, 1974.

PERKINS, V. F. *Film as Film.* New York, 1972.

Thomson, David. *A Biographical Dictionary of Film.* New York, 1976.

Vogel, Amos. *Film as a Subversive Art.* New York, 1975.

Wollen, Peter. *Signs and Meaning in the Cinema.* London, 1969.

Wood, Robin. *Personal Views: Explorations in Film.* London, 1976.

FICTION

Brooks, Richard. *The Producer.* New York, 1951.

Fitzgerald, F. Scott. *The Last Tycoon* (unfinished). New York, 1941.

Lambert, Gavin. *Inside Daisy Clover.* New York, 1963.

Mailer, Norman. *The Deer Park.* New York, 1957.

Raphael, Frederic. *California Time.* New York, 1975.

Schulberg, Budd. *The Disenchanted.* New York, 1950.

———. *What Makes Sammy Run?* New York, 1939.

Vidal, Gore. *Myra Breckinridge.* New York, 1968.

West, Nathanael. *The Day of the Locust.* New York, 1939.

INDEX